FROM GUILT TO SHAME

20|21

Walter Benn Michaels, *Series Editor*

From Guilt to Shame by Ruth Leys

William Faulkner: An Economy of Complex Words by Richard Godden

FROM GUILT TO SHAME

Auschwitz and After

Ruth Leys

PRINCETON UNIVERSITY PRESS

OCM 75390079

PRINCETON AND OXFORD

Copyright © 2007 by Princeton University Press

Published by Princeton University Press, 41 William Street, Princeton,
New Jersey 08540

In the United Kingdom: Princeton University Press, 3 Market Place,
Woodstock, Oxfordshire OX20 1SY

ISBN-13: 978-0-691-13080-4
ISBN-10: 0-691-13080-9

Library of Congress Cataloging-in-Publication Data
Leys, Ruth.
From guilt to shame : Auschwitz and after / Ruth Leys.
p. cm. — (20/21)
Includes bibliographical references and index.
ISBN-13: 978-0-691-13080-4 (hardcover : alk. paper)
ISBN-10: 0-691-13080-9 (hardcover : alk. paper)
1. Guilt—Psychological aspects.   2. Shame—Psychological as-
pects.   3. Holocaust, Jewish (1939–1945)—Psychological aspects.
4. Holocaust survivors—Psychology.   I. Title.
BF575.G8L49 2007
155.9′3—dc22   2006036673

British Library Cataloging-in-Publication Data is available

This book has been composed in Helvetica Neue Typefaces
Printed on acid-free paper. ∞
press.princeton.edu

Printed in the United States of America

10 9 8 7 6 5 4 3 2 1

To Isobel Armstrong, Frances Ferguson, and Meira Likierman

CONTENTS

ACKNOWLEDGMENTS

I AM grateful to several friends and colleagues for their willingness to read all or part of the manuscript of my book and for offering helpful criticisms, many of which I have incorporated into my text. Thanks especially to: Isobel Armstrong, Stefanos Geroulanos, Meira Likierman, David Niremberg, Gabrielle Spiegel, Toril Moi, Hent de Vries, and Allan Young, as well as to my anonymous readers at Princeton University Press who raised many pertinent questions that helped me sharpen my arguments. Alan Fridlund became an invaluable interlocutor at a crucial point in the development of my arguments. Likewise, James Conant steered me toward relevant philosophical literature and gave me superb advice.

I owe a special debt to Walter Benn Michaels and Jennifer Ashton for helping me to think through aspects of the argument of this book, as well as to Michael Fried for his extraordinary intellectual generosity, his ability to make constructive proposals for clarification, and his tenacious readings and rereadings of my work.

I also wish to thank my editor, Hanne Winarsky, for her outstanding support.

I am grateful to the editors of *Science in Context* for permission to reprint material in Chapter 3 which was published in an earlier version in that journal. I am also grateful to the Leo Baeck Institute for the Study of the History and Culture of German-Speaking Jewry in New York for giving me permission to examine some of William Niederland's unpublished psychiatric evaluations of Holocaust survivors housed in its library archives, and to Nils Schott for helping me with the interpretation of some of Niederland's German texts. I am also grateful to the National Endowment of the Humanities for a research fellowship grant in 2001 in support of this project.

I dedicate this book to three extraordinary friends: Isobel Armstrong, Frances Ferguson, and Meira Likierman.

FROM GUILT TO SHAME

INTRODUCTION ██████████████

From Guilt to Shame

W HAT is the logic of torture? In an article on prisoner abuse at Abu Ghraib prison in Iraq, Mark Danner has shown that the methods used to soften up and interrogate detainees by American military personnel can be traced back to techniques developed by the CIA in the 1960s. The best known manual of such procedures, the CIA's *Counterintelligence Interrogation of Resistance Sources,* produced in 1963 at the height of the Cold War, states that the purpose of all coercive techniques of interrogation is "to induce regression." The result of external pressures of sufficient intensity is the loss of those defenses "most recently acquired by civilized man . . . Relatively small degrees of homeostatic derangement, fatigue, pain, sleep loss, or anxiety may impair these functions."[1] The programmatic manipulation and control of the environment, including the use of blindfolds or hooding, sleep and food deprivation, exposure to intense heat and cold, sensory deprivation, and similar methods, are meant to disorient the prisoner and break down resistance. "Once this disruption is achieved," a later version of the manual observes, the subject's resistance is "seriously impaired." He experiences a "kind of psychological shock" as a result of which he is far more open to suggestion and far likelier to comply with what is asked of him than before. Frequently the subject will experience a "feeling of guilt." If the interrogator

[1] Mark Danner, "The Logic of Torture," *New York Review of Books,* June 24, 2004, 71; hereafter abbreviated as "LT." Danner cites from the *KUBARK Counterintelligence Interrogation of Resistant Sources,* July 1963, archived at "Prisoner Abuse: Patterns from the Past," National Security Archive Electronic Briefing Book No. 122, 83. http://www.gwu.edu/~nsarchiv/NSAEBB/NSA-EBB122. KUBARK is a CIA code name.

can intensify those guilt feelings, it will "increase the subject's anxiety and his urge to cooperate as a means of escape."[2] Viewed in this light, Danner remarks, the garish scenes of humiliation documented in the photographs and depositions from Abu Ghraib "begin to be comprehensible; they are in fact staged operas of fabricated shame, intended to 'intensify' the prisoner's 'guilt feelings, increase his anxiety, and his urge to cooperate'" ("LT," 72).

The terms of Danner's analysis imply that there has existed a single logic of torture extending uninterruptedly from the 1960s to the occupation of Iraq, according to which there is no important distinction to be drawn between the emotions of guilt and shame. Yet if we focus on the details of the manuals, reports, and protocols to which he has so usefully drawn our attention, differences become apparent. The CIA's approach to interrogation in 1963 was largely based on a watered-down Freudianism that emphasized the psychic relationship between prisoner and interrogator, especially the tendency of the latter to assume the role of a parental figure with whom the prisoner might unconsciously identify in an ambivalent and guilty manner. The 1963 manual says that its procedures aim not only to "exploit the resistant source's internal conflicts and induce him to wrestle with himself" but also to bring a superior outside force to bear upon his resistance. In other words, by virtue of his role as the sole supplier of satisfaction and punishment the interrogator seeks to assume the stature and importance of a paternal figure in the prisoner's feelings and thoughts. Although there may be "intense hatred" for the interrogator, it is not unusual for the subject also to develop "warm feelings" toward him. Such ambivalence is the basis for the suspect's guilt reactions, and if the interrogator nourishes those feelings of guilt, they may prove strong enough to influence the prisoner's behavior. "Guilt makes compliance more likely."[3] The ultimate goal of the physical abuse and other manipulative techniques described in the manual is thus the production of a docile, compliant, and guilt-wracked prisoner so regressively bonded with his interrogator as to be willing to confess. We might define this 1963 logic of torture as an *identificatory logic of guilt.* According to the manual, hypnosis, suggestion, and narcosis may serve the same purpose, since they too are capable of inducing a regressive identification with the interrogator. Even the efficacity of pain is understood to depend on the prisoner's guilty attitudes. One telling detail in the manual is the advice that if audio and video recording devices are to be used, the subject should not be conscious that he is being recorded—as if the psychological dynamic between prisoner and interrogator conducive to successful interrogation can only develop when the captive is unaware of being seen or overheard by someone other than the interrogator.

[2] *The Human Resource Exploitation Training Manual—1983,* National Security Archive Electronic Briefing Book No. 122, "Non-Coercive Techniques"; http://www.gwu.edu/~snsrchiv/NSA-EBB/NSAEBB122. Also cited by Danner in a more abbreviated form ("LT," 71).

[3] *KUBARK Counterintelligence Interrogation of Resistant Sources,* 1.

Contrast this with the implicit logic of torture at Abu Ghraib forty years later. All the methods that have been described in the current scandal are designed to publicly humiliate and shame the prisoner. An American military pamphlet instructing troops on Iraqi sensitivities warns against shaming or humiliating a man in public, since shaming will cause him and his family to be anti-Coalition. According to the pamphlet, the most important qualifier for all shame is for "a third party to witness the act." It cautions that if an American must do something likely to cause an Iraqi shame, he should "remove the person from the view of others." Acts such as placing hoods over a detainee's head, placing a detainee on the ground, or putting a foot on him should be avoided because they cause Arabs shame. Likewise, the pamphlet says, Iraqis consider a variety of things to be unclean: "'Feet or soles of feet. Using the bathroom around others. Unlike Marines, who are used to open-air toilets, Arab men will not shower/use the bathroom together. Bodily fluids'" ("LT," 72).

As Danner observes, these precepts are emphatically reversed at Abu Ghraib. It is precisely because such methods induce shame that they have been exploited there and at other American interrogation sites, where detainees have been kept hooded and bound, made to crawl and grovel on the floor, forced to put shoes in their mouths, and worse. "And in all of this, as the Red Cross report noted, the *public* nature of the humiliation is absolutely critical: thus the parading of naked bodies, the forced masturbation in front of female soldiers, the confrontation of one naked prisoner with one or more others, the forcing together of naked prisoners in 'human pyramids'" ("LT," 72). The torture carried out at Abu Ghraib almost seems to demand what was counterindicated in 1963, the open use of the camera, because shame depends on the subject's consciousness of exposure. As Danner again notes: "And all of this was made to take place in full view not only of foreigners, men and women, but also of that ultimate third party: the ubiquitous digital camera with its inescapable flash, there to let the detainee know that the humiliation would not stop when the act itself did but would be preserved into the future in a way that the detainee would not be able to control" ("LT," 72). As a "shame multiplier" ("LT," 72) the camera epitomizes the logic of torture at Abu Ghraib, which can be defined as a *spectatorial logic of shame.*[4]

In one sense, the resort to shaming techniques may represent a specific adaptation to the Arab context. But it is also true that the shift from a logic of torture based on guilt to a logic of torture based on shame reflects a more general shift that has taken place in the course of the last forty years from a dis-

[4] In his exposé of the Abu Ghraib scandal, Seymour Hersh reveals that the public humiliation was part of a deliberate American policy to create an army of Iraqi informants, inserted back in the population, willing to do anything, including spying on their associates, in order to avoid dissemination of the shameful photos to family and friends. It was not effective, and the insurgency continued to grow. Seymour Hersh, *Chain of Command: The Road from 9/11 to Abu Ghraib* (New York, 2004), 39.

course of guilt to a discourse of shame. It is not just a question of assuming, as anthropologists used to do, that the Iraqis belong to a more primitive "shame culture" than our own Western "guilt culture." Today, shame (and shameless-ness) has displaced guilt as a dominant emotional reference in the West as well. A major purpose of my book is to examine and evaluate that displace-ment. In his recent study of humiliation and associated emotions, such as shame and embarrassment, William Ian Miller has noted the recent deprecia-tion of guilt and resurgence of interest in shame among the self-help and re-lated disciplines, but disputes the idea that a major paradigm shift has really occurred. He claims that "the makeover makes shame look not at all unlike guilt."[5] I disagree. For all the interest of his study, Miller fails to see what is orig-inal and important about shame theory today, and misconstrues the stakes in-volved in the upsurge of books and articles that take shame as their primary point of reference. I argue instead that the change from a culture of guilt to a culture of shame in Western thinking about the emotions is highly significant and has important consequences.

My story begins with the centrality of guilt to post–World War II assessments of survivors of the concentration camps. The terms used in the CIA's 1963 training manual for the interrogation of resistant detainees bear an uncomfortably close proximity to those used by victims and researchers alike in the same postwar pe-riod to describe the psychodynamics of the tortured and shocked survivors of the Holocaust.[6] Giorgio Agamben has recently observed in this regard that the sur-vivor's feeling of guilt is a *locus classicus* of the literature on the camps.[7] "That many (including me) experienced 'shame,' that is, a feeling of guilt during the im-prisonment and afterward, is an ascertained fact confirmed by numerous testi-monies. It is absurd, but it is a fact," Primo Levi observes in his last (and most

[5] William Ian Miller, *Humiliation and Other Essays on Honor, Social Discomfort, and Violence* (Ithaca and London, 1993), 131.

[6] The CIA's training manual represents an application of the methods of terror, torture, coercion, interro-gation, and "mind control" used against prisoners by the Soviet Union, the Chinese Communists, and the Nazis. Some of the literature on those methods, as well as victim reports, informed the CIA manual; and certain experts, such as Robert J. Lifton and Martin Orne, who worked on thought control and hypnotic regression respectively, received funding support from the military and government agencies interested in developing interrogation techniques. The innocuous-sounding "Society for the Investigation of Human Ecology," which took an active role in sponsoring interrogation research, was a CIA front organization. De-tails can be found in John Marks, *The Search for the "Manchurian Candidate": The CIA and Mind Control* (New York, 1979). See also Ellen Herman, "The Career of Cold War Psychology," *Radical History Review*, no. 63 (Fall 1995): 52–85, for a discussion of the U.S. military's sponsorship of psychological research in the postwar years; and Christopher Simpson's *Science of Coercion: Communication Research and Psy-chological Warfare, 1945–1960* (Oxford, 1994) on the government's effort to enlist communication studies to perfect American propaganda and counterinsurgency programs.

[7] Giorgio Agamben, *Remnants of Auschwitz: The Witness and the Archive,* trans. Daniel Heller-Roazen (New York, 1999), 89; hereafter abbreviated *RA*.

troubled) book about his time in Auschwitz.[8] Similarly the psychoanalyst Bruno Bettelheim, who was imprisoned in Dachau and Buchenwald in 1938–39, writes: "One cannot survive the concentration camp without feeling guilty that one was so incredibly lucky when millions perished, many of them in front of one's eyes . . . In the camps one was forced, day after day, for years, to watch the destruction of others, feeling—against one's better judgment—that one should have intervened, feeling guilty for not having done so, and, most of all, feeling guilty for having also felt glad that it was not oneself who perished."[9] Or in the words of Elie Wiesel, cited by Agamben: "'I live, therefore I am guilty. I am here because a friend, an acquaintance, an unknown person died in my place'" (*RA,* 89). And in a statement also cited by Agamben, Ella Lingens asks: "'Does not each of us who has returned go around with a guilt feeling, feelings which our executioners rarely feel—'I live, because others died in my place?'" (*RA,* 89).

In attempts during the 1960s to explain the phenomenon of survivor guilt, American psychoanalysts such as William Niederland, Henry Krystal, Bettelheim, and others borrowed from the work of Freud, Sandor Ferenczi, and Anna Freud in theorizing that the guilt feelings associated with survival were the result of an *unconscious imitation of, or identification with, the aggressor.* They argued that the humiliated prisoner, in the moment of shock, regressively defends against the persecutor's violence by unconsciously yielding to, or imitatively incorporating, the violent other. And since under camp conditions of abject powerlessness the incorporated aggression cannot be projected onto the aggressor, the violence is turned back against the victim, who experiences it in the form of a self-lacerating conscience. In short, from the start the notion of survivor guilt was closely connected to the theme of imitative identification and to the idea of the victim's defensive, unconscious bond of collusion with the situation of terror. In his highly influential discussion of the "gray zone," where "the two camps of masters and servants both diverge and converge" (*DS,* 42), Primo Levi—no admirer of psychoanalysis—likewise explored the question of the unconscious identification, "mimesis," or imitation of the aggressor that complicitously binds the victim to the violence directed against himself (*DS,* 48).

But it is precisely because of the taint of collusion associated with the notion of survivor guilt that almost from the start objections have been raised against it. To take one influential example, Terrence Des Pres, in his widely admired book *The Survivor* (1976), repudiated both the notion of identification with the aggressor and that of survivor guilt, emphasizing instead the role played in the victim's survival by social bonding, mutual care, and outright resistance. According to Des Pres, if imitation of the SS took place in the camps, as Bettelheim and others

[8] Primo Levi, *The Drowned and the Saved,* trans. Raymond Rosenthal (New York, 1989), 73; hereafter abbreviated *DS.*

[9] Bruno Bettelheim, *Surviving and Other Essays* (New York, 1980), 297–98.

claimed, the imitation was not an unconscious, collusive identification with the enemy but merely a strategic mimicry undertaken consciously by political prisoners in order to obtain positions of power and to assist other victims in the struggle for life.[10] A similar repudiation of the notion of unconscious imitation and survivor guilt marks the more recent literature on trauma. In 1980, when the diagnosis of Posttraumatic Stress Disorder (PTSD) was introduced into the American Psychiatric Association's *Diagnostic and Statistical Manual of Mental Disorders* (*DSM-III*), survivor guilt feelings were regarded as a characteristic symptom of the disorder and were included in the list of diagnostic criteria.[11] But in the revised edition of the manual of 1987 (*DSM-IIIR*), the American Psychiatric Association after considerable controversy downgraded survivor guilt to the status of an "associated" and noncriterial feature of the condition.[12] As we shall see, now that survivor guilt has disappeared from the official list of criteria for PTSD, shame has come to take its place as the emotion that for many investigators most defines the condition of posttraumatic stress.

In a similar movement, literary critic Lawrence Langer, known for his analyses of Holocaust video testimony, has rejected the notion of survivor guilt, not only because he thinks it deflects blame from the real culprits onto the victims themselves, but more generally because it belongs to what he regards as a normalizing, therapeutic, redemptive approach to the misery of the Holocaust that estranges us from the ultimately incomprehensible and unredeemable reality of the camps. This leads him to call for a post-Holocaust revision of ethics that would go beyond the dilemmas and contradictions posed by the unheroic "choiceless choices" that ruled the victims of the Nazis.[13] Although it is not clear what Langer thinks an alternative, post-Holocaust ethics might look like, he hints at one direction to follow when he suggests that "shame" might be a better word than the troubling concept of "guilt" for the anguish experienced by the survivor. Embracing a distinction between guilt and shame that Primo Levi himself does not observe, Langer states that Levi did not enjoy using a word like "guilt" when raising

[10] Terrence Des Pres, *The Survivor: An Anatomy of Life in the Death Camps* (Oxford, 1976).

[11] Nancy C. Andreasen, "Posttraumatic Stress Disorder," in *Comprehensive Textbook of Psychiatry*, vol. 3, 3rd ed., ed., Arnold Kaplan, Alfred Freedman, and Benjamin Sadock (Baltimore, 1980), 1517.

[12] In *DSM-III,* survivor guilt was listed in the "Miscellaneous Category" of symptoms as an optional rather than a necessary feature of PTSD in that patients could have an alternative symptom listed in the manual that likewise qualified them for the disorder. After the demotion of the survivor guilt criterion, the revised manual merely noted under the "Associated Features" of PTSD that "In the case of a life-threatening trauma shared with others, survivors often describe painful guilt feelings about surviving when others did not, or about the things they had to do in order to survive" (*DSM-IIIR*, 249). As I observe in chapter 3, in the discussion leading up to the demotion of the survivor guilt criterion there was disagreement over whether to retain the item as an aspect of the reexperiencing criteria for the disorder, but it was finally eliminated on the grounds that it was not present in all cases of PTSD.

[13] Lawrence L. Langer, *Versions of Survival: The Holocaust and the Human Spirit* (New York, 1982), 36.

the problematic topic of collaboration. In the end, he claims, Levi preferred to speak of "shame" as the "primary legacy of the moral swamp into which German coercion had sunk its prey."[14] Agamben makes a similar gesture when he criticizes the notion of survivor guilt and rejects as "puerile" Levi's self-reproaches for minor wrongs committed by him during his time in the camps. Agamben suggests that the reader's supposed unease with Levi's writings on this topic can only be a reflection of the survivor's embarrassment at being unable to master shame (RA, 88). Agamben's larger claim, which goes far beyond Langer, is that the concentration camps were nothing less than an "absolute situation" that revealed shame to be "truly something like the hidden structure of all subjectivity and consciousness" (RA, 128).

Although Langer and Agamben represent different approaches to the Holocaust and stand for different ideas about shame, the general privilege they accord to shame over guilt can be situated in the context of a broad shift that has recently occurred in the medical and psychiatric sciences, literary criticism, and even philosophy away from the "moral" concept of guilt in favor of the ethically different or "freer" concept of shame. Today's "vogue of shame," to use Christopher Lasch's phrase, is manifest not only in the work of the American Psychiatric Association and books by Langer and Agamben.[15] It is also apparent in such widely disparate texts as Bernard Williams's Shame and Necessity (1993), a study of ancient Greek tragedy and thought; Eve Kosofsky Sedgwick and Adam Frank's Shame and Its Sisters (1995), an anthology of texts by the psychologist Silvan Tomkins (1911–89), who from the 1960s through the 1980s advocated a nonpsychoanalytic affect theory centered on shame; Sedgwick's more recent collection of essays on a variety of topics, including shame, Touching Feeling: Affect, Pedagogy, Performativity (2003); Joseph Adamson and Hilary Clark's literary-critical anthology, Scenes of Shame: Psychoanalysis, Shame, and Writing (1999), which presents a series of studies of the role of shame in nineteenth- and twentieth-century literature, making use of contemporary shame theory; Jacqueline Rose's On Not Being Able to Sleep: Psychoanalysis and the Modern World (2003), which deals with the role of shame in South Africa's Truth and Reconciliation Commission, as well as in the cult of celebrity; Martha C. Nussbaum's Hiding from Humanity: Disgust, Shame, and the Law (2003), a critique of the recent legal use of shaming sanctions; Elspeth Probyn's Blush: Faces of Shame (2005), a cultural studies approach to the psychology and politics of identity; and three somewhat earlier books, Shame: The Power of Caring (1980) by Gershen Kaufman, which was the first text to introduce Tomkins's affect theory into psychotherapy, The Mask of Shame (1981) by psychoanalyst Leon Wurmser, and The Many

[14] Lawrence L. Langer, Preempting the Holocaust (New Haven and London, 1988), 36.

[15] Christopher Lasch, "For Shame: Why Americans Should Be Wary of Self-Esteem," New Republic, August 10, 1992, 29.

Faces of Shame (1987) by Donald L. Nathanson, Tomkins' best-known follower in the psychotherapeutic domain. Each of these works—and there are many others—posits a clear differentiation between guilt and shame in order to make use of shame theory for various philosophical, postpsychoanalytic, postmodernist, and political projects and critiques. It is a measure of how much has changed that the author of a recent biography of Bruno Bettelheim, one of the architects in the United States of the postwar concept of survivor guilt, treats Bettelheim's deeply covered-over feelings of shame, not guilt, as the key to the self-doubt and sense of fraudulence that haunted him throughout his life and career.[16]

The original intuition informing the present book was that the current tendency to privilege shame over guilt could at least partly be understood in terms of the perennial conflict between the "mimetic" and "antimimetic" tendencies internal to trauma theory, as those terms are defined and tracked historically in my *Trauma: A Genealogy* (2000).[17] In that book I argued that from the moment of its invention in the late-nineteenth century, the concept of trauma has been fundamentally unstable, balancing uneasily, or veering uncontrollably, between two antithetical poles or theories. The first, or *mimetic* theory, holds that trauma, or the experience of the traumatized subject, can be understood as involving a kind of hypnotic imitation of or regressive identification with the original traumatogenic person, scene, or event, with the result that the subject is fated to act it out or in other ways imitate it. Trauma is understood as an experience of violence that immerses the victim in the scene so profoundly that it precludes the kind of specular distance necessary for cognitive knowledge of what has happened. The mimetic theory explains the tendency of traumatized people to compulsively repeat their violent experiences in nightmares or repetitive forms of acting out by comparing the traumatic repetition to hypnotic imitation. Trauma is therefore interpreted as an experience of hypnotic imitation and identification that disables the victim's perceptual and cognitive apparatus to such an extent that the experience never becomes part of the ordinary memory system. This means that the amnesia held to be typical of psychical shock is explained as a kind of posthypnotic forgetting.

An aspect of the mimetic theory that should be stressed—and indeed is featured in the CIA's discussion of the resistant source's identification with the interrogator—is that mimesis or unconscious imitation leads to doubts about the veracity of the subject's testimony, since the identificatory process is thought to take place outside of, or dissociated from, ordinary awareness. Because the victim or detainee is imagined as thrust into a state of suggestive-hypnotic imitation, the

[16] Nina Sutton, *Bettelheim: A Life and Legacy* (Boulder, Colo., 1996), 527–29.

[17] Ruth Leys, *Trauma: A Genealogy* (Chicago, 2000).

mimetic theory cannot help worrying about confabulation, or the problem of testimonial authenticity. Finally, since the mimetic theory posits a moment of terrorized identification with the aggressor, prisoners are imagined as incorporating and therefore complicitously sharing the hostility directed toward themselves. The concept of survivor guilt finds its explanation in the mimetic theory by assuming that the identification is always ambivalent because structured by hate and love and hence is inherently rivalrous and guilty.

The second, or *antimimetic* theory, also tends to make imitative identification basic to the traumatic experience, but it understands imitation differently. The mimetic notion that victims of trauma are completely caught up or blindly immersed in the scene of shock is repudiated in favor of the opposite idea that the subject remains aloof from the traumatic experience, in the sense that he remains a spectator of the scene, which he can therefore see and represent to himself. The result is a tendency to relegate the problem of mimesis to a secondary position in order to establish a strict dichotomy between the autonomous subject and the external event. The antimimetic theory is compatible with, and often gives way to, the idea that trauma is a purely external event that befalls a fully constituted if passive subject. Whatever damage there may be to the victim's psychical integrity, there is in principle no problem about his eventually recovering from the trauma, though the process of bringing this about may be long and arduous. And in contrast to the mimetic theory's assumption of an unconscious identification with the aggressor, the antimimetic theory depicts violence as simply an assault from without. This has the advantage of portraying the victim of terror as in no way mimetically collusive with the violence directed against him, even as the absence of hypnotic complication as regards the reliability of his testimony shores up the notion of the unproblematic actuality of the traumatic event.

Des Pres's claim that if the victims of the camps did imitate the SS, they did so only for strategic purposes and always maintained an inner resistance to, or spectatorial distance from, the scene in question conforms to the antimimetic model of trauma. The antimimetic theory also lends itself to various positivistic interpretations of trauma epitomized by the neurobiological theories that have won widespread acceptance today. The American Psychiatric Association's decision in 1987 to remove survivor guilt from the criteria of PTSD may therefore be seen as exemplifying the antimimetic tendency of contemporary American psychiatry to suppress any reference to the mimetic dimension and to enforce instead a strict dichotomy between the autonomous subject and the external trauma. The framers of the definition of PTSD aimed at precisely such a dichotomy for forensic reasons: the division justified the claims of the anti-Vietnam war movement that veterans were suffering from combat-related psychiatric disorders against skeptics who doubted the need for a new diagnostic category. The PTSD committee of *DSM-III* tried to guarantee that strict dichotomy between subject and event by carefully defining the "stressor criterion."[18]

Is it possible that today's shame theory reflects a similar antimimetic tendency? In my book on trauma, I argued that from the end of the nineteenth century to the present there has been a continual oscillation between mimetic and antimimetic theories, indeed that the interpenetration of one by the other, or alternatively the collapse of one into the other, has been recurrent and unstoppable. Put slightly differently, my claim was that the concept of trauma has been structured historically in such a way as simultaneously to invite resolution in favor of one pole or the other of the mimetic-antimimetic oscillation and to resist and ultimately defeat all such attempts at resolution. The wager of the present study is that recent efforts to displace the concept of survivor guilt by that of shame may be understood as yet another manifestation of the fluctuation or tension between the mimetic and the antimimetic paradigms that has structured the genealogy of trauma from the start.

In this book I therefore plan to show that the concept of survivor guilt is inseparable from the notion of the subject's unconscious identification with the other. Conversely, I seek to demonstrate that, in spite of the apparent diversity of approaches proffered by today's theorists, shame theory conforms to the antimimetic pole of trauma theory because it displaces attention from the guilty subject's unconscious yielding to the enemy to the shamed subject's antimimetic consciousness of being seen. As a result, shame theory downplays the mimetic-immersive, interpersonal dynamic central to the formulation of guilt in order to depict shame as an experience of consciousness of the self when the individual becomes aware of being exposed to the diminishing or disapproving gaze of another. In other words, shame enacts a shift from the mimetic to the antimimetic by emphasizing the realm of the specular.

This, however, is not to say that the tension or oscillation between mimesis and antimimesis at work in the guilt-shame debate can be resolved into a simple opposition between a guilt concept governed exclusively and unproblematically by mimetic assumptions and a shame concept governed solely by antimimetic presuppositions. It has been my argument all along that the oscillation between mimetic and antimimetic tendencies in trauma theory can never be fully resolved.

---

[18] They did such a good job that the definition of PTSD was subsequently criticized for ignoring the fact that most people exposed to stressful events do not develop the disorder. In other words, the *DSM-III* definition was faulted for failing to take account of the subjective meaning of the trauma. The *DSM-IV* (1994) revision of PTSD aimed to rectify this shortcoming by explicitly including the "subjective appraisal" of the stressor in the new definition. In short, the antimimetic tendency of American psychiatry never even temporarily succeeded in eliminating the mimetic tendency—and vice versa. The subjectifying innovation of *DSM-IV* can also be understood as a response to entrenched veterans' pension rights for PTSD: the revised definition expanded those rights by allowing the subjective response to even a relatively trivial accident to count in the diagnosis.

Accordingly, we would expect those same tensions to surface within the theorizing of guilt itself, just as we would expect them to manifest themselves in the conceptualization of shame. Thus I shall show that the psychoanalytic explanation of survivor guilt is marked by aporias and inconsistencies that can best be understood as a legacy of unresolved and unresolvable tensions within the theorization of imitation defined simultaneously in mimetic and antimimetic terms. And we shall see that contemporary shame theory, which emphasizes the antimimetic pole of the mimetic-antimimetic oscillation, struggles to maintain a coherent antimimetic position. Nevertheless, I claim that the tension between mimesis and antimimesis that is internal to the conceptualization of both survivor guilt and shame does play out over time in the form of a general shift from a conceptualization of survivor guilt, understood in mimetic terms as involving the subject's unconscious identification with the other, to a conceptualization of shame that transforms passionate identifications into identity and in so doing posits a rigid dichotomy and specular distance between the autonomous subject and the external other. Accordingly, in this book I shall generally be less interested in tracking the inevitable mimetic-antimimetic tensions that arise within the discourses of guilt and shame than in charting the general shift *from* guilt *to* shame.

Moreover, I aim to demonstrate that whereas in the past the theorization of survivor guilt remained within an intentionalist or cognitivist paradigm of the emotions, current shame theory shares the positivist ambitions of the medical sciences by theorizing shame in antiintentionalist (or anticognitivist) terms. By common agreement, guilt concerns your actions, that is, what you do—or what you wish or fantasize you have done, since according to Freud the unconscious does not distinguish between the intention and the deed, the virtual and the actual. Equating intention with the deed, psychoanalysis maintains the link to intention and action that is held to be intrinsic to the notion of guilt.[19] Shame, however, is held to concern not your actions but who you are, that is, your deficiencies and inadequacies as a person as these are revealed to the shaming gaze of the other, a shift of focus from actions to the self that makes the question of personal identity of paramount importance. (It makes no difference to my argument in this regard whether the self is considered a unified, fixed essence or identity or whether,

---

[19] My claim in *Trauma* that, according to Freud's theorization of mimesis, a fundamental tendency toward primary identification precedes and gives rise to desire for an object, does not undo intentionalism. It only undoes a version of intentionalism that accords primordiality to a notion of desire as bound in some essential way to desired objects before some mediator—father, mother, teacher, friend—intervenes to tell what is desirable. If desire is mimetic before it is anything else, this means that it is first mobilized by an identificatory "model" to which it conforms. Thus the child in the famous "fort-da" game discussed by Freud in *Beyond the Pleasure Principle* is not (or not only) playing at losing an object of enjoyment when he throws away the spool but is playing at being his mother, and in so doing is identifying with her. On these points see Mikkel Borch-Jacobsen, *The Freudian Subject,* trans. Catherine Porter (Stanford, Calif., 1988), 26–48.

after Freud, Lacan, or deconstruction, the self is regarded in antiessentialist terms as fragmentary, destabilized, and unfixed.)

Accompanying such a shift of focus to the self, and as an alternative to an intentionalist account of the emotions, many of today's theorists define the affects, including shame, in materialist terms. According to them, shame is the result of inherited, neurophysiological responses of the body that are held to be independent of our intentions and wishes. As I showed in *Trauma,* these same materialist (or literalist) assumptions govern modern trauma theory as well, so that shame theory and trauma theory here overlap. In the works on shame I shall be discussing, the turn to materialism is partly a function of a general displacement of psychoanalysis by postpsychoanalytic and/or biological-evolutionary approaches to the study of human behavior. That displacement has been going on now for more than twenty years and amounts to a major conceptual and methodological paradigm shift. But even in the work of Agamben, for whom the theory of evolution is irrelevant, we find a similar materialist, antiintentionalist approach to shame. The general result is an account of shame that makes questions of agency, intention, and meaning beside the point and privileges instead issues of personal identity and difference.

The success of current shame theory, as I see it, can be explained by its ability to support and reinforce a self-declared postmodernist and posthistoricist commitment to replacing disputes or disagreements about intentions and meaning with an emphasis on who one is, or differences in personal experience. This development is as much a historical phenomenon as it is a theoretical one, and accordingly I conceive of my enterprise as a contribution to our understanding of that history. My book is not intended as a comprehensive study of the vicissitudes of guilt and shame in Western thought.[20] Rather, it is presented as a contribution to the understanding of the changing fortunes of survivor guilt and shame from the post–World War II period to the present. It is an effort to take a step back from the routine, almost somnambulistic way in which notions of shame have recently come to dominate discussions of trauma, violence, and the self in order to examine, in the mode of what might be called a "genealogy of the present," the steps by which the shift from guilt to shame has come about.

Some further remarks are in order. Since four of the five chapters of my book chart responses to survivors of trauma, including centrally survivors of the Holocaust, there is a clear sense in which my book can be understood as a contribution to the field of Holocaust and trauma studies. However, my goal is broader than that. By aiming to grasp the significance of the replacement of postwar notions of guilt by those of shame, my narrative as it unfolds simultaneously loosens

---

[20] For a superb analysis of the emergence of the concept of guilt in Western thought see Jean Delumeau, *Sin and Fear: The Emergence of a Western Guilt Culture, 13th–18th Centuries,* trans. Eric Nicholson (New York, 1990).

the connection to trauma as such—since the most influential writings on shame that I discuss in chapter 4 have little to do with questions of trauma—and expands the scope of the argument. In particular, my objective is to show that with few exceptions *all* the recent shame theorists I discuss, whether they are interested in trauma or not, are alike bound to a set of linked commitments—to antiintentionalism, materialism, and the primacy of personal identity or difference—that decisively alters the terms of the analysis. For what I have come to see is that the conflict between the mimetic and the antimimetic with which I began this project is part of a larger set of oppositions—between intentionalism or cognitivism versus antiintentionalism or anticognitivism, between antimaterialism versus materialism, and between identification versus identity—at work in general questions of interpretation today. What is new is my claim that there is a particular logic at work in the shift from guilt to shame, a logic according to which if you think that the emotions, including shame, are to be understood in nonintentionalist terms, then you are also committed to the idea that they are to be defined in material terms, indeed that they are a matter of personal differences such that what is important is not what you have done, or imagined you have done, but who you are. It seems to me that this logic, pervasive in emotion theory today, is unsound—empirically unsound, because as I shall try to show, the experimental evidence does not support a coherent antiintentionalist position, and theoretically unsound, because it means giving up disagreement about intention and meaning in favor of an interest in simply what an individual person experiences or feels, that is, in favor of questions of personal identity.

My book is not intended as an exhaustive study of psychiatric or institutional responses to survivors of the Holocaust, or as a detailed examination of German reparation law, or as a comprehensive history of psychotherapeutic approaches to the survivor, or as a thorough examination of laboratory experiments that touch on the question of shame, although it engages with aspects of all these topics. It is rather a work of intellectual history in which I focus in a systematic fashion on the shift from guilt to shame that has taken place in the United States in the post–World War II period in an attempt to evaluate the stakes of that change, a change amounting to a major paradigm change in concepts of affect, self, and personal agency.

My study is divided into five chapters. In chapter 1, "Survivor Guilt," I trace the post-Holocaust development of the concept of survivor guilt. I pay special attention to the contributions of those psychoanalysts who, encouraged by West Germany's new reparation laws, which recognized emotional disability as a basis for a compensation claim, tried to help victims of the Nazis make claims for restitution by establishing a "survivor syndrome" diagnosis that linked the victim's characteristic symptoms of persistent depression and guilt-ridden anxiety to his or her disastrous experiences during the war. In the course of my analysis I note that many of the figures I discuss, including Primo Levi, do not make a clear distinction between guilt and shame, treating the latter as a variant of the former—the present tendency to treat guilt and shame in binary terms is a recent development (I myself do not believe that these emotions are necessarily mutually exclusive). I also discuss some of the difficulties those same analysts experienced in theorizing survivor guilt coherently in mimetic-identificatory terms. I suggest that revisionist modifications in the Freudian approach to the traumatized subject introduced by Robert Jay Lifton, a psychiatrist recognized for his 1968 study of survivors of Hiroshima, disarticulated the concept of survivor guilt from that of identification with the aggressor in such a way that the connection between guilt and aggression was dissolved or at least attenuated and more traditional notions of individual responsibility and consciousness began to take over. I show that Lifton's ideas about guilt were taken up by critics who were opposed to the whole idea of a "survivor syndrome," with the result that his ideas were soon put to uses that were fundamentally hostile to the psychoanalytic enterprise.

Chapter 2, "Dismantling Survivor Guilt," centers on critiques of the concept of survivor guilt by Terrence Des Pres and others in the political context of the postwar controversy launched in the 1960s by Hannah Arendt and others over the question of Jewish "complicity" in the Holocaust. In his book *The Survivor* (1976), Des Pres claimed that the notion of survivor guilt ended up blaming camp prisoners because it implied they were collusive with perpetrator violence. Instead, Des Pres proposed a sociobiological definition of survivors as ethical and caring persons who, thanks to their biological endowment, had emerged from the camps with their integrity and minds intact. His critique belongs to that general movement in the human sciences in America that during the 1970s and 1980s displaced psychoanalysis from its previous position of importance. In particular, Des Pres crystallized a tendency in the wake of the Eichmann trial to question the authority of the Freudians to give a just portrait of the survivor. At the center of Des Pres's attack on the notion of survivor guilt was his account of survivors as prisoners who, if they were obliged to imitate the enemy for self-protection, did so not in the mode of an unconscious identification with the aggressor but in the mode of a conscious mimicry that concealed the victims' true wishes and feelings. Des Pres's recasting of imitation in antimimetic terms as deliberate simulation permitted a reevaluation of survivors not as neurotic or ill but as capable of resisting power by performatively disguising their true intentions. At the same time, by reinterpreting survival in terms of a biological "talent for life," Des Pres treated the human being's capacity for intentions as a function of his or her biological-corporeal endowment—in other words, he interpreted survival in materialist terms. Des Pres made use of Erving Goffman's dramaturgical ideas to support his arguments. Similar approaches to imitation governed sociological and psychoanalytic critiques of the notion of survivor guilt in the 1970s and 1980s.

Shame is not yet the dominant motif of the works I examine in this chapter, but the account of survival and the self that they offer helped set the stage for shame theory's rise to influence.

In chapter 3, "Image and Trauma," I turn to the American Psychiatric Association's decision in 1987 to drop survivor guilt as one of the diagnostic criteria for PTSD. The third, 1980 edition of the American Psychiatric Association's *Diagnostic and Statistical Manual* (*DSM-III*), which officially introduced the diagnosis of Posttraumatic Stress Disorder (PTSD), represented a revolution in the approach of American and hence worldwide psychiatry. Psychoanalytic norms that for thirty years or more had dominated the field were abandoned in favor of a more positivist and ostensibly atheoretical description and classification of mental disorders. The introduction of PTSD stimulated a large number of research projects designed to further clarify and operationalize the disorder. In this chapter I explore the importance of the concept of the traumatic "image" to the ongoing process of reformulation. In particular, I argue that the reconceptualization of PTSD in the 1980s around the *traumatic image*, defined as an externally caused mental content or "icon" uncontaminated by any mimetic, fictive, or fantasmatic dimension, made the notion of survivor guilt, which depended for its rationale on a now-discredited Freudian theory of identification with the aggressor, an incoherent element in the theory of posttraumatic stress, so that its elimination from those criteria made sense. This doesn't mean that the notion of survivor guilt completely disappeared from the ordinary or daily language of trauma, only that within psychiatry it now lacked any obvious theoretical justification. I therefore link the demise of survivor guilt in trauma theory to the coalescence of the question of traumatic violence around the concept of image. I shall focus on the work of several trauma theorists, including Mardi J. Horowitz, whose use of stress-inducing films to operationalize and objectivize trauma contributed to the formulation of posttraumatic stress. The chapter ends with a brief discussion of the ways in which shame has come to take the place of survivor guilt in recent discussions of PTSD.

In chapter 4, "Shame Now," I examine a variety of recent texts on shame in order to exhibit and critically assess the fundamental logic of shame theory today. In the course of my discussion I shall take into account a wide range of psychological, biological, and literary-critical works. I shall pay special attention to the postmodernist, postpsychoanalytic writings of literary critic Eve Kosofsky Sedgwick, in my view the most brilliant and articulate of recent shame theorists. Sedgwick is indebted to the work of psychologist Silvan Tomkins, who proposed an "affect program theory" of the emotions that defined the affects, including shame, in biological, antiintentionalist terms. Although Sedgwick presents the intentionalist or cognitivist theory of the emotions as the entrenched position she wants to challenge, I see things rather differently. In fact, the opposite seems to me true: versions of Tomkins's "affect program theory"—especially those associated with the work of Tomkins's followers Paul Ekman and Carroll E. Izard—have dominated modern psychological, if not philosophical, work on the emotions for many years now, and Sedgwick's recent commitment to Tomkins's work suggests that the influence of such theory has now spread to the humanities as well.

In this chapter the larger implications of my argument begin to emerge. Since neither Tomkins, Ekman, or Izard formulate their work on the affects in terms of trauma theory, the theme of trauma, which up to this point has marked my discussion of survivor guilt, recedes, at least for the moment (it returns in chapter 5). At the same time, my discussion broadens to include a discussion and critique of the general emotion theory associated with the work of Silvan Tomkins, and of the experiments performed by Ekman and others to support the new materialist approach to shame. This chapter, arguably the heart of my book, contains a detailed, critical (though by no means exhaustive) assessment of the arguments and evidence adduced in support of the antiintentionalist position in emotion theory. My aim is not only to say what I think is wrong or incoherent about the Tomkins-Ekman-Izard approach to the affects but to analyze the identitarian consequences of that approach as those consequences are especially made evident in the work of Sedgwick and her followers. The overall purpose of the chapter is thus to critique the antiintentionalist, materialist paradigm that governs modern shame theory and that has displaced the intentionalist paradigm that had previously informed the concept of survivor guilt.

In chapter 5, "The Shame of Auschwitz," I return to the theme of the Holocaust in order to analyze Giorgio Agamben's influential effort to dislodge the notion of survivor guilt from its position of importance in the literature of the Nazi camps in favor of a highly personal, but in the end representative, notion of shame. My goal is to demonstrate the similarities between Sedgwick's materialist and antiintentionalist approach to shame and Agamben's ideas. In other words, I aim to show that, in spite of an apparently very different intellectual agenda, Agamben's hostility to the idea of survivor guilt and his concomitant valorization of shame are based on similar ideas about the absence of intention and meaning in shame that we find developed by Sedgwick and many recent affect theorists. This entails a brief discussion of Agamben's ideas about testimony, in the course of which I shall also draw attention to the similarities between his materialist ideas about language and those of trauma theorists Shoshana Felman and Cathy Caruth.

One last point, which brings me back to where I began. Many Americans, including myself, would not hesitate to declare that they experience intense shame for the prisoner abuse scandal at Abu Ghraib. Nothing that is said critically about contemporary shame theory in the pages that follow is meant to criticize the view that shame can be an appropriate response to such situations.

Survivor Guilt

The Slap

ON THE eve of the evacuation of Auschwitz at the end of the war, Paul Steinberg nearly slapped a dying man. By then a well-protected, eighteen-year-old "veteran" whose cool and calculating survival techniques had both impressed and chilled fellow prisoner Primo Levi, Steinberg had been asked to help keep order in the barracks. Sensing that a Polish Jew "at end of his road" was defying his command to get out of his bunk and make his bed, Steinberg raised his hand to hit him. At the last moment, he tells us, he held back so that his hand just grazed the dying man's cheek. The memory of that banal incident, he reports in a memoir, haunted him all his life. The contagion had done its job and he had not escaped corruption. "In that world of violence, I'd made a gesture of violence, thus proving that I had taken my proper place there." As he observed, the Khmer Rouge had massacred their own brothers and sisters, the French soldiers had tortured people in Algeria, the Hutus had hacked the Tutsis to death, and he had slapped an old Polish Jew. During the 1960s, when trying to break free of his memories by drafting a novel in which his alter ego witnesses a scene that climaxes in a slap, Steinberg reports that he began to feel he was going mad—specifically, he feared that he would end up imitating the suicide that he regarded as the logical ending for his fictive hero. And toward the conclusion of his memoir, reflecting on Levi's portrait of him in the camps as a cold fish ferociously determined to do anything to stay alive, Steinberg expresses regret that, since Levi was now himself dead by suicide, he no longer has the chance to persuade Levi to change his verdict by showing him that there were "extenuating circumstances." "I'll never know whether I have the right to ask clemency of the jury," Steinberg ends. "Can one be so guilty for having survived?"[1]

In the figure of the slap, Steinberg condenses the central themes of this chapter: the sheer contagiousness of violence and the self-destructive guilt of the survivor. As he intuitively recognizes, survivor guilt is inseparable from the imitation of the aggressor. The victim becomes contaminated by the aggression directed against himself by identifying with it and passing on its sting.[2] "Domination is propagated by the dominated," Adorno wrote after the war with specific reference to the tendency of camp prisoners to identify with their executioners.[3] In memoir after memoir, survivors have repeatedly testified to the complicitous and guilty effects of that contagion. Yet throughout a long history, the notions of survivor guilt and identification with the aggressor have repeatedly caused trouble. Lawrence Langer has praised Levi for defending his fellow camp sufferers against unjust charges growing out of "stereotyped notions" of their ordeal, and for clearly defining the criminality of the killers and their supporters in language that "leaves the nature of their crimes unmistakable."[4] According to Langer, among the stereotyped ideas about survival that Levi criticized were notions of the nobility of suffering and romantic concepts that attributed survival to a blend of will, resistance, and inner discipline. Langer credits Levi with proposing instead the "sober and more practical principle" that survival depended on various degrees of collaboration with the enemy (PH, 35). He quotes Levi: "'Before discussing separately the motives that impelled some prisoners to collaborate to some extent with the Lager authorities, however, it is necessary to declare the imprudence of issuing hasty moral judgement on such human cases. Certainly, the greatest responsibility lies with the system, the very structure of the totalitarian state; the concurrent guilt on the part of the individual big and small collaborators (never likeable, never transparent!) is always difficult to evaluate'" (PH, 35).

Yet in broaching the question of collaboration and guilt in Levi's work, Langer fails to observe that when Levi discusses collaboration as a paradigm of the "incredibly complicated internal structure" of the Lager, "where the two camps of masters and servants both diverge and converge," he is explicitly considering the problem of the "servile imitation" of the victor that swept Paul Steinberg into complicity with the violence directed against him.[5] For in remarks Langer does not

---

[1] Paul Steinberg, *Speak You Also: A Survivor's Reckoning,* trans. Linda Coverdale with Bill Ford (New York, 2000), 125–31. Steinberg appears as "Henri" in Levi's chapter "The Drowned and the Saved," in *Survival in Auschwitz: The Nazi Assault on Humanity*, trans. Stuart Woolf (New York, 1993), 98–100.

[2] Elias Canetti's phrase, of course, from *Crowds and Power* (New York, 1984), 227.

[3] Theodor Adorno, *Minima Moralia: Reflections from a Damaged Life* (Thetford, Eng., 1978), 183.

[4] Lawrence L. Langer, *Preempting the Holocaust* (New Haven and London, 1988), 35; hereafter abbreviated *PH*.

[5] Primo Levi, *The Drowned and the Saved* (New York, 1989), 42; hereafter abbreviated *DS*.

cite, Levi reflects on the tendency of the oppressed to identify with their oppressors. "Finally, power was sought by the many among the oppressed who had been contaminated by their oppressors and unconsciously strove to identify with them," he observes. "*This mimesis, this identification or imitation, or exchange of roles between oppressor and victim, has provoked much discussion. True and invented, disturbing and banal, acute and stupid things have been said, it is not virgin terrain; on the contrary it is a badly plowed field, trampled and torn up*" (*DS*, 48, my emphasis). In the next paragraph Levi goes on to state that, although he does not know whether there lurks a murderer in the depths of his unconscious, he does know that he was neither a guilty victim nor a murderer. Yet he does not quit the ambiguous terrain of collaboration, identification, and guilt, as it seems Langer would like him to do, for he adds:

> I know that in the Lager, and more generally on the human stage, everything happens, and that therefore the single example proves little. Having said all this quite clearly, and reaffirmed that confusing the two roles [of victim and perpetrator] means wanting to becloud our need for justice at its foundation, I should make a few more remarks.
>
> It remains true that in the Lager, and outside, there exist gray, ambiguous persons, ready to compromise. The extreme pressure of the Lager tends to increase their ranks; they are the rightful owners of a quota of guilt (which grows apace with their freedom of choice), and besides this they are the vectors and instruments of the system's guilt. (*DS*, 49)

Among the gray and ambigous persons Levi goes on to discuss is the "symbolic and compendiary figure" (*DS*, 68) of Chaim Rumkowski, the Jew who presided over the Lodz ghetto in Poland, and whose imitation or identification with the rhetorical style of Hitler or Mussolini, perhaps deliberate, perhaps unconscious (*DS*, 50), was so complete, Levi suggests, that he must have come to believe he *was* a messiah, "a savior of his people, whose welfare, at least at intervals, he must certainly have desired" (*DS*, 64). "Paradoxically," Levi comments, "his identification with the oppressor alternates, or goes hand in hand, with an identification with the oppressed, because, as Thomas Mann says, man is a mixed-up creature. He becomes all the more confused, we might add, the more he is subjected to tensions: at that point he evades our judgment, just as a compass goes wild at the magnetic pole" (*DS*, 64). Levi goes on to note that a story like this is "not self-contained" but rather sums up in itself the entire theme of the gray zone and "leaves one dangling. It shouts and clamors to be understood, because in it one perceives a symbol, as in dreams, and the signs of heaven" (*DS*, 66–67). The urgency and threat that emanates from Rumkowski's story is that "we are all mirrored in Rumkowski, his ambiguity is ours, it is our second nature, we hybrids molded from clay and spirit. . . . Willingly or not we come to terms with power, forgetting that we are all in the ghetto, that the ghetto is walled in, that outside the ghetto reign the lords of death, and that close by the train is wait-ing" (*DS*, 69).[6]

It is evident from these passages that Levi's concept of the gray zone is inti-mately connected to the notion of mimetic identification, and that when he says that the mimetic identification of the oppressed with the oppressor has already provoked "much discussion," he is acknowledging his familiarity with at least some of the large body of literature on the notion of mimetic identification and the concentration camp victim that Langer, in his haste to align Levi with his own hostility to psychological and clinical approaches to the survivor, is unwilling to engage. Moreover, if, as Levi tells us, "invented," "banal," and "stupid" things have been said about identification or imitation, it is also the case that for him "true," "disturbing," and "acute" things have been said about it as well.[7] Indeed, as he himself stated, a number of his short stories take identification with the ag-gressor and survivor guilt as their theme.[8] Furthermore, as anyone who studies the matter discovers, the theme of identification is inseparable from that of sur-vivor guilt, a subject on which Levi also wrote with feeling. When writing on this topic Levi did not make a clear distinction between guilt and shame: although he titled his most important discussion of this topic "Shame," he treats guilt and shame as synonymous terms. (Later, in chapter 4, I shall suggest ways in which Levi's apparent inability to distinguish between guilt and shame might be re-solved.) "What guilt?" Levi asks in *The Drowned and the Saved.* And answers: "When all was over, the awareness emerged that we had not done anything, or not enough, against the system into which we had been absorbed" (*DS*, 76–77). Speaking next about the question of resistance in the Lagers, he observes that on a rational plane, there should not have been much for the survivor to be ashamed of,

[6] For a brilliant fictional re-creation of Rumkowski's life and times see Leslie Epstein, *King of the Jews* (New York, 1979).

[7] For Levi's criticisms of psychoanalysis see *The Drowned and the Saved,* 84–85; Levi, *The Voice of Memory: Interviews, 1961–1987,* ed. Maro Belpoliti and Robert Gordon, trans. Robert Gordon (New York, 2001), 223–24 (hereafter abbreviated *VM*); and Miriam Anissimov, *Primo Levi: Tragedy of an Optimist* (Woodstock, N.Y., 1999), 374, 399.

[8] "I feel in my stomach, in my guts, something I haven't quite digested, connected to the theme of the *Lager* . . . After all the polemic about the identification between victim and oppressor, the theme of guilt, the extreme ambiguity of that place, the grey band that separated the oppressed from the oppressors. I've published a number of short stories in *La Stampa* and all of them have these themes in mind" (Levi, *The Voice of Memory,* 131). In one essay Levi analyzed Jack London's famous *The Call of the Wild* (1903), the story of the kidnapping of a domesticated dog, Buck, from his owner's splendid estate in Santa Clara to Yukon, where he becomes a starved member of a sled team working for gold prospectors in the gold rush of 1897. In his desire for primacy Buck successfully challenges the authority of the chief dog by killing him in a fight and becomes the new, brutal team leader. By using the term "Kapo" to describe the now vi-ciously powerful dog, Levi treats London's story as an allegory of what he had witnessed in Auschwitz (Primo Levi, "Jack London's Buck," in *The Mirror Maker: Stories and Essays* [New York, 1989], 149–53).

but shame persisted nevertheless, especially for the few bright examples of those who had the strength and possibility to resist. I spoke about this in the chapter, "The Last," in *Survival in Auschwitz*, where I described the public hanging of a resistor before a terrified and apathetic crowd of prisoners. This is a thought that then just barely grazed us, but that returned "afterward": you too could have, you certainly should have. And this is a judgment that the survivor believes he sees in the eyes of those (especially the young) who listen to his stories and judge with facile hindsight, or who perhaps feel cruelly repelled. Consciously or not, he feels accused and judged, compelled to justify and defend himself. (*DS*, 77–78)

"More realistic," is how Levi characterizes the even more oppressive *self*-accusation of having "failed in terms of human solidarity" (*DS*, 78). He states in this connection that if few survivors feel guilty about acts of commission—about having deliberately damaged, robbed, or beaten a companion—"almost everybody feels guilty of having omitted to offer help" (*DS*, 78). He remembers with "a certain relief" that he once tried to give courage to an eighteen-year-old Italian who had just arrived in the camp; but he also remembers with "disquiet" that much more often he "shrugged his shoulders impatiently" at other requests, because he had deeply assimilated the principal rule of the place, which made it "mandatory that you take care of yourself first of all" (*DS*, 78–79).

At this juncture Levi tells the story of how, at a time when the absence of drinkable water in the camp made thirst a horrible torment, in the cellar where he had been assigned to work, he found, in a two-inch pipe running along the wall, less than a liter of water, which he was able to extract and share with his closest friend, Alberto. But he did not share the water with another friend, Daniele, who glimpsed the truth and many months later reproached Levi: "Why the two of you and not I?" (*DS*, 80–81). In apparent contradiction of his former claim that he was a "guiltless victim" Levi now admits to a paradoxical sense of shame. He is unable to decide whether that shame is justified but reports that until Daniele's death after the war the veil of that act of omission stood between the two of them. Levi asks: "Are you ashamed because you are alive in place of another? And in particular, of a man more generous, more sensitive, more useful, wiser, worthier of living than you? You cannot block out such feelings" (*DS*, 81).[9] Levi rejects the opinion of a friend who claimed that Levi's survival was not the work of chance but of Providence, marking him as man of the elect preordained for some good, and in a passage that returns to the theme of collaboration and is among the bleakest he ever wrote, he declares:

Such an opinion seemed monstrous to me. It pained me as when one touches an exposed nerve, and kindled the doubt I spoke of before: I might be alive in the place of an-

---

[9] For Levi's torments over the incident see also Levi, *The Voice of Memory*, 254; and Anissimov, *Primo Levi: Tragedy of an Optimist*, 162–63.

other, at the expense of another; I might have usurped, that is, in fact, killed. The "saved" of the Lager were not the best, those predestined to do good, the bearers of a message: what I had seen and lived through, proved the exact contrary. Preferably the worst survived, the selfish, the violent, the insensitive, the collaborators of the "gray zone," the spies. It was not a certain rule (there were none, nor are there certain rules in human matters), but it was nevertheless a rule. I felt innocent, yes, but enrolled among the saved and therefore in permanent search of a justification in my own eyes and those of others. The worst survived, that is, the fittest; the best all died" (*DS*, 82).

But just as Langer sidesteps the mimetic-identificatory dimension of Levi's thought, so he rejects the associated concept of survivor guilt. "The question of 'survivor guilt' continues to haunt us like a ghost that will not die," he comments. "The psychological community, especially in America, has made the idea an unchallenged premise about survival experience. But in an unpublished paper . . . Norwegian psychiatrist and Auschwitz survivor Leo Eitinger argued that 'most survivors had the same self-reproaches one can hear in all cases of losses: If I had done this or that or if I had not done this or that, perhaps he or she would have lived today.' Such 'guilt,' which Eitinger prefers to call self-reproach, is not specific to survivors but represents a common human response" (*PH*, 202–3, n. 9).[10] How Eitinger's remarks are meant to tell against the notion of survivor guilt is not clear—if anything they seem to confirm its basic premises, for we shall see that it is because Freud regarded identification with the aggressor as a standard psychic defense against loss that the notion could be applied to the survivor's experiences.

Langer is hostile to the idea of survivor guilt in part because it seems to him that it deflects blame from the real culprits onto the victims themselves (*PH*, 133–34, 141, 169, 183). More generally, Langer rejects the notion of survivor guilt because he thinks it encourages a tendency to psychologize the victim by focusing attention on his inner conflicts at the expense of condemning the perpetrators and the violent world they created. He includes the entire language of trauma and the psychological sciences in his critique (*PH*, 68). (When Langer privileges the notion of shame over guilt in Levi's writings, the idea seems to be that shame is preferable to guilt because it shifts attention to questions of public humiliation and away from issues of subjective state or complicity.) For Langer, the situation of extremity is one of such radical coercion that the victim's behavior is entirely determined by external assault, and notions of moral "choice" and "responsibility" cease to have any meaning: "Powerless men, virtually unarmed, were forced by circumstances and the egoism of the survival impulse to choose uncertain life over certain death. Their 'choice' certified the doom of the Jews. Who can blame

[10] Langer cites an unpublished paper Eitinger presented at a conference sponsored by the U.S. Holocaust Memorial Museum Research Center in December 1993.

them? Who can praise them? 'Choice,' 'blame,' and 'praise' join that expanding list of free words that died at Auschwitz, leaving no successors."[11] Or as he also puts it: "Is the choice between two horrors any choice at all?" (*VS*, 43). And again: "[T]he Nazi mind created a world where meaningful choice disappeared and the hope for survival was made to depend on equally impossible alternatives" (*VS*, 47).[12]

According to these formulations, the only alternative to the condition of radical constraint in extremity is the situation of an individual who, outside extreme conditions, lacks curbs of any kind and is therefore in full possession of freedom. What seems hyperbolic or "metaphysical" about Langer's stark opposition between, on the one hand, the camp prisoner's complete passivity, and on the other hand, the free individual's pure spontaneity, is that it not only makes the camps radically discontinuous with other situations—indeed he claims that the Holocaust is so disconnected from what went before that it "stops" history (*VS*, 45)—but that it also imagines life outside the camps in completely idealized terms, as if outside the Lager people are never confronted with constraints or forced to make difficult choices between dire alternatives. Moreover, the same dichotomy between utter passivity and perfect freedom means that, rejecting the notion of the victim's guilt feelings as paradoxical or contradictory, Langer can only conceptualize guilt in terms of objective actions and is incapable of taking seriously the possibility that someone may be objectively innocent *and* nevertheless feel guilty. His commitment to the idea that in extremity the camp prisoner's actions are entirely determined by external circumstances and his denial of the relevance of the psychological sciences make him deny the existence of that unconscious fantasy of yielding to those in power that, according to Ferenczi and other psychoanalytic theorists, comes to the rescue of the victim in situations of helplessness.

Langer praises Levi for accepting the inevitability of collaboration under conditions of harsh oppression (*PH*, 35) in terms suggesting that Levi fully endorsed a similar dualism of determinism versus spontaneity. But in his reflections on the meaning of survivor guilt, Levi is more nuanced than Langer. Levi argues emphatically that the executioners should never be confused with the victims and that the perpetrators deserved to be brought to justice. Moreover, he recognizes that the behavior of the mass of camp prisoners was rigidly preordained by a daily struggle for life which reduced moral choices to "zero," with the result that some survived only by luck. He speaks with compassion in this regard of the "extreme

[11] Langer, *Versions of Survival: The Holocaust and the Human Spirit* (New York, 1982), 95; hereafter abbreviated *VS*.

[12] Cf. Langer's *Holocaust Testimonies: The Ruins of Memory* (New Haven and London, 1991), where he says that the legacy of the Holocaust not just for the victims but for us as well is the destruction of human agency; identity is thus forged by "circumstances rather than by values" (199).

case" (*DS*, 50) of the members of the *Sonderkommandos* or "Special Squads" at Auschwitz and other extermination camps—those prisoners, largely Jews, who were forced to run the crematoria and whose "state of compulsion following an order" thwarted the "need and our ability to judge" (*DS*, 58). But that does not prevent Levi from acknowledging as an ineluctable fact of survivor experience the existence of a noncontradictory combination of objective innocence and subjective feelings of guilt.

When an interviewer raised the "delicate question" of the identification between victim and executioner and the survivor's feeling of guilt, Levi replied that all survivors came out of the Lager with a sense of "unease" and to this unease "we applied the label 'sense of guilt'" (*VM*, 253). It was not that the survivor felt the guilt that should be felt by the executioner, he explained. But to some degree, he believed, "all of us or most of us have felt a certain unease at the thought that so many died who were at least as worthy as us, if not more so . . . It is the feeling of being alive in some one else's stead . . . Then there is also a sense of guilt for perhaps not having done everything one could have done, for instance, putting up more resistance . . . In any case, *the fact of being victims is not contradicted by these feelings of guilt*" (*VM*, 254, my emphasis).[13]

Levi's insight—that for the survivor being a victim does not preclude the experience of guilt—is compatible with psychoanalysis, which recognizes something that is missing from Langer's discussion of the survivor, namely, a third term between the purely objective and the purely subjective, or between external reality and inner consciousness—call it psychic reality or the unconscious—that serves to collapse the distinction between actually doing something bad and unconsciously wishing or intending to do so, and thus allows for the coexistence in the survivor of objective innocence and a subjective feeling of culpability. In other words, Levi's insight is compatible with the psychoanalytic notion of survivor guilt.

She Demanded to Be Killed Herself and
Bitten to Death

Some commentators have objected that the notion of survivor guilt was simply a projection onto the survivor of American psychoanalysts' own feelings of guilt for having lived through the war in the safety of the United States. Although this seems much too simplistic, it is true that the idea of survivor guilt as a theoretical-therapeutic concept owes its importance in the United States largely to postwar psychoanalysis, as well as to the impact of the West German indemnification laws which, starting in 1953, for the first time permitted survivors to

---

[13] All emphases in quotations are in the original unless otherwise noted.

claim compensation for medical damages resulting from the Nazi persecution. A number of physicians helped victims prepare legal claims and in the process of interviewing and dealing with hundreds of cases began the task of conceptualizing the psychological consequences of the trauma of the Holocaust. Many specialists, especially those representing the West German authorities, were committed to organic approaches to mental illness, and hence dismissed victims' claims to distress as *Rentenneurose*—neuroses produced simply by the patient's desire for a pension. To the dismay of many American psychoanalysts, other experts in both Germany and the United States exploited psychoanalytic theory in order to argue that, since an individual's personality was formed by the age of six, the problems of the survivor could not be attributed to the concentration-camp experience.[14] These forensic issues played an important role in the emerging literature on the survivor, as the psychiatrists and psychoanalysts most closely involved in assisting patients with their restitution claims made it their task to prove the existence of a specific disorder, variously called "repatriation neurosis," "concentration camp syndrome," or "survivor syndrome," that could be shown to be directly associated with the trauma of the camps.[15] They also struggled to conceptualize the psychodynamics of the survivor syndrome, which in the intensity and severity of its symptoms seemed to go beyond received understandings of the traumatic neuroses and indeed to challenge many established psychoanalytic concepts.

One of the principal architects of the concept of survivor guilt was the American psychoanalyst William G. Niederland, a figure largely neglected today except for occasional references to his influential studies of Freud's famous Schreber case.[16] In 1961 Niederland wrote a pioneering and much cited article on emotional disorders in survivors of the Holocaust that set the stage for extensive discussions throughout the 1960s of the psychiatric consequences of the Nazi per-

[14] For an especially outspoken condemnation of the reparation process see K. R. Eissler, "Perverted Psychiatry?" *American Journal of Psychiatry* 123 (1967): 1352–58.

[15] For the development of these terms see especially Elmer Luchterhand, "Early and Late Effects of Imprisonment in Nazi Concentration Camps: Conflicting Results in Survivor Research," *Social Psychiatry* 5 (1970): 104; and *Massive Psychic Trauma,* ed. Henry Krystal (New York, 1968), hereafter abbreviated as *MPT;* George M. Kren, "The Holocaust Survivor and Psychoanalysis," in *Healing Their Wounds: Psychotherapy with Holocaust Survivors and Their Families,* ed. Paul Marcus and Alan Rosenberg (New York, 1989), 3–21; and Anna Ornstein, "Survival and Recovery," *Psychoanalytic Inquiry* 5 (1985): 99–130. From large literature on the West German reparation process, I have been particularly impressed by Christian Pross's brilliant discussion, *Paying for the Past: The Struggle over Reparations for Surviving Victims of the Nazi Terror* (Baltimore, 1988). It is worth emphasizing that psychiatrists and psychoanalysts needed to come up with a diagnosis that had credibility as a disease entity in the compensation process, since Germany did not pay for loss of freedom or property or any other damages suffered by non-German Jews: only demonstrable physical or mental damage to health entitled them to reparations.

[16] For the link between Niederland's work on the Holocaust survivor and his work on the Schreber case, in which he emphasized the role of traumatic reality or the "kernel of truth" in the production of the patient's psychotic symptoms, see *MPT,* 127; and Robert Jay Lifton, *Death in Life: Survivors of Hiroshima*

secution. The West German restitution authorities frequently denied a claim for compensation on the grounds that there was no causal relationship between the claimant's present sufferings and his or her disastrous experiences during the war. In one case, the claim of a victim who been brutally mistreated during the course of almost six years of imprisonment in various concentration camps and had lost his parents and almost all his other relatives to extermination (amounting to nearly eighty people) was summarily rejected on the grounds that "[t]he claimant was nineteen years of age when he was first exposed to the procedures of the Nazi persecution. It cannot be assumed that their psychic working through in a person can give rise to lasting anxiety symptoms or other psychological manifestations. It must therefore be denied that there are any disturbances in the claimant attributable to the emotional experiences connected with the persecution." (*MPT*, 10) In outspoken condemnation of the West German restitution authorities Niederland set out to describe the array of disorders that could regularly be observed in survivors and that he believed could be directly attributed to their Holocaust experiences.[17]

Those disorders included a clinical picture or psychological "imprint" ("PS,"

(Chapel Hill and London, 1991), 513; hereafter abbreviated *DL*. Niederland (1904–93), the son of an orthodox rabbi, was born in Germany and trained in medicine before fleeing the Nazis in Germany and setting up a private psychiatric practice in Milan, Italy. After the signing of the Italian-German military alliance in 1939, he fled once again, first to a refugee camp in England and then to New York. There he underwent formal psychoanalytic training, maintained a private practice, and served on the psychiatric staffs of various institutions, all of which had programs for the treatment and rehabilitation of survivors of the Nazi persecution. For a valuable discussion of Niederland's life and work see Wenda Focke, *William Niederland: Psychiater Der Verfolgten, Seine Zeit, Sein Leben, Sein Werk, Ein Porträt* (Würzburg, 1992).

[17] William G. Niederland, "The Problem of the Survivor. Part I: Some Remarks on the Psychiatric Evaluation of Emotional Disorders in Survivors of Nazi Persecution," *Journal of the Hillsdale Hospital* 10 (1961): 233–47; hereafter abbreviated "PS." In addition to studying Niederland's published writings, I have been able to examine several of the many unpublished psychiatric evaluations Niederland prepared for the United Restitution Organization in New York and other agencies, located in the archives of the Leo Baeck Institute for the Study of the History and Culture of German-speaking Jewry, New York. In those evaluations, Niederland challenged the West German restitution authorities who had denied pension benefits to claimants on the grounds that the latter had suffered from constititutional or endogenous or hereditary problems *prior* to the persecution, and hence that the camp experience could not have played a causal role in the claimants' presenting difficulties. In response, Niederland emphasized the patients' normality and good health before the persecution and attempted to link their symptoms of depression, anxiety, sleeplessness, nightmares, social isolation, and various psychosomatic and other disorders to their specific experiences of persecution. He especially stressed the centrality of survivor guilt. Thus in the earliest evaluation I have seen, dating to 1961, Niederland observed that the claimant's partly conscious, partly unconscious "survivor guilt" (*Ueberlebensschuld*) appeared as a psychopathic symptom only *after* the survivor's liberation from the camps, when it became clear to her that her relatives had not survived. I have also consulted William Niederland's *Folgen der Verfolgung: Das Uberlebenden-Syndrom, Seelenmord* (Frankfurt am Main, 1980), which includes several of Niederland's psychiatric evaluations.

236), variously named "postconcentration camp syndrome," "chronic reactive depression," or "depression due to uprooting," characterized by a "pervasive depressive mood with morose behavior and a tendency to withdrawal, general apathy alternating with occasional short-lived angry outbursts, feelings of helplessness and insecurity, lack of initiative and interest, prevalence of self-deprecatory attitudes and expressions" ("PS," 237). In extreme cases, Niederland described a "'living corpse'" appearance he attributed to the fact that most survivors had lived among the dead and dying for years, that they were in a sense themselves "walking or prospective corpses" and had survived only because they had been able to live the existence of a "'walking corpse'" while their fellow inmates had succumbed ("PS," 237). In addition, Niederland described a "severe and persevering guilt complex, of far-reaching pathological significance" ("PS," 237), to which he devoted a large part of his article. Like other victims of trauma, survivors of the camps also suffered from a host of cognitive, memory, sleep, psychosomatic, and other disorders, including anxiety and agitation resulting in insomnia, nightmares, fears of renewed persecution that often culminated in paranoid ideas, personality changes, and fully developed psychotic or psychoticlike disturbances with delusional or semidelusional symptoms, morbid brooding, complete inertia, stuporous or agitated behavior. Here also depressive features usually dominated the clinical picture.[18] He deliberately omitted mental symptoms due to organic brain damage, cerebral concussion, and other forms of maltreatment.[19]

Niederland emphasized the importance in many cases, especially from the

---

[18] Niederland later took pride in coming up with the term "survivor syndrome." "As you may know," he wrote in 1981, "I coined the the very term 'survivor syndrome' as early as 1961 and introduced it as a new clinical entity in the professional literature with my further publications . . . In DSM-III it has now become the 'Delayed Stress Syndrome,' in a little different wording and phrasing." Letter to Dr. Gary Leter, March 4, 1981, William G. Niederland Papers, Library of Congress Manuscript Division, Container 2, Folder L.

[19] Norwegian and Danish authors tended to attribute the concentration camp syndrome to biological causes, such as organic brain damage or the effects of starvation, rather than to psychological traumata of the kind emphasized by American psychiatrists such as Niederland. Indeed, Leo Eitinger, a physician and survivor of various concentration camps, including Auschwitz, and participant in the Norwegian research efforts, claimed that his group of researchers was unable to find in the surviving Norwegian prisoners any of the guilt feelings described by so many American experts. He attributed the differences to the different fates of Norwegian and Jewish survivors: as non-Jews the former had been treated brutally but had not faced extermination and were moreover treated as heroes on their return, whereas Jewish survivors had experienced greater hardships, had lost everything, and faced a hostile world on liberation. The debate can be followed in Leo Eitinger, *Concentration Camp Survivors in Norway and Israel* (Oslo, 1964); and Leo Eitinger, "The Concentration Camp Syndrome: An Organic Brain Syndrome?" *Integrative Psychiatry* 3 (1985): 115–26, with comments by Lawrence G. Kolb, Niederland, and others. In the latter publication, Niederland stated: "Certainly organic damage may well be a factor and must be taken into account. However, the 'survivor syndrome' results from the overwhelming psychological traumatization sustained during the concentration camp experience, life in agonizing and precarious hideouts, total loss of family members, and so on" (123).

point of view of compensation claims, of a relatively symptom-free interval be-tween the liberation or later discharge from Displaced Persons hospitals in Eu-rope and the development of new symptoms, usually after a period of months or years following the patient's arrival in the United States. Legitimate indemnifica-tion had often been denied because of the lack of symptoms during this interval. But Niederland regarded such a symptom-free interval as characteristic of the psychical effects of persecution, especially among those victims who were the only or near-only survivors of their families and who consequently carried within themselves a terrible burden of guilt, first from the loss through extermination of their loved ones and then from their ever-present conscious or unconscious dread of punishment for having survived when those loved ones did not. Nieder-land suggested that as long as such survivors could tell themselves during the years after liberation that some of their missing family members might still miracu-lously reappear, and as long as they were exposed to the many adjustment prob-lems and hardship difficulties following their arrival in America, such patients re-mained relatively free of symptoms and self-punishing tendencies. But when in the end they had to recognize that there was no hope that the lost relatives would return, and when they finally appeared to be settled and even adjusted to their new lives, they might break down with some of the symptoms he had described. Niederland claimed that failure to appreciate the significance of the symptom-free interval, as well as the role of denial and memory disturbances, meant that inex-perienced or impatient medical examiners were prone to miss the crucial ele-ments in the traumatization picture and to deny the role of persecution in such cases.

To illustrate his findings, Niederland described the case of a woman, born in Poland, who had been a victim of the Nazis. After surviving the ghetto, forced la-bor, and several concentration camps, including Auschwitz, where she had lost her parents and four siblings, at liberation she had married and in the late 1940s had arrived in the States where, apparently healthy, she had settled in Brooklyn with her husband and two children. In 1952 the woman had suddenly fallen ill with serious psychotic problems after the outbreak of a small fire in the basement of her apartment house. The fire had been promptly extinguished, but the patient had had to be hospitalized. The patient's claim for compensation had been re-jected by the German authorities on the grounds that " 'true mental diseases are of endogenous origin' " ("PS," 240), which is to say that her symptoms were un-connected to her victimization. But Niederland on appeal argued that the pa-tient's symptoms could be directly attributed to her camp experiences:

> [T]he patient's acute *breakdown occurred when she saw the smoke* of the fire coming
> from the basement through the window. She then wanted to throw her children out of the
> window in order *to rescue them from the danger of the invading smoke and fire,* person-

ified by her delusionally as the invading Nazis. She said she could not look at fire or smoke, since *it reminded her of the death of her parents in the Auschwitz gas chambers.* She accused herself of having caused her parents' death, became hallucinatory, afraid of her dead sister, and *demanded to be killed herself and bitten to death.* It thus became clear that . . . the outbreak of the disease in 1952 was . . . dynamically connected with her persecution experiences, since the full delusional content centering about smoke, gas, fire, death, killing, and being killed was directly derived from and pointed to the patient's life under Nazi rule, with most of her delusional fantasies focused on the Auschwitz crematorium. There both her parents as well as her four brothers and sisters had been put to death, while she—also first in Auschwitz and then in other camps—had survived. ("PS," 240)

For Niederland the case was exemplary precisely because it revealed the psychodynamics of survivor guilt and its relation to the symptom-free interval. According to him, the belatedness of the survivor's symptoms, erupting as they did only after a period of years and as a consequence of a precipitating external event, was characteristic of the survivor syndrome. He suggested that the victim had suffered from such an intolerable burden of guilt for surviving that she had made every effort to repress her feelings. The hardships and uncertain living conditions through the first years of liberation, and the subsequent difficulties of emigration, had also bolstered her attempt at repression. The repression was reinforced by the magically sustained expectation or hope that some of her dead family members might still return. But when the guilt erupted into consciousness, in this case owing to the precipitating event of the basement fire, it manifested itself in feelings of self-accusatory depression, inner misery, and pain, as well as in feelings of being persecuted, attacked, and hated.[20] In the patient's extraordinary demand that she be killed and bitten to death, Niederland felt that the victim's enormous tragedy became strikingly apparent. Without being able to prove it, "because no physician would or perhaps should go to such exploratory depths in these tortured people without inviting catastrophe" ("PS," 242), he daringly sug-

[20] William G. Niederland, comments as a discussant of a paper by Klaus D. Hoppe, "The Psychodynamics of Concentration Camp Victims," *Psychoanalytic Forum* 1 (1966): 8; hereafter abbreviated "PC." Psychoanalysts and psychiatrists offered a variety of explanations for the "symptom-free interval." These included the idea that the missing "bridge symptoms" could be reconsructed in all cases; the absorption of such "bridge symptoms" by masochistic traits or somatic complaints; the absence of such a symptom-free interval in child survivors with the consequent suggestion that its presence in adults was due to the greater strength of adult egos in the liberation period; and the role of fantasies about the return of deceased relatives in delaying the full impact of survivor guilt (*MPT,* passim). For skeptical views of the symptom-free interval and the further suggestion that the symptoms were entirely a product of the psychiatrist's "suggestions," see Elmer Luchterhand, "Early and Late Effects of Imprisonment in Nazi Concentration Camps," *Social Psychiatry* 5 (1970): 105; and Isaac Kanter, "Social Psychiatry and the Holocaust," *Journal of Psychology and Judaism* 1 (1986): 55–66.

gested that the reference to biting was an almost direct allusion to cannibalism, "possibly the mode of survival which alone helped the patient to stay alive" ("PS," 242). He quoted the words of Paul Friedman, one of the first psychiatrists to survey the postconcentration camp scene in Europe: "'One cannot live for years in a world in which cannibalism becomes a reality, in which one is forced at the point of a gun to eat one's own feces, without profound internal adjustments . . . without [being] reverted to a primitive, narcissistic stage of development'" ("PS," 242).[21] "The factor of *guilt,* usually is an ongoing and unsettling process . . . in the whole survivor pathology. The apparently paradoxical problem of guilt in survivor populations . . . has perhaps not been sufficiently considered in the dynamics of these patients, much less in the forensic-psychiatric evaluation of their conditions for the German compensation courts," Niederland commented. "It is indeed one of the most bitter ironies in this situation, so replete with tragedy and bitterness, that feelings of guilt accompanied by shame, self-condemnatory tendencies and self-accusations should be experienced by the *victims* of the persecution, and apparently much less (if at all) by the perpetrators of it . . . [F]rom my work with hundreds of persecution survivors, I know their feelings of guilt and shame are of the most profound order and stand at the bottom of many of their clinical manifestations" ("PC," 80).[22]

In a series of subsequent articles, Niederland repeatedly drew attention to the role of guilt in the survivor's emotional problems. For example, in a paper of 1964 criticizing the German indemnification process, he reviewed the growing American and European psychiatric literature on the survivor syndrome and again related the characteristic depressive and psychotic symptoms to the patient's persecution ex-

---

[21] Niederland cites Paul Friedman, "Some Aspects of Concentration Camp Psychology," *American Journal of Psychiatry* 105 (1949): 601–5, but the reference to cannibalism comes from a related paper by Friedman, "The Effects of Imprisonment," *Acta Medica Orientalia* 7 (1948): 164. For another early postliberation report of cannibalism among Belsen inmates see M. Niremberski, "Psychological Investigation of a Group of Internees at Belsen Camp," *Journal of Mental Science* 92 (1946): 66.

[22] I note that, as is true of other analysts concerned with Holocaust survivors at this time, Niederland does not appear to distinguish between guilt and shame. It is a sign of Freud's influence that Niederland and others provide relatively systematic accounts of the psychodynamics of guilt based on Freud's ideas, but that the notion of shame remains unthematized and untheorized by them, in fact seems to be used—when it is used—as almost synonymous with guilt. However, among the sources on which Niederland drew for his analysis of the survivor syndrome was an article by Stanley Rosenman who, in a discussion of natural disasters that took the pervasiveness of guilt feelings in the victims as a given, explained survivor guilt as a result of the victim's tendency to unconsciously assimilate the external traumatic force or event to the father or other significant figure with whom the subject then identifies, thereby incorporating the aggression in the mode of a chastising superego. Rosenman distinguished shame from guilt by interpreting shame in spectatorial terms as the emotion experienced at the exposure of some shameful aspect of the self to the gaze of the other. We shall see these distinctions resurfacing in recent discussions of shame (chapter 4). Stanley Rosenman, "The Paradox of Guilt in Disaster Victim Populations," *Psychiatric Quarterly* 30 (1956): 181–221.

periences. He described the case of a survivor of Auschwitz who had been liberated in 1945 at the point of death and had come to America five years later. His most outstanding symptom of which the patient himself complained was a state of "confusion between past and present." Thus on the occasion of Jewish holidays the patient would become so haunted by thoughts of a hanging he had witnessed at Auschwitz that although he knew the event had happened many years before in Europe, he nevertheless became uncertain as to whether or not it was also happening again in New York. Similarly, when walking through the snowy streets, the same patient would start to think obsessively of the murderous forced march from Auschwitz he had taken in the winter of 1944–45 in the company of thousands of other victims, many of whom had died of exposure or were shot as stragglers by the guards. Thinking of these events, he became increasingly confused about the pastness of the march, and felt as if it were happening all over again. Niederland regarded the patient's depressive ruminations as typical manifestations of survivor guilt.[23] In 1968 Niederland named chronic depressive states, covering the spectrum of conditions from masochistic character changes to psychotic depression, as among the manifestations of the survivor syndrome, stating that the incidence and severity of depression correlated closely with survivor guilt. In arguing for the necessity of recognizing the emergence under extreme conditions of a "survivor syndrome" distinct from the more familiar traumatic neuroses of war, he stressed the need for a sharper focus on the "all-pervasive guilt" of the victim, as well as a sort of "*hyperacusis to guilt*" on the part of the analyst who thus needed to be alert to the patients' defenses and denials.[24]

Survivor guilt was also a major theme in a series of workshops on the effects of massive trauma, especially the trauma of the Nazi camps, organized at Wayne State University in Detroit throughout the 1960s by Niederland and Henry Krystal, the latter himself a survivor. Participants included many of the major American and European figures in the field. From those workshops, whose findings were published in two influential books in 1968 and 1971, something of a consensus began to emerge about the incidence of the survivor syndrome and the dynamics of survivor guilt. On the basis of randomly selected, statistically evaluated case records obtained from the psychiatric examination of survivors (mostly, but not all

[23] William G. Niederland, "Psychiatric Disorders among Persecution Victims: A Contribution to the Understanding of Concentration Camp Pathology and Its After-Effects," *Journal of Nervous and Mental Disease* 139 (1964): 460; hereafter abbreviated "PD."

[24] William G. Niederland, "Clinical Observations on the 'Survivor Syndrome,'" *International Journal of Psycho-Analysis* 49 (1968): 313–15; hereafter abbreviated "CO." See also idem, "Ein Blick in die Tiefen der 'unbewaltigen' Vergangenheit und Gegenwart, anlasslich der Besprechung von Walter von Baeyer, Heinz Hafner, und Karl Peter Kisker, *Psychiatrie der Verfolgten*," *Psyche* 20 (1966): 466–76; idem, "Diskussionsbeitrag zu E. de Wind: Begegnung mit dem Tod," *Psyche* 22 (1968): 442–46; and idem, "Psychiatrie der Verfolgten und Seelischer Verfolgungsschaden," in *Ergebnisse fur die Medizin*, vol. 2, *Psychiatrie*, ed. Uwe Henrik Peters (Zurich, 1980), 1055–67.

of them, persons interviewed for the purposes of applying for compensation), Krystal and Niederland reported that survivor guilt was a major pathogenic force (found in 92 percent of cases). They and others also elaborated their understanding of the nature of the psychic defenses involved.[25]

Identification with the Aggressor

If it is true that survivors paradoxically feel remorse for surviving, why is this so? Why do survivors feel guilty? Today's critics of the concept of survivor guilt rarely ask that question, because they are more interested in emphasizing the inadequacy of the concept, in order to dismiss it, than in investigating its rationale. Yet it is a question that psychoanalysts in the postwar years tried to address and that steers us directly into questions of mimesis and mimetic identification of the sort raised by Levi in *The Drowned and the Saved.*

According to Niederland and others, survivor guilt was the product of a massive psychic regression in concentration camp victims as they tried to cope with the brutality and terror of the camps. The claim was that after an initial period of shock, disorientation, and depersonalization, prisoners survived by a "robotization" or "automatization" of psychic functions, involving a mesmerized suppression of self-reflection, volition, and judgment, and a trancelike regression to auto-

[25] See *MPT,* 331. See also Henry Krystal and William G. Niederland, eds., *Psychic Traumatization: Aftereffects in Individuals and Communities* (Boston, 1971); hereafter abbreviated *PT.* Between them, these two books provide an important overview of the pertinent European and American literature in the 1950s and 1960s. Especially useful is Klaus D. Hoppe's survey of publications in English and German, "The Aftermath of Nazi Persecutions Reflected in Recent Psychiatric Literature" (*PT,* 169–204). I have also consulted: V. E. Frankl, *Ein Psychologie erlebt das Konkentrationslager* (Vienna, 1946); J. Tas, Psychical Disorders among Inmates of Concentration Camps and Repatriates," *Psychiatric Quarterly* 25 (1951): 679–90; E. Federn, "The Endurance of Torture," *Complex* 4 (1951): 34–41; J. Rickman, "Guilt and the Dynamics of Psychological Disorder in the Individual," in *Selected Contributions to Psychoanalysis* (London, 1957); W. von Baeyer, "Erlebnisreaktive Storung und ihre Bedeutung für die Begutachtung," *Deutsche medizinische Wohschsch* 83 (1958): 2317–21; U. Venzlaff, *Die Psychoreaktiven Storung nach Entschadigungspflichtigen Ereignissen* (Berlin, 1958); H. Bensheim, "Die K. Z. Neurose rassisch Verfolgter," *Nervenartz* 31 (1960): 462–71; Edgar C. Trautman, "Psychiatrische Untersuchungen an Uberlebenden der Nationalsozialistischen Vernichungslager 15 Jahre nach der Befreiung," *Nervenartz* 32 (1961): 545–51; G. E. Winckler, "Probleme der Psychiatrischen Begutachtung der Opfer der Nationalsozialistischen Verfolgten," *Medizinische Welt* 22 (1961): 1226–32; H. Paul and H. Herberg, eds., *Psychische Spaetschaeden nach Politischer Verfolgung* (Basel, 1963); W. R. von Baeyer, H. Hafner and K. Kisker, *Psychiatrie der Verfolgten* (Berlin, 1964); U. Venzlaff, "Mental Disorders Resulting from Racial Persecution Outside of Concentration Camps," *International Journal of Social Psychiatry* 10 (1964): 177–82; E. de Wind, "The Confrontation with Death," *International Journal of Psychoanalysis* 49 (1968): 302–5; E. Simenauer, "Late Psychic Sequalae of Man-Made Disasters," *International Journal of Psychoanalysis* 49 (1968): 306–9.

matic modes of action, feeling, and behavior.[26] For Niederland and his colleagues, that state of hypnotized, "puppet-like" obedience implied a regression, or return, to primordial forms of psychic defense, involving the inmates' tendency to yield unconsciously to their persecutors by fantasmatically identifying with them. "The suspension of superego functions is also an unconscious imitation of the persecutors," Niederland wrote (*MPT*, 31). Here was the famous—or according to its critics, infamous—concept of "*identification with the aggressor*" by which psychoanalysts tried to explain the effects of terror on the camp victim. The idea was that under conditions of violent threat and powerlessness the inmates' only psychic solution was not to resist but to give in to the threatening situation—by identifying with or fantasmatically incorporating the oppressor.

The concept of identification with the aggressor has a long history going back to the earliest years of psychoanalysis. In 1896, in a letter to Wilhelm Fliess, Freud interpreted one of his dreams soon after his father's death as stemming from "the tendency to self-reproach that regularly sets in among the survivors."[27] The following year he commented that:

> Hostile impulses against parents (a wish that they should die) are also an integral constituent of neuroses . . . These impulses are repressed at periods when compassion for parents is aroused—at times of their illness or death. On such occasions it is a manifestation of mourning to reproach oneself for their death (so-called melancholia) or to punish oneself in a hysterical fashion, through the medium of the idea of retribution, with the same states [of illness] that they have had. The identification which occurs here is, as can be seen, nothing other than a mode of thinking and does not make the search for the motive superfluous.
>
> It seems as though this death wish is directed in sons against their fathers and in daughters against their mothers.[28]

Freud's statement touches on all the issues that have been fundamental to the notion of survivor guilt: the idea that survivor guilt originates in hostile impulses or

[26] " 'As the bread is distributed one can hear, far from the windows, in the dark air, the band beginning to play,' " Primo Levi recalled in a passage partly quoted by Niederland ("PD," 462). " 'Our comrades, out in the fog, are marching like automatons; their souls are dead and the music drives them, like the wind drives dead leaves, and takes the place of their wills. There is no longer any will: every beat of the drum becomes a step, a reflected contraction of exhausted muscles . . . They are ten thousand and they are a single grey machine: they are exactly determined; they do not think and they do not desire, they walk . . . Even those in Ka-Be recognize this departure and return from work, the hypnosis of the interminable rhythm, which kills thought and deadens pain.' " Levi, *Survival in Auschwitz: The Nazi Assault on Humanity* (New York, 1993), 52.

[27] *The Complete Letters of Sigmund Freud to Wilhelm Fliess, 1887–1904,* trans. and ed. Jeffrey Moussaieff Masson (Cambridge, Mass., 1985), 202.

[28] Ibid., 250.

wishes against the powerful father or his substitute, which is to say the idea that survivor guilt is a phenomenon of aggression; the idea that out of fear of the father, those hostile impulses are repressed and turned against the ego, to be experienced in the form of guilt; the connection between survivor guilt and melancholia, or failed mourning; crucially for our purposes, the idea that the survivor tends to identify with the parent and that the identification is a mode of self-punishment; and, finally, the question of whether that identification as a mode of thinking is a primordial response to loss, or whether it requires a further explanation in terms of motives—a question that raises the general problem, so central to Freud's work, of how to characterize the relationship between identification (or mimesis) and desire.[29] These same issues are at work in Freud's account of the origin of guilt in *Civilization and Its Discontents* (1930). "A considerable amount of aggressiveness must be developed in the child against the authority which prevents him from having his first, but none the less his most important, satisfactions, whatever the kind of instinctual deprivation that is demanded of him may be; but he is obliged to renounce the satisfaction of this revengeful aggressiveness," Freud writes. He continues:

> He finds his way out of this economically difficult situation with the help of familiar mechanisms. By means of identification he takes the unattackable authority into himself. The authority now turns into his super-ego and enters into possession of all the aggressiveness which a child would have liked to exercise against it . . . [T]he original severity of the super-ego does not—or does not so much—represent the severity which one has experienced from it [the object], or which one attributes to it; it represents one's own aggressiveness towards it. If this is correct, we may assert truly that in the beginning conscience arises through the suppression of an aggressive impulse, and that it is subsequently reinforced by fresh suppressions of the same kind.[30]

In 1936 the concept of identification with the aggressor entered the psychoanalytic mainstream when Anna Freud, in her influential book *The Ego and the Mechanisms of Defense*, elaborated on Freud's discussion of identification and guilt by defining "identification with the aggressor" as one of the ego's most potent weapons in dealing with threat. She described the case of a young boy whose facial grimaces involuntarily imitated his teacher's angry expression. The boy identified himself with the teacher's anger and copied his expression as he spoke, though the imitation was not recognized. Through his

---

[29] These themes are explored in detail in my *Trauma: A Genealogy* (Chicago, 2000). See also Ruth Leys, "Death Masks: Kardiner and Ferenczi on Psychic Trauma," *Representations* 53 (Winter 1996): 44–73.

[30] Sigmund Freud, *Civilization and Its Discontents* (1930), in *The Standard Edition of the Complete Psychological Works of Sigmund Freud,* trans. and ed. James Strachey (London, 1953–74), 21: 129–30.

grimaces, Anna Freud suggested, the child was assimilating himself to the dreaded external object. The prototype for this psychic operation was the oedipal schema, according to which the child makes use of his capacity to identify with the father as a way of resolving his oedipus complex: by imitating the father's hostility to his oedipal desires, the child incorporates the father's anger and thereby makes the latter's aggression its own. As she stated: "A child introjects some characteristic of an anxiety object and so assimilates an anxiety experience which he has just undergone . . . By impersonating the aggressor, assuming his attributes or imitating his aggression, the child transforms himself from the person that is threatened into the person who makes the threat." She observed that at first the introjected parental anger is not formed into self-criticism but instead, through the supplementary mechanism of projection, is turned back onto the external world. Identification with the aggressor is thus succeeded by a hostile aggression toward others: "The moment the criticism is internalized, the offense is externalized." Later, however, the introjected father-figure contributes to the formation of the child's ego-ideal, or superego, the transgression of whose prohibitions thereafter arouses a punishing sense of guilt.[31]

Even before Anna Freud, Sandor Ferenczi made the idea of the mimetic imitation or incorporation of the aggressor central to his account of the traumatic experience. "The early-seduced child adapts itself to its difficult task with the aid of complete identification with the aggressor," he wrote in 1932 of the sexually traumatized child made helpless by a powerful adult. Distinguishing the subject's identificatory response from its libidinal relation to objects, Ferenczi appealed to Freud's observations on identification to propose that the child's mimetic-hypnotic imitation, or trancelike incorporation, of the aggressor served as the model for the traumatized adult's defense against extreme danger.[32] Similarly, in 1940 the American psychoanalyst Clara Thompson followed up on Anna Freud's and Ferenczi's observations by describing identification with the aggressor as a characteristic mode of defense against danger in certain psychotic or quasipsychotic adults. Distinguishing between conscious "imitation" and largely unconscious "identification," she suggested that both imitation and identification could be found in individuals living in countries ruled by dictators where nonconformity could be punished by death. She observed that many people under such conditions conformed outwardly to their oppressors but kept their own inner counsel. As she put it: "They think otherwise." On the other hand, there were other individuals who "converted" to the reigning ideology through fear. Closing their minds to

[31] Anna Freud, *The Ego and the Mechanisms of Defense* (1936; New York, 1966), 110–18.

[32] *The Clinical Diary of Sandor Ferenczi,* ed. Judith Dupont (Cambridge, Mass., 1988), 190. For a detailed discussion of Ferenczi's ideas about identification see Leys, *Trauma: A Genealogy,* chaps. 4–5.

any critical attitude toward the regime, they resembled the psychotic patients Thompson had treated who out of fear had completely identified with the hostile aggressor.[33]

Bruno Bettelheim was the first to apply the concept of identification with the aggressor directly to the victims of the Nazis when, on the basis of his own experience as an inmate in Dachau and Buchenwald before the war, in an influential article of 1943 he claimed that as part of the adaptation to camp life, older prisoners were forced into regressive forms of dependency on their oppressors, including a tendency to identify with them. In a statement that would subsequently arouse the hostility of numerous critics, he asserted that so great an amount of prohibited aggression accumulated in older prisoners that they slowly accepted, "as an expression of their verbal aggression, terms which definitely did not originate in their previous vocabularies, but were taken over from the very different vocabulary of the Gestapo. From copying the verbal aggressions of the Gestapo to copying their form of bodily aggression was one more step, but it took several years to make this step . . . The identification with the Gestapo did not stop with the copying of their outer appearance and behavior. Old prisoners accepted their goals and values, too, even when they seemed opposed to their own interests. It was appalling to see how far formerly politically well-educated prisoners would go in this identification."[34]

The same theme was developed by several authors writing about survivors soon after the war. "Through identification with the tormentor, the prominents tried to free themselves from such anxieties and to gain security," wrote Hilde Bluhm in an article of 1948 on the survivors of the camps. "For losing one's self in a powerful enemy, being 'eaten up' by him, means overcoming one's own help-

[33] Clara M. Thompson, "Identification with the Enemy and Loss of the Sense of Self," in *Interpersonal Psychoanalysis: Papers of Clara M. Thompson* (New York, 1956), 139–49. Thompson reported on six cases of institutionalized psychotics with desperate early lives who repeated their patterns of uncritical identification with Thompson herself. None of them recovered. In making her observations about the effects of dictatorship on the psyche, Thompson was possibly thinking of the experience of the Hungarians under a fascist government, for she had lived in Budapest on and off between 1927 and 1932 in the course of undergoing an analysis with Ferenczi.

[34] Bruno Bettelheim, "Individual and Mass Behavior in Extreme Situations," *Journal of Abnormal and Social Psychology* 38 (October 1943): 417–51. The psychoanalyst Ernst Federn, who was imprisoned with Bettelheim in Dachau and Buchenwald, recalled that "Bettelheim and I had noticed the degree to which the mechanism of defence that Sandor Ferenczi and Anna Freud have described as identification with the aggressor could be observed amongst the camp inmates. Who made this observation first I cannot tell today, but it was a significant one. What Anna Freud had described of children and what every nursery-school teacher can confirm can also be found among adults and most clearly when they are in a regressed state of mind. In other words Bettelheim, myself and later Brief [Dr. Brief, a psychoanalyst also interned at Buchenwald] found confirmation of two important psychoanalytic findings. Under severe mental strain man regresses and develops infantile mechanisms of defence" (*Witnessing Psychoanalysis: From Vienna back to Vienna via Buchenwald and the USA* (London, 1980), 5.

lessness and participating in his omnipotence . . . It was a means of defense of a rather paradoxical nature: survival through surrender; protection against the fear of the enemy—by becoming part of him; overcoming helplessness—by regressing to childish dependence."[35] The concept of identification with the aggressor was likewise deployed by Elie Cohen, a survivor of Auschwitz and the death marches, who followed Anna Freud, Bettelheim, Bluhm, and others in claiming in his book *Human Behavior in the Concentration Camps* (1953) that "only a very few of the prisoners escaped a more or less intensive identification with the SS."[36]

When in the 1960s Niederland and other psychoanalysts invoked the concept of identification with the aggressor to explain the symptoms of the survivor syndrome, they therefore did so in the confidence that the concept would be comprehended. For example, at one of the workshop meetings on massive trauma a case was described of a woman who had fallen ill with various delusional ideas centering on the Nazi persecutions only *after* obtaining a reparation pension. It was suggested that accepting money from the German government was linked in the victim's mind to her formerly suppressed "survivor guilt" about the death of her five-month-old child during a death march:

> The patient felt that she was responsible for the death of the child because while they were on the march she was permitted by the German soldier to enter a peasant house and feed the baby. The peasant woman offered to take the child from the patient and return him after the war. The patient refused the offer; a few days later the child died in her arms. In the spring of 1962, the patient developed another manic episode . . . Once again she was delusional but appeared to be preoccupied primarily with her trip to Israel . . . she made repeated reference to a certain sum of money for the trip . . . When this was followed up, it turned out that *the amount that she was about to spend was exactly the same sum of money that she had received recently from the German government as*

[35] Hilde Bluhm, *American Journal of Psychotherapy*, 2 (1948): 24–25; she cited the work of Ferenczi, Anna Freud, Thompson, and Bettelheim.

[36] Elie Cohen, *Human Behavior in the Concentration Camps* (London, 1953), 177. Many years later, in an article on German guilt, Cohen—who had worked as a physician at the Dutch camp of Westerbork and at Auschwitz, where his wife and child were gassed—testified to his own feelings of guilt: "Do I have guilt feelings? I don't feel guilty for having survived while so many were murdered. Among them were my wife and child. That Germans gassed them like mad dogs filled me with anger against the German people. I feel guilty, however, since I worked for the Germans: In the transit camp of Westerbork I was a transport physician and in Auschwitz an inmate physician, and I assisted in selections to the gas chamber. My own explanation is: I wanted to live and for that I did much. Today I find that I crossed the norms of humanity. But that is easily said." Elie Cohen, "Die Schuld der Deutschen," in *Das Echo des Holocaust,* ed. Helmut Schreier and Matthias Heyl (Hamburg, 1992), 21–22, cited by Raul Hilberg, *Sources of Holocaust Research: An Analysis* (Chicago, 2001), 173–73. See also E. A. Cohen's earlier *The Abyss: A Confession,* trans. James Brockway (New York, 1973); and idem, "The Post-Concentration Camp Syndrome: A Disaster Syndrome," *Science and Public Policy* 8 (1981): 244, where Cohen mentions survivor guilt as one of the characteristic symptoms of the survivor syndrome.

restitution. It was pointed out to her and she had become aware of her guilt for having received some money, an interpretation which ultimately stated she had been paid for her child's death . . . Obtaining a pension brings identification with the aggressor nearer to consciousness, and with it guilt over survival priorities. Survivor guilt, the result of universal ambivalence, often makes the acceptance of any compensation a traumatic event for the survivor. (*MPT*, 37–38)

In the economic terms proposed by Freud, the concept of identification with the aggressor implied that in adapting to terror the prisoner suffered a breach in her "protective shield" against stimuli, with the result that she experienced a sudden paralysis of the functions of the ego through which perception, recognition, orientation, and mastery were achieved. The consequence was a regressive mode of adaptation to the traumatic situation that, on the model of the infant's earliest ties to the world, paradoxically made the victim unconsciously imitate or hypnotically yield to the traumatic scene. Niederland and his colleagues thus proposed that the trauma of the Nazi persecution produced a fundamental fragmentation or dissociation of the ego, involving an identificatory mode of defense more primordial than repression and an inhibition of the ego consequent on a mimetic incorporation of the traumatic situation or person.[37] The behavior of the survivor in this regard was compared to that of brainwashed soldiers coming out of prisoner-of-war camps in Korea: "[I]n turning the aggression against the self and assuming a position of identification with the aggressor, the patient's behavior resembled that of brain-washed soldiers, who after a prisoner-of-war experience tended to identify with their captors" (*MPT*, 38). Today this phenomenon is called the "Stockholm Syndrome," after Swedish victims of a kidnapping who ended up identifying with their captors.[38]

Survivor Guilt

For postwar analysts concerned with the survivor, then, the concept of identification held the key to the victim's depressive remorse and pathological conscience. It is all the more necessary to emphasize this, because the connection between identification and guilt—which is to say between mimesis and guilt—has been almost completely lost sight of by recent authors, who tend to discuss the two notions separately, as if they bear no relation to each

[37] Niederland remarks at one point that the automatization of the ego in trauma "went beyond the known defenses of denial and repression" (*MPT*, 318).

[38] Martin Symonds, "Victim Responses to Terror: Understanding and Treatment," in *Victims of Terrorism,* ed. F. M. Ochberg and D. A. Soskis (Boulder, Colo., 1982), 94–103; and Thomas Strentz, "The Stockholm Syndrome: Law Enforcement Policy and Hostage Behavior," in *Victims of Terrorism*, 149–63.

other. For example, in rejecting both the idea of identification with the aggressor and that of survivor guilt, Terrence Des Pres in his influential study of the survivor—to be discussed at length in chapter 2—treats the two notions separately, wholly ignoring the conceptual links between them. Nor does the philosopher Giorgio Agamben, whose work I shall discuss in chapter 5, mention the connection between the notion of survivor guilt and the theme of identification.

Identification with the aggressor did not mean a literal return to childhood behavior but a return to modes of psychic defense that Freud considered developmentally primordial or foundational for the subject. "Many concentration camp inmates regressed to the earliest phase of compliance and submission during their imprisonment," Klaus Hoppe wrote with reference to the ideas of Bettelheim, Cohen, and others. "They elevated their SS guards to parental images with whom they would identify, and whom they would imitate at times."[39] Gustav Bychowski, who interviewed more than forty patients referred to him by the United Restitution Organization for his expert opinion, observed that the most common symptom was an "apathetic depression of hopelessness and resignation" marked by aggression and remorse. "The problems of aggression in the survivors are related to the mechanism of identification with the aggressor," he remarked. "Under these circumstances, one can develop hostility to one's fellow victims. Such individuals have been unable to undo this identification, and now find themselves isolated from their present environment. The price of survival through identification with the aggressor is a serious characterological derangement, corruption of the superego, or tendency to severe depression" (*MPT*, 85).

According to these authors, identification with the aggressor temporarily solved the problem of the rage victims felt toward their tormentors, rage they could not express without fear of immediate reprisal. By unconsciously identifying with those in power, inmates became ruthless like them and thereby diverted the hostility directed against themselves onto other helpless victims. Identification with the aggressor thus helped explain the well-known fact, documented by Primo Levi and many others, that in the camps prisoners often became the target of each other's sadism to the extent that they sometimes had as much to fear from each other as from their masters.[40] Identification with the aggressor also ex-

[39] Klaus Hoppe, "Persecution and Conscience," *Psychoanalytic Review* 52 (1965): 107.

[40] Levi observed in this regard that one of the shocks for the new arrival in the camps was the discovery that, contrary to the idea that victims and persecutors could be divided into two starkly opposed blocks, the enemy was all around "but also inside, the 'we' lost its limits . . . One entered hoping at least for the solidarity of one's companions in misfortune, but the hoped for allies, except in special cases, were not there; there were instead a thousand sealed off monads, and between them a desperate covert and continuous struggle. This brusque revelation, which becomes manifest from the very first hours of imprisonment, often in the instant form of concrete aggression on the part of those in whom one hoped to find future allies, was so harsh as to cause the immediate collapse of one's capacity to resist. For many it was

plained the phenomenon of survivor guilt. For according to Niederland and his associates, the incorporated aggression of the parental figure or his substitute, which was at first projected outward against other victims, was subsequently turned against the victim himself. Survivor guilt was thus a disorder of aggression in which the mimetically absorbed, threatening figure of the other haunted the victim in the form of a self-lacerating, melancholic conscience. In Niederland's formula of the guilt-ridden survivor: "*I* live—*they* died, i.e., *they,* unconsciously, were sacrificed by *me*" ("PD," 471).

Niederland especially emphasized the role of selections in exacerbating the survivor's guilt feelings, because every selection of another inmate meant that the prisoner's own chances of survival were at least temporarily prolonged. In 1964 he remarked that among the survivors whom he had seen as patients, not one who had gone through the selections referred to them without expressions not only of acute fear and stark disgust, but also of intense guilt. In the camps, he observed, the majority of the patients had lost their parents, mates, children, siblings, and friends, while they themselves had remained alive. From an adaptational point of view, the ego of the survivor was confronted with an unresolvable conflict which in many cases had remained unmitigated. The intensity and persistence of this guilty conflict became clear to him, he stated, when he learned during the examination of survivors of "their belief, at times their semidelusional conviction, that they could have prevented the mass murder of their families by depriving themselves of some chance of survival" ("PD," 466). As he also put it: "The selections by which prisoners lost their remaining love objects were ultimately responsible for their own survival, as a result of which there evolved the insoluble intrapsychic conflict now manifest as survivor guilt" (*MPT,* 32–33). Like many others, Niederland acknowledged the ways in which the victims' forced participation in the Nazi machine as slave laborers or other role exacerbated their psychic dilemmas.

Hillel Klein, a child survivor and physician active in the treatment of Holocaust survivors in Israel, described a patient suffering from an incurable disturbance bordering on the psychotic with obsessive thoughts and suicidal depression who accused herself of killing an admired and envied older brother because the latter had been beaten to death after he had decided, on her advice, not to go on a transport but to stay with her in the camp, as she secretly wished him to do. Klein mentioned the patient's ambivalence toward her brother who, according to him,

---

lethal, indirectly or even directly: it is difficult to defend oneself against a blow for which one is not prepared" (*DS*, 38). Many other authors commented on the ruthless struggle for life in the camps and the absence of solidarity among the prisoners. See for example Curt Bondy, "Problems of Internment Camps," *Journal of Abnormal and Social Psychology* 38 (1943): 453–75; and Herbert A. Bloch, "The Personality of Inmates of Concentration Camps," *American Journal of Sociology* 52 (1946–47): 335–41.

had served as a substitute parent for his sister and hence as an oedipal figure. He attributed the patient's self-punishing feelings and atonement for his death in the form of a compulsive illness to these dynamic factors. He noted that during treatment the therapist had to remember again and again that the patient's guilt feelings had their origin in a tragic and cruel reality. In the patient's chaotic world it seemed that all her sadomasochistic fantasies had come true: "The patient hadn't killed her brother and hadn't even indirectly caused his death, but her ambivalent feelings toward him—feelings of envy and dependence—express themselves in the need for self-punishment in the form of recurring obsessions: 'I killed him.' She says about her brother: 'I thought I would die of hunger if he would leave me and go to another camp. Therefore, I advised him to stay. And so I killed him'" (*MPT*, 239).[41]

"The patient hadn't killed her brother and hadn't even indirectly caused his death." As psychoanalysts for the most part understood, the patient's sense of responsibility for the death of others was not necessarily based on reality but was of a magical, unconscious kind. The patient described by Klein had not really caused her brother's death: she felt guilty because she had experienced a moment of relief at her own safety when he was killed, a moment of relief tantamount to the fulfillment of an unconscious, hostile wish. As Freud observed in *Civilization and Its Discontents,* a person feels guilty not only when he has done something that he knows to be "bad," but also when he has not actually *done* the bad thing but has only recognized in himself "an *intention* to do it,"—an unconscious intention, moreover, which the subject equates with the deed itself: "The distinction . . . between doing something bad and wishing to do it disappears entirely, since nothing can be hidden from the super-ego, not even thoughts . . . The super-ego torments the sinful ego with the same feeling of anxiety and is on the watch for opportunities of getting it punished by the external world."[42] "Murder begins with the intention to kill," Derrida has observed of Freud's psychoanalytic logic. "The unconscious does not know the difference here between the virtual and the actual, the intention and the action (a certain Judaism also, by the way), or at least does not model itself on the manner in which the conscious (as well as the law or the morals accorded to it) distributes the relations of the virtual, of the intentional,

[41] Henry Krystal makes a similar statement: "The problem of aggression is one of the most difficult areas in psychotherapy with survivors, insofar as the aggression occurred under circumstances so horrendous that it is almost impossible for the psychotherapist to prove to the patient that he did not 'cause' the destruction and that his fantasies were not actually endowed with omnipotent power . . . [T]he circumstances of the persecution can be viewed as a seduction of the survivor into psychically participating in all impulses that he would have otherwise managed to repress or sublimate or deal with in more normal ways. There is no doubt that the persecution experience created a psychic situation in which infantile fantasies were revived and lent the feeling of reality" (*MPT*, 133).

[42] Freud, *Civilization and Its Discontents*, 125.

and of the actual. We will never have finished, we have not in truth begun, drawing all the ethico-juridical consequences from this."[43]

In an influential paper on guilt whose theses would reverberate throughout American discussions of the survivor, the philosopher Martin Buber drew a distinction between ontic or existential guilt on the one hand and psychological or "neurotic guilt" on the other, in terms suggesting that neurotic guilt was not authentic or real. According to Buber, the "significant actuality" of human existence transcends the task and methods of the psychotherapist. "Within his methods," Buber wrote, "the psychotherapist has only to do with guilt feelings, conscious and unconscious . . . But within a comprehensive service to knowledge and help, he must himself encounter guilt as an ontic character whose place is not the soul but being."[44] There was, he said, no place for guilt in the ontological sense in Freud's psychoanalysis, which occupied itself more with the effects of repressed childhood wishes or "youthful lusts gone astray" than with the inner consequences of a "man's betrayal of his friend or his cause" ("GGF," 117). As he also put it: "There exists real guilt, fundamentally different from all the anxiety-induced bugbears that are generated in the cavern of the unconscious. Personal guilt, whose reality some schools of psychoanalysis contest and others ignore, does not permit itself to be reduced to the trespass against a powerful taboo" ("GGF," 120).

In an intelligent reply, however, the philosopher Herbert Fingarette suggested that Buber's invocation of a metaphysical distinction between the two forms of guilt was from the outset a "fatal misstep" based on the very psychologism to which it was in spirit opposed. Fingarette observed that instead of arguing for the unity of human suffering, whether neurotic or otherwise, Buber had divided the human world in two, assigning to the psychotherapeutic technician the "merely psychological realm" and turning his own attention to the spiritual realm. The proper perspective, Fingarette claimed, was to recognize that (with exceptions that he did not pursue) "*all* guilt with which we deal should properly taken as real guilt, as real as any other guilt, and real in every sense of 'real.'" This did not mean equating fantasy and actuality: Fingarette observed that it was a worse crime to commit a real murder than it was to fantasize committing one. But—charging most psychotherapists with making the error of tacitly assuming that only actions and their effects, viewed literally and not symbolically, were what counted morally—he went on to emphasize that the distinctive character of neurotic guilt was not its *unreality* but its source in unconscious infantile conflicts: what was inauthentic about neurotic guilt was not the guilt itself but the subject's tendency to consciously assign it to one source, when its origin lay in desires and

[43] Jacques Derrida, *Archive Fever: A Freudian Impression*, trans. Eric Prenowitz (Chicago and London, 1996), 65–66.

[44] Martin Buber, "Guilt and Guilt Feelings," *Psychiatry* 20 (1957): 115; hereafter "GGF."

aims that were in conflict with his being's moral order. Neurotic guilt was thus the guilt of a person afraid of, and secretly untrue to, his own adult commitments. Here Fingarette noted the originality of Freud's ethical insight in this regard:

I shall state a general thesis . . . When stated bluntly, the general thesis still often appears novel and radical. Yet this very thesis is fundamental to twentieth century dynamic psychiatry and, equally, to the historical moral insights of the major civilizations. The thesis, briefly, is this: moral guilt accrues by virtue of our wishes, not merely our acts. Of course, legal guilt depends primarily upon our acts, though we should note that even here the assessment of motive plays a role. But the question of moral guilt does not wait for acts: it is in profound degree a question of what one harbors in one's heart. This is the gist of Freud's basic concept of "psychic reality." In the psychic economy, the wish is omnipotent. To wish, psychologically, is to have done. Hence a person suffers guilt for his wishes, even his unconscious wishes. This insight . . . is not in opposition to the central insights of the great moral teachings.[45]

This point can be illustrated by the example of a young woman who had had sexual fantasies to the point of hallucination that she had sexually abused her three-year-old nephew and had compulsively sought reassurance from those around her that certain acts had not taken place. In his hostility to Freud's theory of fantasy and his commitment to the reality of sexual abuse, Jeffrey Masson has cited this case as evidence that sexual impulses, which may and often do lead to sexual acts, are always real. But, as Jacqueline Rose has observed in defense of the Freudian theory of fantasy, Masson's argument simply leaves the woman in the position of being charged with an actual crime of which she accuses herself, when her far more painful reality leaves her suspended between fantasy and the reality of the event.[46] We may put it that Freud's account of conscience and morals cuts through the dichotomy of either assuming that the survivor is guilty in actuality or denying his painful feelings as merely imaginary or unreal.

It is on the basis of considerations such as these that analysts in the postwar years could sympathetically approach the survivor's horrifying sense of complicity in events beyond his objective control. In the words of Joost Meerloo, himself a survivor who immediately after the war, as High Commissioner for Welfare for the Netherlands, had dealt with Dutch victims and also had examined camp survivors for compensation purposes: "One of the hidden thoughts of every inmate had been: 'If my neighbor gets killed before I do, I get another chance to live.' The former camp inmates showed guilt and anxiety because their unconscious murder-

---

[45] Herbert Fingarette, "Real Guilt and Neurotic Guilt," *Journal of Existential Psychiatry* 2 (1962): 145–58. Fingarette's observations found their way into the survivor literature—for example, in Klaus D. Hoppe's "Persecution and Conscience," the author cites Fingarette's paper in order to reject Buber's separation of "so-called" authentic guilt from neurotic guilt (114).

[46] Jacqueline Rose, *Sexuality in the Field of Vision* (Thetford, Norfolk, 1986), 13–14.

ous wishes had been stirred up. I could report to you the strangest and most tragic acts of betrayal between parents and children and brothers and sisters" (*MPT*, 74). He reported that many former inmates had had to battle against gnawing feelings of self-reproach because they survived while their loved ones did not. "I have seen several cases of survivors who *had* to go through an outburst of increased mourning and depression several years later when some acquaintance or relative died. Through these depressions, which were often suicidal, they tried to purify themselves of past death wishes; now they went through the mourning rituals they were forbidden to perform during the camp years" (*MPT*, 74).[47]

As this last quotation suggests, for the post-Holocaust analysts confronted with the difficulties of the survivor, the survivor syndrome was a disease of mourning, which is to say, a form of melancholia. This was Meerloo's interpretation, as it was that of Krystal and Niederland, who jointly observed in a passage that must be quoted in its entirety:

> Survivor guilt is a form of pathological mourning in which the survivor is stuck in a magnification of the guilt which is present in every bereaved person. The ambivalence, or more precisely, the repressed aggression toward the lost object prevents the completion of the work of mourning (Freud, 1917). Hidden in the self-reproach of many younger patients is their repressed rage against the now murdered parents who failed to protect them from the persecutions to which the survivors were subjected.
>
> Closely connected to the persistence of survivor guilt and pathological mourning is the unconscious identification with the aggressor on the part of the survivors. We feel that some unconscious identification with the aggressor may have been indispensable to survival. The violent, often sudden destruction of the survivor's whole world makes the acknowledgment and working through of such identifications most threatening. To own up to death wishes in regard to a whole destroyed civilization is more than most people can do. Neither can the therapist assure the patient that his wishes did not have magic powers, since the most fantastically destructive genocide of history did, in fact, become part of their lives. Thus, the survivor finds himself in an insoluble conflict. The only workable, but unsatisfactory, solution is afforded by repression, an ego split in which identification with the aggressor was repressed and walled off by counter-

[47] As Dr. Alexander Szatmari put it: "Normal psychoanalytic practice familiarizes us with the notion that, on an infantile level, the patient experiences the departure of his mother as a desertion and that the abandoned child is likely to feel that he has caused the mother to forsake him, because of his 'bad' aggressive impulses—either as a punishment or by causing her destruction. As a result of the magical thinking due to the ego regression of our patients here, however, there is a tendency to view the death of the mother, father, sister, or brother as their direct responsibility; the event is obviously viewed through the aperture of early infantile aggression. This happens again in many of the nightmares, where the guilt repeats and fortifies itself, maintaining the repetitive pattern of the regression. It can be considered as a dread of one's own aggressive omnipotent impulses, similar to the world destruction fantasy of the schizophrenic" (MPT, 132).

cathexis. Since, in view of the magnitude of the trauma, the repression mechanism seems to have failed in a certain number of cases . . . the conscious awareness of such identification with the aggressor may add to the enormous burden of unconscious guilt and drive the victim into further self-isolation, brooding withdrawal, self-contempt and self-exclusion from human society, or in the case of total denial and projection, into psychotic illness" (*MPT*, 343–44).

What this passage shows is that for Niederland and his associates, survivor guilt conformed to the model of pathological mourning, or melancholia, as described by Freud in "Mourning and Melancholia" (1917), according to which survivors react to the loss of a loved object (whether through an actual death, or through some other unknown or unconscious loss) by identifying with or incorporating it. The reproaches and denigrations that melancholics direct against themselves are not really self-criticisms but reproaches leveled against the object with which they are now identified. The "shadow of the object" falls upon the subject's ego, as Freud puts it, because instead of displacing its affects onto a libidinal object that substitutes for the one that has been lost, the ego reverts to the more primordial identificatory method of object choice by incorporating the object while simultaneously entering into "dissension with itself," which is to say, with its ego-ideal or superego.[48] Ambivalence—or "more precisely," as Krystal and Niederland note, the repressed aggression toward the lost object—holds the key to the survivor's failed mourning and melancholic's guilt. For if the subject's objects are loved they are also hated, and this hate is what must be repressed and displaced through the mechanism of identification and incorporation. Freud explains the "riddle" of the melancholic's or survivor's tendency to suicide in the same identificatory-mimetic terms.[49]

But the statement by Krystal and Niederland just cited also suggests certain aporias in their understanding of the relations between identification and guilt. The authors observe that identification with the aggressor is "closely connected" to survivor guilt and pathological mourning. The tentativeness of this formulation hints at the authors' difficulty in articulating the precise relationship between the two concepts. Most analysts represented the subject's identification with the aggressor as a consequence of the survivor's loving and hostile oedipal impulses toward the lost love object. For example, in discussing the case of a survivor of Auschwitz whose father had been killed there, the Dutch analyst Eddy de Wind traced the patient's feelings of guilt back to his "death wishes towards the father

---

[48] Mikkel Borch-Jacobsen, *The Freudian Subject* (Stanford, Calif., 1988), trans. Catherine Porter, 183; hereafter abbreviated *FS*.

[49] Thus in "Mourning and Melancholia," Freud suggests that the melancholic subject can actually kill himself only if he can treat himself as an object: the suicidal subject kills the other or object in the self with which he is fantasmatically identified and has therefore "become" (Freud, "Mourning and Melancholia" [1917], in *The Standard Edition*, 14:243–58).

in the oedipal phase of his development" (*PT*, 97). On this formulation, the patient's oedipal wishes, which found such horrific confirmation in the death of his parents in the camp, produced a regressive tendency to unconscious identification with the SS, the father-substitute. Identification was thus defined as a mechanism of defense motivated by oedipal desire, a mechanism that was thought to come to the subject's aid as a means of coping with his own murderous impulses that had been simultaneously revived and repressed at the time of the loved and hated parent's death.

In treating identification as a secondary effect of the ambivalence of oedipal desire in this way, psychoanalysts were being true to a certain reading of Freud's intentions. But in his various discussions of identification, Freud also characterized the relationship between identification and desire differently. On this alternative account, identification is not a mode of relationship to objects secondary to desire, but *is itself primary, indeed foundational.* "Identification is known to psychoanalysis as the earliest expression of an emotional tie with another person," Freud stated in 1921, remarking that it is "already possible before any sexual-object choice has been made."[50] Or as he also observed in *Moses and Monotheism*: "[I]dentification is a preliminary stage of object-choice, in that it is the first way— and one that is expressed in an ambivalent fashion—in which the ego picks out an object."[51] But this is to say that identification subtends the subject's relation to the object from the start—prior to the oedipus complex and indeed *"right up to the Oedipus complex itself"* (*FS,* 183). For Freud, a devouring, cannibalistic incorporative violence defines the subject's relation to the "other" from the very beginning, which means that the ambivalence of the mimetico-identificatory relationship is inescapable: identification with the father-aggressor can never fully purge the child's aggression toward the loved object since, according to Freud himself, hatred and rivalry inhere in the processes of identification that are constitutive of subjectivity itself. There is an important sense, then, in which Freud's own texts undermined the oedipal logic on which the notion of survivor guilt appeared to depend.[52]

The ensuing difficulties could not be resolved. For example, in an exchange with Niederland, Klaus Hoppe conceded the importance of survivor guilt but rejected its role as the single most pathogenic factor in the survivor syndrome on

---

[50] Sigmund Freud, "Identification," in *Group Psychology and the Analysis of the Ego* (1921), *Standard Edition*, 18:105.

[51] Sigmund Freud, "Mourning and Melancholia," in *The Standard Edition*, 23: 249.

[52] These issues have been searchingly examined by Mikkel Borch-Jacobsen in *The Freudian Subject* and "The Freudian Subject: From Politics to Ethics," in *The Emotional Tie: Psychoanalysis, Mimesis, and Affect,* trans. Douglas Brick (Stanford, Calif., 1992), 15–35. They are also fundamental to my *Trauma: A Genealogy*, where I show that the primordiality of mimetic identification in Freud's own theorizing of trauma plays havoc with his oedipal theory of desire and constantly undermines his therapeutic project.

the grounds that, from a genetic or developmental point of view, guilt feelings were characteristic of the phallic (or oedipal) phase, whereas most victims appeared to regress to preoedipal stages—as if the absence of a coherent theoretical account of the origin of survivor guilt in preoedipal processes inevitably called into question its centrality as a symptom of the survivor syndrome.[53] Possibly it was in response to these same theoretical difficulties that in 1981 Niederland himself came to reject the classical oedipal rationale for survivor guilt, foregrounding instead the survivor's identification with the victims, or dead loved ones:

> The guilt feelings and guilt anxieties in an unresolved grief situation, psychoanalytically speaking, are usually considered as being based on early hostility and death wishes with regard to family members wiped out in the course of the holocaust . . . I cannot accept this explanation. It is true that masochistic tendencies are operative in many of them, but in the great majority it is the survival itself that stands at the core of the inner conflict. The holocaust survivor identifies himself with the beloved dead whom he feels he should join in death, so much so that the phenomenological attitude in a number of my patients, with respect to their tactiturn behavior, pale complexion, shuffling gait, etc., often is that of being walking corpses themselves.
>
> On the basis of my long-standing research, I have reason to believe that the survival is unconsciously felt as a betrayal of the dead parents and siblings, and being alive constitutes an ongoing conflict as well as a source of constant feelings of guilt and anxiety.[54]

What are the implications of Niederland's argument, which seems to downplay the hostility and aggressivity toward the dead loves ones that are usually held to central to survivor guilt? His remarks so closely echo the views of Robert Jay Lifton about the origin of survivor guilt as to suggest a convergence of viewpoints. In the concluding section of this chapter I shall briefly analyze Lifton's views on survivor guilt, in order to evaluate the stakes of Niederland's and Lifton's shared perspective, and to set the stage for my discussion in the next chapter of Terrence Des Pres's assault on the entire idea of the survivor syndrome and the concept of survivor guilt.

The Dead

When psychoanalysts began to help survivors make reparation claims against the West German government, they were struck by the lack of fit between the victim's difficulties and classical psychoanalytic categories and ap-

---

[53] Klaus D. Hoppe, "Author's Response," after discussion of his paper "The Psychodynamics of Concentration Camp Victims," *Psychoanalytic Forum* 1 (1966): 85.

[54] William G. Niederland, "The Survivor Syndrome: Further Observations and Dimensions," *Journal of the American Psychoanalytic Association* 29 (1981): 421.

proaches. The familiar diagnosis of "traumatic neurosis," according to which the symptoms of acute trauma were transitory and impermanent, did not seem adequate to the multitude, severity, and persistence of the clinical symptoms observed. Niederland confessed that he had had "tremendous difficulty" in formulating and reducing the survivor experience into words (*MPT*, 63) and other analysts, such as Bettelheim and Krystal (*MPT*, 25), voiced the same frustration.[55] New nosological and conceptual approaches seemed called for, which is why Niederland's description of the "survivor syndrome" and "survivor guilt" found ready acceptance. Moreover, the classical psychoanalytic emphasis on infantile fantasy struck some commentators as insufficient, which is why, again, Niederland's effort to link the clinical symptoms of trauma more directly to the external circumstances behind the patient's depressions, psychoticlike actions, and delusions also found support. Still, no one was fully satisfied with the solutions proposed.

The time was ripe for Robert Jay Lifton's "cultural" or "formative-symbolic" approach to these questions. As a result of his revisions, the link that had hitherto bound the concept of survivor guilt to the psychoanalytic notion of identification with the aggressor was loosened, and in its place was installed a psychiatry focused on death. In the process, the concept of survivor guilt itself was changed, even transformed. Lifton was so successful in imposing his ideas that not only does Niederland appear to have been influenced by them, but we shall see that when Des Pres launched his attack on the whole idea of survivor guilt, he focused on Lifton's ideas, not Niederland's.

Lifton's main contribution to the topic of survivor guilt was his claim that survivor guilt was a function of the survivor's identification with the dead. This was the central theme of his famous studies of Japanese survivors of the atom bomb, which culminated in his widely admired book, *Death in Life: Survivors of Hiroshima* (1968).[56] In that book, he generalized his findings to include the burgeoning literature on the concentration camp survivor; indeed, in 1965 Lifton participated in one of the workshops on massive traumatization organized by Niederland and Krystal (*DL*, 572, n. 25; see also *MPT*, 168–203, where Lifton's paper, "The Survivors of the Hiroshima Disaster and the Survivors of Nazi Persecution" was presented to one of the workshops on massive trauma and discussed).

In his writings on the survivor, Lifton characterized the latter's encounter with death as the most striking psychological effect of the nuclear explosion, both in the immediate aftermath and as a pervasive phenomenon. The encounter was so intense, he argued, that it could not be endured for long, with the result that a process of defensive numbing or "psychic closing off" soon occurred, designed

---

[55] Bruno Bettelheim, *The Informed Heart: Autonomy in a Mass Age* (New York, 1960), 12–21.

[56] Robert Jay Lifton, *Death in Life: Survivors of Hiroshima* (Chapel Hill and London, 1991; originally published, 1968); hereafter abbreviated *DL*.

to protect the subject from the overwhelming confrontation. But that defensive numbing could not fully succeed, with the result that the survivor experienced not only a profound identification with the dead, but also persistent feelings of guilt and shame (I will return in a moment to Lifton's coalescence of these two emotions). According to Lifton, the survivor's intimate identification with the dead tended to suffuse his entire identity: *"For survivors seem not only to have experienced the atomic disaster, but to have imbibed it and incorporated it into their beings, including all of its elements of horror, evil, and particularly of death.* They feel compelled virtually to merge with those who died . . . And they judge, and indeed judge harshly, their own behavior and that of other survivors on the basis of the degree of respect it demonstrates toward the dead."[57]

Lifton thematized the experience of identification, guilt, and shame in terms of one incident or "image" with which survivors identified, leaving them with a profound feeling of self-condemnation. One Hiroshima survivor, who was haunted by the image of the gaze of the dead, recalled: " 'I saw disappointment in their eyes. They looked at me with great expectation, staring right through me. It was very hard to be stared at by those eyes' " ("PE," 469). In Lifton's interpretation: "He felt, in other words, accused by the eyes of the anonymous dead and dying, of wrong-doing and transgression (a sense of guilt) for not helping them, for letting them die, for 'selfishly' remaining alive and strong; and 'exposed' and 'seen through' by the same eyes for these identical feelings (a sense of shame)" ("PE," 469). Nor according to Lifton was the survivor's close identification with the dead and subsequent guilt and shame limited to the Japanese *hibakusha*, or bomb survivors, for these were characteristic of any response to disaster ("PE," 494, n. 21). In Lifton's revisionist interpretation, identification with the dead, the haunting death image, guilt, and shame, formed a single clinical-theoretical ensemble, somewhat remote from Freud's psychoanalytic approach, the main elements of which, for our purposes, can be summarized as follows:

1. The confrontation with death is the central event of human experience. According to Lifton, Freud in his brilliant one-sidedness had reduced the fear of death to the fear of castration, thereby relegating death anxiety to a secondary phenomenon and ignoring the individual's actual psychological experience of death. Freud had contended that one cannot imagine or represent one's own death. " 'It is indeed impossible to imagine our own death; and whenever we attempt to do so we can perceive that we are in fact still present as spectators,' " Lifton cites Freud as having stated in a famous passage in 1915. " 'Hence the psychoanalytic school could venture on the assertion that at bottom no one be-

---

[57] Robert Jay Lifton, "Psychological Effects of the Atomic Bomb in Hiroshima: The Theme of Death," *Daedalus* 92 (1963): 482–83; hereafter abbreviated "PE."

lieves in his own death or, to put the same thing in another way, that in the unconscious every one of us is convinced of his own immortality.' "[58] What Freud suggests here is that the moment I try to think of my own death I become a viewer of myself and hence miss precisely what is at stake in death: the cessation of my being in the world. Imagining or representing my own death thus becomes a way of overcoming the threat of nonbeing by preserving myself as an eyewitness, which means that in imagining or representing my death I occlude the very relation to nonbeing that is inseparable from death itself.[59] For Freud, the place of the dead is unoccupiable for us except by misrecognition: death sets an absolute limit on identification. Lifton denies this. "[O]ur own death—or at least our own dying—is not entirely unimaginable" ("ODDS," 202). It might be true that death can be imagined "only with a considerable degree of distance, blurring, and denial" ("DDS," 202), but that only makes it all the more necessary for us to grasp the symbolic forms by which humans confront and attempt to master death.

2. Guilt and shame are inherent in the survivor's identificatory encounter with death. Lifton treats these two affects as virtually identical. By a maneuver sanctioned by the latest psychoanalytic and anthropological studies, Lifton recasts Japan, which had previously been defined as a "shame culture," as a "guilt culture" comparable to guilt cultures in the West. But if Lifton assimilates shame to guilt, in a contrary movement he redefines guilt itself in the specular terms that, as will emerge in chapter 4, are usually associated with the notion of shame. Thus if for Lifton identification is the key to the survivor's relation to death, identification is at once immersive or mimetic *and* specular or antimimetic because structured by the accusing gaze of the dead. (We shall find the same double or mimetic-antimimetic account of identification in Lifton's work on the Buffalo Creek disaster, to be discussed in chapter 3.) He writes:

> "Identification guilt" is based upon the tendency to judge oneself through the eyes of others, as revealed by the great significance the internalized image of the accusing eyes of the dead had for Hiroshima survivors. This pressure of identification with others is stressed in East Asian and other non-Western cultures (where it is frequently referred to as a shame sanction), in contrast to the Western emphasis upon internalized conscience and upon inner evil and sinfulness. But the distinction is far from absolute. For we have

[58] Robert Jay Lifton, "On Death and Death Symbolism: The Hiroshima Disaster," *Psychiatry* 27 (1964): 202; hereafter abbreviated "ODDS." Lifton was quoting from Freud, "Thoughts for the Times on War and Death" (1915), in *The Standard Edition*, 14:289. In his paper, Lifton suggested that the Hiroshima survivor's identification with the dead strikingly resembled Niederland's description of the Holocaust survivor as presenting a "living corpse" appearance, and that the issue of "survivor priority" was central to the camp survivor's experience ("ODDS," 201, n. 24).

[59] As Lifton observed, the philosopher Maurice Merleau-Ponty had said something similar: " 'Neither my birth nor my death can appear to me as *my* experiences . . . I can only grasp myself as 'already born' and 'still living'—grasping my birth and death only as pre-personal horizons' " (cited by Lifton, "ODDS," 202).

seen that identification guilt can become thoroughly internalized and function as conscience. And the Western sense of sin is itself based on a process of identification,
whether with one's parents, with others who mediate society's rules, or with the image of
Christ.

Both guilt and shame, in their various forms, are fundamentally related issues of human connection, and the eye symbolism retained by Hiroshima survivors transcends the
somewhat arbitrary distinctions we tend to make between the two. (*DL*, 496)

From this perspective, being stared at by the dead signified both the survivor's
guilt, in the sense of being accused of wrongdoing, and his shame, in the sense
of being "exposed" as someone who selfishly wanted to live. "But the basic psychological process taking place is the survivor's identification with the owners of
the accusing eyes as human beings like him for whom he is responsible, his internalization of what he imagines to be their judgment of him, which in turn results in
his 'seeing himself' as one who has 'stolen life' from them" (*DL*, 496).[60]

3. Guilt has little to do with Freud's theories about the sexual-aggressive
drives, which Lifton rejects as mechanical. Rather, it is an expression of the survivor's sense that, however unwittingly, he or she has participated in a total human breakdown. Unlike Fingarette, Lifton endorses Martin Buber's claim that authentic guilt concerns the inner consequences of a man's actual betrayal of his
friend or cause. "Martin Buber took the right direction when he spoke of guilt as
existing when 'the human order of being is injured,' and the guilty person as 'he
who inflicted the wound.' Buber's imagery of injury and wound suggests the idea
of threat to the integrity of the individual or social organism. And indeed, Buber
relates death and guilt still more specifically by suggesting that certain forms of
action or inaction cause one to be 'again and again visited by the memory of . . .
guilt,' and to be possessed by pain that 'has nothing to do with any parental or
social reprimand' or with any social or religious 'punishing power.' "[61] Thus for
Lifton, the injury that the survivor of Hiroshima or the camps has inflicted on another human being is not essentially a matter of the survivor's guilt-inducing hostile wishes against the dead parents (*DL*, 489), but of his participation in, and dis-
tantiation from, the general breakdown of meaning associated with the traumatic
disaster: "We can therefore define guilt in general as an image-feeling of responsi-

[60] For the inseparability of guilt and shame see also "PE," 492, n. 11; *DL*, 36; and Lifton, *History and
Human Survival: Essays on the Young and Old, Survivors and the Dead, Peace and War, and on Contemporary Psychohistory* (New York, 1971), 385, n. 21. Lifton cites the work of Gerhart Piers and Milton B.
Singer, *Shame and Guilt: A Psychoanalytic and Cultural Study* (Springfield, Ill., 1953); Erik H. Erikson,
Childhood and Society (New York, 1963); and more specifically for Japan, George De Vos, "The Relation
of Guilt toward Parents to Achievement and Arranged Marriage among Japanese," *Psychiatry* 23 (1960):
287–301.

[61] Robert Jay Lifton, *The Broken Connection: On Death and the Continuity of Life* (New York, 1983),
137; hereafter abbreviated *BC*.

bility or blame for bringing about injury or disintegration, or other psychological equivalents of death . . . Freud dealt mostly with hypertrophied and pathological susceptibility to guilt—with 'neurotic guilt'—derived from early life. The term *static guilt* is used here for these patterns to emphasize the deadening immobilization of the self . . . But Freud had no provision for the energizing and transforming aspects of guilt, here called *animating guilt*" (*BC*, 139). As he also writes: "The extreme experience . . . demonstrates that guilt is immediately stimulated by participation in the breakdown of the general human order and by separation from it. This is true whether we employ the Western cultural idiom of sin and retribution or the East Asian one of humiliation and abandonment. Death, especially when inappropriate and premature, is the essence of breakdown and separation. In identifying so strongly with the dead—in forming what we have called the identity of the dead—the survivor seeks both to atone for his participation in that breakdown, and to reconstitute a form or order around that atonement" (*DL*, 497).

In particular, guilt concerns conflicts over "death timing," since the survivor simultaneously wishes to outlive his parents and wants them to live forever—indeed according to Lifton ambivalence is nothing but the experience of contradictory wishes concerning death timing (*DL*, 490). Guilt is thus a question of the survivor's "unconscious sense of an organic balance" which makes him feel that his survival has been "purchased" at the cost of another's, to the point that he may even feel that he as actually killed the other person, no matter how inappropriate that feeling is (*DL*, 490). "*For the survivor can never, inwardly, simply conclude that it was logical and right for him, and not others, to survive. Rather, I would hold, he is bound by an unconscious perception of organic social balance which makes him feel that his survival was made possible by others' death: If they had not died, he would have had to; and if he had not survived, someone else would have.* This kind of guilt, as it relates to survival priority, may well be that most fundamental to human existence" ("ODDS," 200). Lifton acknowledges that feelings of relief and even joy at surviving when others have died may contribute to the survivor's sense of guilt. In a more classically Freudian vein, he even concedes that the survivor's guilt might be "accentuated" by previous death wishes toward parents or siblings ("ODDS," 200). But he rejects Freud's emphasis on the sexual-aggressive drives, or life and death instincts, employing instead a descriptive approach that thematizes the historical-symbolic images and forms by which human beings negotiate their confrontation with death.

4. Survivor guilt does not have any inherent connection with aggression. If survivor guilt is fundamentally an identificatory phenomenon, it is less a matter of the survivor's hostile identifications with the violent or powerful father-aggressor than of a remorseful identification with the dead and impotent victim. Lifton acknowledges the existence of identification with the aggressor, but downplays it (*DL*, 498, 511) in order to emphasize a less psychoanalytic account of guilt as a feeling of responsibility for the dead, a feeling that for many survivors makes bearing witness a permanent task. In a roundtable discussion of guilt in 1972, presided over by Lifton and Leslie Farber, Dr. Joel Kovel objected to the absence in Lifton's approach to guilt of any reference to the aggressivity inherent in Freud's account: "No mention was made . . . of what Freud said was the principal problem in the development of guilt—both in terms of objective guilt and in guilt feeling, although he didn't distinguish [them]—the problem of aggression. Freud saw aggression as an independent, self-subsisting instinct in man. This is a very problematic concept, of course, but something on the order of guilt feeling can be an extremely important aid to explanation so long as it's kept tied to the problem of aggression, because it is aggression that will generate both the act of destruction and the feeling that one is being destructive."[62] This is what Lifton's approach to survivor guilt tends to deny.

One consequence of Lifton's shift of emphasis is that the notion of the survivor's abject complicity with the perpetrator's violence, implicit in the notion of identification with the aggressor, is downplayed. Concern about the ways in which theories about the survivor's identification with the aggressor could be seen as "blaming the victim" surfaced in psychoanalytic circles even before Des Pres and others made it the center of their critique (see chapter 2). Thus echoes of the controversy over Raul Hilberg's discussion of the Jewish failure to resist the Nazis and Hannah Arendt's remarks in *Eichmann in Jerusalem* about the cooperation of the Jewish leadership in the ghettoes of the East can be found in the workshop discussions of massive traumatization during the 1960s and early 1970s.[63] It would not be going too far, I think, to suggest that Lifton's account of the survivor's identification with the dead served to defuse worries that psychoanalytic theories about survivor guilt amounted to accusing Jews of abject complicity in their fate. On Lifton's revised approach, if survivors feel guilty, they do so because of their identification with the dead victims, not because of their psychic collusion with violence.

5. The kind of guilt that matters is not the static, compulsive, self-punishing guilt of the neurotic, but the animating, creative guilt of the kind that has the po-

---

[62] Leslie H. Farber and Robert Jay Lifton, "Questions of Guilt," *Partisan Review* 39 (1972): 523; hereafter abbreviated "QG."

[63] "Hillberg [sic] (1962), in trying to understand the Jewish reaction to overcompliance to their Nazi enemies, has suggested that 1500 years of ghetto existence and persecution by the Christian Church-State had modified the reaction to threatened genocide to the extent that resistance and revenge became impossible, and only appeasement, overcompliance and evasion were available as modes of action . . . Involved here is a process of suggestion in which the individual becomes convinced that he *deserves* to be killed and/or that any resistance is pointless. Should the execution be called off at the last minute, we may discover the prisoner to be psychologically damaged . . . He may . . . present a picture of a 'break in the life-line' and 'collapse of the personality,' as observed in concentration camp survivors" (*MPT*, 5). For another reference to the Hilberg-Arendt dispute see *PT*, 121.

tential to change and transform the patient. The distinction between neurotic and animating guilt was elaborated by Lifton during his engagement with antiwar Vietnam veterans in the 1970s, work that entailed a shift of attention from the victims of the atom bomb and the camps to a more explicit confrontation with the role of the perpetrator. As Lifton recognized, the guilt Vietnam veterans tended to acknowledge and that fueled the antiwar movement was not so much a function of their experiences as victims and survivors of atrocity but of their participation as "slaughterers" in what they now saw as an unjust and evil war. In Lifton's conceptualization, animating guilt belongs less to the domain of the unconscious and the conflictual than to the domain of the individual's moral and legal culpability for the murder of others, including innocent civilians. According to Lifton, this guilt becomes an energizing "anxiety of responsibility" when it encourages persons to take responsibility for the wrongs they have committed by identifying with the victims and other groups and by agitating for political change.[64]

The overall result of Lifton's shift of emphasis from neurotic to "real" guilt was to give survivor guilt a positive value as that which leads to recognition of the interdependency of human life in terms remote from Freud's ideas. "In Freudian theory the idea of guilt is built around parricide and the Oedipus complex: guilt is seen most fundamentally as an expression of something like parricide," Lifton wrote. "What I'm suggesting is a theory of guilt in which guilt comes into the world, so to speak, not around the Oedipus complex, biologically or genetically transmitted and re-stimulated within each generation or family life, but rather, simply around the issue of life and death itself insofar as we take responsibility for death and dying or for symbolic modes of killing and destroying aspects of others, whether literally their bodies or something more metaphorical in them or in our selves" ("QG," 518).[65] In a recent interview Lifton has suggested that bearing witness is one way the camp survivor can transmute the pain and guilt of

---

[64] As Ben Shephard has pointed out, the work of Niederland and others helped create a new professional model of the psychiatrist as patients' advocate, helping a group of wronged victims win reparation of various kinds. It also helped create the idea that victims of extreme conditions could be afflicted by a special "syndrome," characterized by symptoms such as delayed emotional aftereffects, survivor guilt, and depression. Chaim Shatan and others were struck by the the resemblance between the emotional problems of the returning Vietnam veteran and the concentration camp survivors. In 1972 Shatan invited Niederland to give a workshop presentation called "The Guilt and Grief of Vietnam Veterans and Concentration Camp Survivors." Niederland was ambivalent about drawing parallels between the two groups. See C. Shatan, "The Grief of Soldiers: Vietnam Combat Veterans' Self-Help Movement," *American Journal of Orthopsychiatry* 43 (1973): 640–53; idem, "Stress Disorders among Vietnam Veterans: The Emotional Content of Combat Continues," in *Stress Disorders among Vietnam Veterans*, ed. C. Figley, (New York, 1978), 456–47; H. Glover, "Survival Guilt and the Vietnam Veteran," *Journal of Nervous and Mental Diseases* 172 (1984), 393–97; and Ben Shephard, *A War of Nerves* (London, 2000), 361.

[65] For a similar discussion see Robert Jay Lifton, *The Broken Connection: On Death and the Continuity of Life* (New York, 1983), 132–46.

survival into responsibility.[66] In short, through his work with the Vietnam veterans, Lifton came to elaborate a notion of guilt that is much closer to traditional ideas about responsibility than to Freud's psychoanalytic concepts. Not surprisingly, when his ideas were taken up by critics of the concept of the survivor guilt, such as Des Pres, they were put to uses that were fundamentally hostile to the psychoanalytic enterprise.

[66] Cathy Caruth, "An Interview with Robert Lifton" in *Trauma: Explorations in Memory*, ed. Cathy Caruth, (Baltimore, 1995), 138.

Dismantling Survivor Guilt

"Radical Nakedness"

IN 1976, the concepts of survivor guilt and identification with the aggressor were subjected to an attack widely held to be so persuasive that there is an important sense in which they never fully recovered their former prestige. In his critique, *The Survivor: An Anatomy of Life in the Death Camps*, Terrence Des Pres aimed to wrest the image of the camp survivor as a broken psychopathological "case" from the psychoanalysts in order to celebrate the victim's extraordinary talent for life and moral endurance.[1] Des Pres's success is at first sight surprising. His sociobiological premises seem naive and his portrait of survivors as generally admirable individuals devoid of debilitating resentment or emotional harm appears too simplistic. Since the 1960s the notions of survivor guilt and identification with the aggressor had been at the center of the clinical understanding of the victims of the camps without arousing serious controversy.[2] Yet with few exceptions, critics now applauded Des Pres's work in such glowing terms as to suggest that a fundamental paradigm shift was in the air.

Des Pres was a literary critic who based his arguments largely on a reading of

---

[1] Terrence Des Pres, *The Survivor: An Anatomy of Life in the Death Camps* (Oxford, 1976); hereafter abbreviated *TS*.

[2] A point made by George M. Kren, "The Holocaust Survivor and Psychoanalysis," in *Healing Their Wounds: Psychotherapy with Holocaust Survivors and Their Families*, ed. Paul Marcus and Alan Rosenberg (New York, 1989), 7. Some sociologists had criticized Bettelheim earlier, but their work did not attract much attention until Des Pres's attack.

texts, not on interviews with survivors themselves.[3] He made use of a variety of materials, including fiction (novels by Camus, Malamud, and Solzhenitsyn), memoirs by survivors of both Nazi and Soviet concentration camps, certain sociological-anthropological writings, and biological-sociobiological analyses of animal behavior. Among the works mentioned in his book was Hannah Arendt's *Eichmann in Jerusalem* (1963). The reference to Arendt provides a clue to one of the contexts in which the production and reception of Des Pres's book needs to be situated, namely, the divisive controversy that, starting in 1963, had erupted in America and elsewhere over Arendt's notion of the "banality of evil" and her discussion of the role of the *Judenraten* in the fate of the Jews. In his monumental study, *The Destruction of the European Jews* (1961), on which Arendt relied heavily, the historian Raul Hilberg had also stressed the part played in the disaster by the "cooperation" of the ghetto leaders. In reaction against Arendt's and Hilberg's emphasis on the passivity and collusiveness of at least certain victims of the Nazis, a movement had begun that sought to portray the survivor in less pathological, more positive terms.[4] Recently, Susan Neiman has claimed that Arendt's argument in her Eichmann report was quite different from what it has usually been taken to be, suggesting that Arendt's work can be read as "the best attempt at theodicy postwar philosophy has produced." By this she means that Arendt sought to demonstrate that if under conditions of terror most people will comply but, in Arendt's words, "'*some people will not*,'" then humanly speaking "'no more is required, and no more can reasonably be asked, for this planet to remain a place fit for human habitation.'"[5] Des Pres's work on the survivor may be viewed similarly as a modern, quasireligious theodicy that sought to justify the persistence of virtue in an evil world. As he stated, the goal of his book was to "see what goodness might be found in the worst possible world."[6] Des Pres acknowledged the savagery of the camps and the fact that death was a certain outcome for huge num-

---

[3] At one point, Des Pres mentions talking to survivors about suicide in the camps (*TS*, 86), but he does not report their words, nor does he seem to have systematically interviewed survivors. Anna Ornstein is therefore mistaken when she describes Des Pres's findings as "empirical" because based on interviews with survivors. See Anna Ornstein, "Survival and Recovery," *Psychoanalytic Inquiry* 5 (1985): 114.

[4] For a discussion of the role played by Arendt's Eichmann report and Hilberg's work in the debate over Jewish passivity see especially Peter Novick, *The Holocaust in American Life* (Boston, 1999). See also Lawrence Douglas's discussion of the issue of Jewish collaboration in *The Memory of Judgment: Making Law and History in the Trials of the Holocaust* (New Haven, 2001).

[5] Susan Neiman, *Evil in Modern Thought: An Alternative History of Philosophy* (Princeton, 2002), 300, 302, citing Arendt's *Eichmann in Jerusalem: A Report on the Banality of Evil* (New York, 1963), 233; see also Susan Neiman, "Theodicy in Jerusalem," in *Hannah Arendt in Jerusalem*, ed. Steven E. Ascheim (Berkeley, 2001), 81.

[6] Terrence Des Pres, "The Bettelheim Problem," *Social Research* 46 (1979): 646. Des Pres justifies his use of a "kind of archaic, quasi-religious vocabulary" because "only a language of ultimate concern can be adequate to facts such as these" (*TS*, vi).

bers of prisoners. But he wanted to qualify the view of the camps as "all against all" by emphasizing the "small deeds of courage and resistance, of help and mutual care" that took place there (*TS*, 99). According to him, if modern totalitarianisms had not succeeded in completely destroying human morality and conscience, this was because men and women possessed built-in moral resources on which under extreme conditions they could rely in order to maintain themselves as free, ethical individuals.

One of the most original if dubious components of Des Pres's argument was his use of the newly emerging science of sociobiology to explain survival in terms of biologically evolved behavior patterns designed to keep life going in even the most dire circumstances. For Des Pres, survival in the concentration camps essentially depended on a "biologically determined 'talent'" for life or "bank of knowledge embedded in the body's cells"—a biological gift which ensured that even under the most extreme conditions men and women tended to preserve themselves in ways recognizably human, just as other animals, plants, and even bacteria also tend to preserve themselves: "The key to survival behavior may thus lie in the priority of biological being" (*TS*, 193). The survivor's biological endowment, not culture, ensured that resistance, dignity, goodwill, trust, and decency survived the totalitarian assault. Setting up a stark opposition between civilization and extremity, he offered a materialist vision according to which life in the camps had no symbolic or psychological meaning but was lived at a purely corporeal level. Des Pres thus claimed that the camp inmate's life was lived in a mode of "radical nakedness" (*TS*, 179) because it was lived completely outside the norms of everyday life.[7]

This meant that psychoanalysis was useless for explaining the camp inmate's behavior. According to Des Pres, the phenomenon of civilization was based on the processes of sublimation and symbolization. Civilization thus defined involved the transcendence of primal needs through systems of technical and symbolic mediation. Freedom to mediate facts and "instill new significance, to create and multiply meanings" was its essence (*TS*, 157). As a "theory of culture" and of man in the civilized state, Des Pres acknowledged the considerable interpretive power of psychoanalysis when it was applied to actions that were complex because "symbolic, mediated, and therefore at a sufficient remove from necessity" (*TS*, 155). Psychoanalysis correctly understood that under conditions of culture nothing could be taken at face value: in ordinary life people acted for all sorts of reasons, some known and others unconscious. Behavior therefore required interpretation; indeed, "interpretation validates experience, hence the usefulness of the psychoanalytic approach" (*TS*, 157).

---

[7] Des Pres had been a Junior Fellow in the Harvard University's Society of Fellows, where he would have had the chance to converse with the biologist E. O. Wilson, whose book, *Sociobiology: The New Synthesis* (1975), informs Des Pres's study.

But in the camps the multiplicity of motives that gave civilized behavior its depth and complexity was lost and the purpose of action became simply to keep life going: "When men and women must respond directly to necessity—when defilement occurs at gun-point and the most undelayable of needs determines action, or when death itself is the determinant—then behavior has no 'meaning' at all in a symbolic or psychological sense" (*TS*, 155–56). Survivors act as they do "because they must—the issue is always life and death—and at every moment the meaning and purpose of their behavior is fully known" (*TS*, 157). Extremity was thus a situation in which men and women lived "*without accommodation*" because they were "stripped of spiritual as well as physical mediations, until literally nothing was left to persist through pain and time but the body itself" (*TS*, 181). In such conditions there could be no disagreement about the meaning of prisoner behavior in the camps because in an abrupt process of "desublimation" (*TS*, 182) the inmate was reduced to his immediate material existence. "In extremity everything depends on the body" (*TS*, 183)—a body that thanks to evolution knew how to act spontaneously and correctly, which is to say, how to act in a recognizably human and ethically responsible way.

It was Des Pres's commitment to a kind of materialism, his emphasis on the radical nakedness of the camp experience, that made irrelevant not only any appeal to unconscious motives and feelings in the explanation of the survivor's behavior but to the notion of interpretation as such. The critic Lawrence Langer has proposed similar ideas. It is true that Des Pres adopted a form of immanence that Langer disputes. According to Des Pres, under conditions of extremity "meaning no longer exists above and beyond the world; it re-enters concrete experience, becomes immanent and invests each act and moment with urgent depth" (*TS*, 69). Using sociobiology to explain victim behavior, Des Pres imagined not the end of morality for the prisoners but its naked exhibition, its revelation as a biological-material "instinct" for goodness and social cooperation.[8] Langer rejects Des Pres's reliance on traditional ethical concepts, such as dignity, to describe the response to atrocity, and his idealization of the inmates' behavior, because Langer thinks the very springs of moral existence were destroyed by the Nazi system of genocide. Yet for Langer, too, the death encounter resists symbolization and metaphorization and hence is "strictly physical."[9] He says of survivor Charlotte Delbo's haunting dream in which she says she felt again the "'*real* thirst'" she experienced when at Auschwitz-Birkenau that "the nightmare [Delbo] describes is not a metaphor but a reality. Nothing is disguised, and no one is needed to analyze its concealed meanings"—as if her dream was a literal transcription of events

---

[8] There is, in fact, a Spinozian element to Des Pres's work, as J. L. Cameron noted in his review of *The Survivor,* "Living through Hell," *New York Review of Books,* March 4, 1976, 20.

[9] Lawrence Langer, *Versions of Survival: The Holocaust and the Human Spirit* (New York, 1982), 55; hereafter abbreviated *VS.*

and the camp survivor's experience one of unmediated, material factuality.[10] Agamben claims much the same thing when he reflects on the concentration camp as a space of exception. *"Inasmuch as its inhabitants have been stripped of every political status and reduced completely to naked life,"* he writes, *"the camp is also the most absolute biopolitical space that has ever been realized—a space in which power confronts nothing other than pure biological life without any mediation . . .* [T]he essence of the camp consists in the materialization of the state of exception and the consequent creation of a space for naked life as such."[11]

Des Pres, Langer, and Agamben are thus committed to a version of the literalism and materialism that, as I argued in *Trauma: A Genealogy*, informs more recent discussions of massive stress—and with the same problematic results. In that book, I argued that there is a marked tendency in recent trauma theory to treat the traumatic event as something that leaves a "reality imprint" in the brain, an imprint that in its insistent literality testifies to the existence of a timeless historical truth unaffected by suggestive-mimetic factors or unconscious-symbolic elaboration. Modern trauma theorists are thus bound to the epistemological-ontological claim that the symptoms of trauma, such as repetitive nightmares and flashbacks, are literal or material replicas of the trauma and that, as such, they stand outside all interpretation or representation. In my book on trauma I subjected such claims to an extensive critique. My point here is that we find in the earlier example of Des Pres a similar tendency to literalism and materialism. In his case, one might sympathize with his desire to resist, say, the crudeness of the psychoanalytic claim that the camp inmate's anguish at being forced to live in his own excrement and filth was due to a conflict between his horror at the forced breaching of cultural taboos and his regressive, infantile desire to subvert them (*TS*, 67). But when he goes on to argue that what made excremental assault so unbearable to the victim was that the "symbolic stain" became a condition of "literal defilement" and that the evil caused a "real 'loss of the core of the personal core of one's being'" (*TS*,

---

[10] Lawrence L. Langer, *Holocaust Testimonies: The Ruins of Memory* (New Haven, 1991), 8); hereafter abbreviated *HT*. "When decisions determined by the desire to continue *being* are described with a vocabulary of value, the quality of that being is inevitably distorted," Langer writes elsewhere (*VS*, 124). Langer's attempt to distinguish between "heroic" versus "deep" (or "unheroic," or "humiliated," or "anguished") memory relies on this distinction between meaning *versus* the unmediated or "naked" fact or truth. So does his belief that oral testimony can give us a glimpse of the literal or naked truth of the camps, a truth that is stripped of all values. He regards Elie Wiesel's description of man in Auschwitz as a "starved stomach" as a perfect image of life in extremity (*HT*, 25), where not only life but also language is reduced to "physical substance, the thing itself" (*HT*, 46). Langer goes further than Des Pres in imagining that in extremity the victim's behavior is completely determined by material "circumstances" rather than values or meaning (*VS*, 124), so that he lacks all choice.

[11] Giorgio Agamben, *Means without End: Notes on Politics,* trans. Vincenzo Binetti and Cesare Casarino (Minneapolis, 2000), 40.

69), he is offering an interpretation of camp behavior that is itself open to challenge. In his literalism and materialism he assumes that excremental contact is inevitably humiliating or shameful to every human being in every context. Yet it could be argued that for some or indeed many individuals, what is humiliating or shameful is not fecal contact *per se* but the feeling of powerlessness associated with excremental assault. In other words, it could be that it is precisely the meaning of the overall situation that determines the victim's reaction.[12]

The Survivor as Witness

To defend his position Des Pres needed to argue that the camp prisoner's mind was divested of any hidden or psychic content in order to make it performatively one with a body destined by evolution to maintain an ethically coherent life. He therefore undertook to refute two well-entrenched psychoanalytic assumptions—that survivors suffered from guilt for outliving dead relatives, friends, and fellow prisoners, and that under extremity they tended to identify with their tormentors (which is why, according to the Freudian theory of the superego, they felt guilty). He treated Lifton's writings on the victims of Hiroshima as the "most developed" work on survivor guilt; Bruno Bettelheim, in his capacity as the most famous of the Freudians associated with the notion of identification with the aggressor, was Des Pres's other target. We shall see that neither concepts of identification nor of guilt and shame are alien to Des Pres's work, but that in his hands they take on a decidedly unpsychoanalytic meaning.

It was shrewd of Des Pres to focus on Lifton's contributions to the notion of survivor guilt, rather than those of Niederland, whose work he did not mention, for as has emerged Lifton had already shifted the focus of attention away from the survivor's identification with the aggressor to the survivor's identification with the dead victim in ways that suited Des Pres.[13] For Des Pres, too, wanted to situate the question of guilt in the context of the survivor's relationship with the dead—but with a difference. Des Pres's essential claim was that the testimony of the survivor was rooted in an instinctive "will to bear witness" (*TS*, 133) whose

[12] This argument has been made by Maury Silva, Rosaria Conte, Maria Miceli, and Isabella Poggi in "Humiliation: Feeling, Social Control, and the Construction of Identity," *Journal for the Theory of Social Behavior* 16 (October 1986): 269–83. For critiques of Des Pres's sociobiological ideas see J. M. Cameron, "Living Through Hell," 19–20; and Leon Rappoport, "Survivors of the Holocaust," *Journal of Psychohistory* 4 (1977): 359–67.

[13] The work of Niederland and others was however discussed by Ernest Rappaport, whose papers Des Pres valued (see below). Des Pres also cited the classical work of Auschwitz survivor Elie A. Cohen, *Human Behavior in the Concentration Camp* (1954), trans. M. H. Braaksma (New York, 1954), in which the author applied the notion of identification with the aggressor to explain aspects of the inmate's behavior.

source was the survivor's knowledge that he or she could not have survived without the help of countless dead others. In Des Pres's view, the survivor's imperative to tell the story therefore represented a debt to the dead based not on some obscure psychological process but on a literal identification or identity with them: "It is not an exaggeration, nor merely a metaphor, to say that the survivor's identity includes the dead" (*TS*, 38). For Des Pres the survivor's identification with the dead was radically misunderstood if it was taken as evidence of something "suspect" in the survivor's behavior: "Observers call it 'survival guilt,' a term much used and almost wholly negative in emphasis" (*TS*, 39). He criticized Lifton for claiming that survivors had a need to justify their survival in the face of the death of loved ones, that the survivors' incorporation of the dead created guilt over survival, and that their tendency to be haunted by the dead was clear proof of neurosis. Rejecting the theory of survivor guilt on the grounds that it attributed blame for his sufferings to the victim himself, Des Pres defined the survivor instead as a person who insisted on the need to remember and be heard by a psychiatric system that was mistakenly determined to scapegoat him: "We join in a 'conspiracy of silence,' and undermine the survivor's authority by pointing to his guilt. If he is guilty, then perhaps it is true that the victims of atrocity collaborate in their own destruction; in which case blame can be imputed to the victims themselves. And if he is guilty, then the survivor's suffering, all the sorrow he describes, is deserved; in which case a balance between *that* pain and our own is restored. Strategies like these are commonly employed against survivors. Most simply, of course, the imputation of guilt is a transfer from spectator to victim" (*TS*, 41).[14]

This last passage suggests that Des Pres shared with many other commentators a misconception about the psychoanalytic notion of guilt, confusing the survivor's unconscious intention or fantasy to commit aggression, or to identify with the oppressor, with actual complicity in murderous events. Bettelheim registered this objection when he complained that by asserting that the survivor is *not* guilty, Des Pres obfuscated the real issue, since "nobody in his senses has ever charged he *was* guilty": the real issue was that the survivor nevertheless *felt* remorse.[15] The Freudian claim was that the feeling of guilt might be entirely fantasmatic and hence radically dissociated from any actual crime. However, Des Pres

---

[14] "By saying men and women died like sheep we say that they collaborated in the administration of their own deaths, and therefore *they* are responsible for the crimes that occurred. And because survivors are obsessed with a need to bear witness, to 'let the world know,' as they say, we have concluded that this abnormal behavior can only be fueled by guilt . . . Conscience is thereby reduced to confession, concern to fixation; and to madmen such as these we need not listen. For if the survivor is guilty he or she is infected and must be shunned . . . Terrible events are thus reduced to acts of self-infliction. Violence has its origin and outcome in those to whom it happens, and the moral symmetry of the universe is upheld" (Terrence Des Pres, "Victims and Survivors," *Dissent* 23 [1976], 49).

[15] Bruno Bettelheim, *Surviving and Other Essays* (New York, 1979), 297.

argued that since the will to bear witness arose in the *initial* stage of adjustment to extremity, before guilt had had time to accrue, the will to testify had the force of a "task" that preceded any notion of guilt (*TS*, 39). He cited the following passage from a letter sent to him by a survivor, Ernest A. Rappaport:

> I feel no guilt in being a survivor, but I feel that I have a task to fulfill. We may call it the sur-
> vivor task, and it is a part of my ego ideal, not of my superego. This task crowded into my
> thinking when I participated for the first time at the roll call of the captives in the concen-
> tration camp Buchenwald thirty-four years ago when I had no guarantee whatsoever that
> I would be a survivor. (*TS*, 40)[16]

Rappaport also published two papers on the trauma of the concentration camps that Des Pres regarded as crucial to his case: "These are important articles, and much of my argument against the current concept of survival guilt is based on Dr. Rappaport's observations."[17]

Des Pres's enthusiasm for Rappaport's ideas is curious, for his papers make an odd impression.[18] Disjointed and clumsily organized, they exhibit some of the same difficulties in mastering trauma that the author was trying to analyze at the level of theory. Nevertheless, they are of considerable interest for the light they throw on the stakes involved in Des Pres's reevaluation of the survivor. Although in the course of his postwar career as a psychoanalyst in Chicago, Rappaport interviewed other survivors as part of the German reparation process ("SG," 45), his primary subject was himself. Like Niederland and others, whose work on the survivor syndrome he acknowledged, Rappaport was troubled by the inadequacy of existing diagnoses, such as "traumatic neurosis," to capture the experience of massive trauma. But he took his concerns in a different direction. He rejected the thesis that the survivor unconsciously "incorporates" the violence directed against himself. He was especially critical of Bettelheim's claims along these lines,

---

[16] The letter, the only one from a survivor quoted throughout the entire book, is unattributed but on internal evidence was undoubtedly written by Rappaport, who was in Buchenwald at the same time as Bettelheim.

[17] Des Pres, "Survivors and the Will to Bear Witness," *Social Research* 40 (1973): 682–83, note; hereafter abbreviated "S."

[18] Ernest A. Rappaport, "Beyond Traumatic Neurosis: A Psychoanalytic Study of Late Reactions to the Concentration Camp Trauma," *International Journal of Psychoanalysis* 49 (1968): 719–31, hereafter abbreviated "BTN"; and idem, "Survivor Guilt," *Midstream* 17 (1971): 41–47, hereafter abbreviated "SG." For a recent mention of Rappaport's essays see Robert Krell's essay, "Psychiatry and the Holocaust," in Robert Krell and Marcus I. Sherman, *Medical and Psychological Effects of Concentration Camps on Holocaust Survivors*, vol. 4, *Genocide: A Critical Bibliographic Review* (New Brunswick, N.J., 1997), 6. Condemning the failure of postwar psychiatry, especially psychoanalysis, to deal appropriately with the survivor, Krell praises Rappaport's work as a "particularly compelling" critique of Bettelheim's and other psychoanalytic theories of the survivor. But Krell does not seem to be aware of Des Pres's reliance on Rappaport's work.

which he dismissed as the product of an insufficiently distanced personal experience and as likely to encourage an anti-Semitic tendency to blame the victim ("BTN," 723). For Rappaport, what made his experience of the camps traumatic was the guilty indifference of bystanders who, having themselves been exempted from the trauma of the camps, refused to listen to the witnesses from hell ("BTN," 720). What the victim himself felt was not guilt, Rappaport claimed, but frustration at being unable to tell his story.

As he reported, while in Buchenwald he had managed to purchase on the black market a counterfeit Shanghai visa that had enabled him to leave the camp and emigrate. As he was leaving Germany, he had been taken off the train and threatened with further punishment by German agents if he should subsequently dare to speak out about the atrocities he had experienced and witnessed. Although this threat had strengthened his determination to publicize his experiences, somehow he had been unable to do so. According to Rappaport, this was the theme of the anxious, repetitive dreams that had haunted him personally for so many years, for in his dreams all sorts of obstacles, including the SS, got in his way. Rappaport thus interpreted his repetitive dreams as frustrated attempts to publicize his camp experience. He observed that at a recent discussion of an earlier version of one of his papers, the psychoanalyst Otto E. Sperling attributed Rappaport's long delay in publishing his ideas to obvious superego warnings: " 'If I were his superego,' " Rappaport reported Sperling as saying, " 'I would have been impatient too. I would have asked him, 'why do you wait until the last moment to write this paper? It is now twenty-four years since those things happened. What will you do if you die before you write the paper?' " ("BTN," 730). Sperling thus interpreted Rappaport's dilatoriness as a response to a prohibition, specifically, the Nazi ban against his bearing witness to his ordeal. As Rappaport noted: "He interpreted my procrastination on the basis of his hypothesis of the parasitic superego of the enemy which he assumed was introjected by the Gestapo command to keep silent about the camp when they took me off the train at the border station. It has derived from his concept of the trauma as a command which he had also used to interpret the lack of resistance of the Jewish victims of Nazi persecution" ("BTN," 729). In other words, Sperling interpreted Rappaport's dreams and inability to publish an account of his camp experiences in classically mimetico-traumatic terms as due to the victim's unconscious identification with the threatening aggressor and his incorporation of the Nazi prohibition against testifying.[19]

[19] Sperling made his comments on Rappaport's paper at the annual meeting of the American Psychoanalytic Association in Los Angeles, in May 1964. Rappaport appears to be referring to Otto E. Sperling's paper, "The Interpretation of Trauma as a Command," *Psychoanalytic Quarterly* 19 (1950): 352–70, based in part on the analysis of concentration camp inmates, where, in line with Ferenczi's earlier observations on trauma, the author suggested that trauma produced an identificatory incorporation of the stimulus, conceived as a hypnotic command. The result was that the victim incorporated the enemy's superego

But Rappaport refused Sperling's interpretation, asserting that it was the "trauma after trauma" ("BTN," 730) of not being heard after the war that weakened his determination to write.[20] He thus attributed his failure as a witness not to any unconscious determinants but to a deficit due largely to the trauma of the world's indifference to his sufferings:

> The dreams are repetitive dreams and are the ego's attempt at subsequent mastery not of the trauma but of the task to alert the world and to become a witness for the prosecution before the tribunal of history. The feeling of urgency is so great that the mind is flooded with camp memories which attach themselves at random to any theme of daily life regardless of its significance. I have the inclination to forget, but there is the consciousness of a mission of which I keep reminding myself . . . I keep on, at least unconsciously, to struggle against the defeat of civilization . . . There is no childhood prototype in the unconscious of experiences of this sort . . . The danger to life was actually much less of a trauma than the abandonment by a faithless and indifferent inhumanity and the utterly degrading and humiliating conditions in the camp . . . In conclusion, one can say that the regenerative powers of the ego are not limitless, that the human spirit can be broken beyond repair, and that the damage can go "beyond" a traumatic neurosis . . . The camp experience is so far outside normal experience and so far from the usual categories of thinking and feeling that it not only has no prototype as a derivative from childhood memories in the unconscious; it can never be deleted from memory. ("BTN," 729–30)

I take Rappaport to be claiming that his repetitive dreams were not symbolic representations of infantile inner conflicts, as classical psychoanalysis would assume, or more direct representations of the actual trauma of the camps, as Niederland's revised account of the traumatic neuroses would claim. Rather, they represented the dreamer's determination to testify to his experience of the camps. If he was nevertheless thwarted in his goal, this was because his traumatized ego has been damaged and above all because of the world's defensive

---

injunction, thereby acquiring a parasitic superego, rather in the way hypnotic incorporation and repetition occurred under conditions of fright. He mentioned as the most striking contemporary example of this phenomenon the great number of prisoners of concentration camps who espoused the doctrines of their torturers, citing in this regard the work of Bettelheim and others on the tendency of concentration camp victims to identify with the enemy.

[20] Rappaport continued: "Instead, there was a fear of appearing perhaps 'abnormal' and of having not worked through my own inner conflicts. Even Sperling who opened his discussion with declaring how necessary it was that I wrote this paper, referred to my 'conflict' about faith in humanity and accusations about humanity's lack of interest as a reflection or revival of a conflict with a parent figure in my childhood. Unfortunately—not in particular for me, but for humanity—it is considered an attribute of normality to retain a resigned or acquiescent silence in the face of crime" ("BTN," 730). See also Yael Danieli, "Psychotherapists' Participation in the Conspiracy of Silence About the Holocaust," *Psychoanalytic Psychology* 14 (1984): 23–42.

apathy. The net effect of Rappaport's interpretation was to deny the dynamics of the Freudian unconscious by treating the dream at the manifest level of meaning, by transferring the notion of survivor guilt from the victim to the bystander, and by regarding the victim's memories of the camp experience as intact and veridical— in brief, by depathologizing the victim and placing blame for his psychological difficulties largely on the resistance he encountered when he did not go along with the "'preferred attitude of forgetting'" (TS, 41).

Des Pres followed Rappaport in interpreting the survivor's behavior in terms of a "task" (TS, 40). He found further support for his view in Lifton's recent effort, already discussed in the previous chapter, to rethink survivor guilt as a problem less of neurosis than of an "energizing or animating guilt" or "anxiety of responsibility" expressive of the victim's intense concern with the historical record and need to render significant the deaths he had seen (TS, 40).[21] "At which point—and this is the conclusion I draw from Lifton's work—the idea of guilt transcends itself," Des Pres commented. "As the capacity for response to deeds and events; as care for the future; as awareness of the interdependency of human life, it becomes simply conscience. Ernest A. Rappaport has reached a similar conclusion" (TS, 40). In other words, Des Pres accepted the relevance of guilt to the survivor, but endorsed a notion of guilt that, shorn of any psychoanalytic-dynamic attributes, reverted to the quasireligious idea of a conscience. Thus for Des Pres, what was wrong with the theory of survivor guilt was precisely that it belonged to a symbolic-interpretive system that he felt served to deny the brute reality of the camps. As civilized human beings, people living "safe and at ease" were not prepared to hear what the survivor had to say because their spiritual well-being depended on "systems of mediation which transcend or otherwise deflect the sources of dread." They used such mediations to deflect attention from those "primal negations of human value," evil, and "human insufficiency" that they would rather ignore (TS, 41–42).

The only guilt whose existence Des Pres was prepared to admit was the survivor's "real guilt" (TS, 43) as a transgressor of existing norms and disturber of the peace who wished to speak the truth about unspeakable things, a guilt that was only redoubled when out of self-doubt he betrayed his task of bearing witness. "The final guilt is not to bear witness. The survivor's worst torment is not to be able to speak" (TS, 43).[22] What the survivor knew and "civilized people" preferred

[21] Des Pres cites Robert J. Lifton's "Questions of Guilt," Partisan Review 39 (Winter 1972): 514–30 (already discussed in chapter 1).

[22] Des Pres's valorization of the act of testifying contrasts with the claim of Shoshana Felman, Dori Laub, and some other recent theorists of trauma that the radical nature of the camp experience precluded all witnessing; for them, silence—or the impossibility of testifying—becomes the mark of trauma, a point that will be further elaborated by Agamben (see chapter 5). See Shoshana Felman and Dori Laub, Testimony: Crises of Witnessing in Literature, Psychoanalysis, and History (New York, 1992).

to ignore was that "life lives upon life" (*TS*, 43), that is, that survival depended on the general sacrifice of others. Des Pres observed that the philosopher Karl Jaspers had defined "collective" or "metaphysical guilt" as the lack of absolute solidarity with the human being as such. He quoted Jaspers as stating: " 'This solidarity is violated by my presence at a wrong or a crime. It is not enough that I cautiously risk my life to prevent it; if it happens and I was there, and if I survive where the other is killed, I know from a voice within myself: I am guilty of being still alive' " (*TS*, 43).[23] Des Pres noted that in a famous passage Levi had referred to this same feeling when he spoke on liberation of " 'the shame . . . the just man experiences at another's crime; the feeling of guilt that such a crime should exist, that it should have been introduced irrevocably into the world of things that exist, and that his will for good should have proved too weak or null, and should not have availed in defense' " (*TS*, 43).[24] But he denied there was anything metaphysical about Levi's perception, which he argued stemmed rather from the survivor's awareness of the "empirical fact" that each person's existence depended on the work, sacrifice, and often death of others. That awareness, that sense of responsibility for the other, was not unique to survivors and ought not to be imputed to them as if theirs was a special case (*TS*, 44).

In one passage Rappaport himself made use of the notion of survivor guilt to describe the case of a severely depressed survivor whose marriage while hiding from the Nazis "saved her from suicide out of guilt that she had not accompanied her parents on the road to death" ("BTN," 726). But Des Pres simply asserted: "With very few exceptions, the testimony of survivors does not concern itself with guilt of any sort" (*TS*, 44). He proposed that the attention of survivors was directed wholly at the scenes of horror they could never forget, scenes they felt morally compelled to record in a story whose content, moreover, had to be accepted "at face value"—that is, as the literal or objective truth (*TS*, 44). Consistent with his biological materialism, Des Pres even conceptualized the survivor's testimony in corporeal-material terms. Just as the mangled body revealed a mangled soul, he suggested, so in the presence of the horror of the camps mind and body recoiled in "a single expression of shock" (*TS*, 46): "The whole body screams, and this 'last vestige of human dignity,' as Nadezhda Mandelstam suggested, is life's own cry of dread and care, of recognition and refusal and appeal to resistance. On the surface men go numb, but deeper down the scream is there, 'like a flame imprisoned in my bones,' as Chaim Kaplan puts it" (*TS*, 46). On this basis, Des Pres defined conscience as a kind of objective-corporeal reaction:

[23] Des Pres cites from Karl Jaspers, *The Question of German Guilt,* trans. E. B. Ashton (New York, 1947), 71.

[24] Des Pres cites from Primo Levi's *The Reawakening*, trans. Stuart Woolf (Boston, 1965), 182.

This response, this *response-ability*, is what I wish to call "conscience"—conscience in its social form; not the internalized voice of authority, not the introspective self-loathing of the famed Puritan or "New England" conscience. And not remorse. If bearing witness were an isolated private act, a purely subjective event, then perhaps the theory of guilt would serve. But as we have seen, the survivor's behavior is typical, and more, it is integral to conditions which reach beyond personal involvement. Horrible events take place, that is the (objective) beginning. The survivor feels compelled to bear witness, that is the (subjective) middle. His testimony enters public consciousness, thereby modifying the moral order to which it appeals, and that is the (objective) end. Conscience, in other words, is a social achievement . . . Through [the survivor] the events in question are verified and their reality made binding in the eyes of others. The survivor-as-witness, therefore, embodies a socio-historical process founded not upon the desire for justice (what can justice mean when genocide is the issue?), but upon the involvement of all human beings in common care for life and the future . . . Survivors do not bear witness to guilt, neither theirs nor ours, but to objective conditions of evil. (*TS*, 46–49)

The terms of Des Pres's overall analysis are almost identical to those used by Langer in the latter's somewhat later critique of survivor guilt. There is the same tendency to a stark dualism between the objective and the subjective, or between the external and the internal, a dualism that excludes any recourse to a third or middle term, such as unconscious fantasy, to explain the idea of survivor guilt; the same tendency to imagine that the victim's experience is not an object of interpretation; the same tendency to deny any complexity of motive in the camps and indeed any inner psychological life; and the same tendency to reduce the prisoner's behavior to his material conditions of existence. The survivor is viewed less as an individual whose mode of life needs to be understood and interpreted than as a new kind of material object, identity, or type of person ("S," 688).

Dramaturgies of the Self

Des Pres's criticism of the concept of survivor guilt entailed a parallel critique of the notion of identification with the aggressor. The argument had already been made by Rappaport when he rejected Sperling's interpretation of his inability to publicize his camp experiences. Rappaport was particularly indignant about the use of the psychoanalytic concept of regression to describe prisoner behavior. Niederland had characterized the camp prisoner in terms of "regression to sadomasochistic and oral narcissistic levels, emotional detachment rapidly progressing to depersonalization and derealization," suggesting that overwhelming terror induced in the victim a turning back to earlier modes of psychic defense, involving self-estrangement or depersonalization and a trancelike state of automatic obedience and identification. He had suggested that regression entailed a defensive, psychic "flight from reality" or emotional numbing that helped survivors preserve life and cope with the daily horror. He had focused in this regard on the regressive effects of the total suppression of the victim's anger against the Nazi rulers, as well as the personality disintegration caused by starvation and physical treatment, the loss of personal identity, the abrogation of causality, and other factors; and he had emphasized the victim's necessary compliance with amoral and degrading commands if he or she wished to stay alive, a compliance that inevitably produced superego conflicts because their realization often came about at the expense of other persons, or meant working as a slave laborer to support the enemy.[25]

Rappaport rejected these ideas. Accusing his psychoanalytic colleagues of anti-Semitism for speaking of the inmate's regressive tendency to unconsciously identify with the aggressor, he substituted instead the claim that, if the camp prisoner did imitate the behavior of the SS, the imitation was only a dissimulation: "The criteria of conduct in a concentration camp were irrational but no captive could escape the necessity to make at least a pretense of identification with the standard behavior. To speak of 'sadomasochistic regression' i.e., of the need of the masochist to provoke the sadist, 'the interdynamics of Nazis and concentration camp Jews,' of a complicity of the victim with the aggressor is a sad commentary reflecting anti-Jewish tendencies even among psychoanalysts" ("SG," 43).[26] He therefore suggested that imitative identification occurred in the camp as a conscious strategy of survival.[27]

[25] Niederland, "Psychiatric Disorders among Persecution Victims," *Journal of Nervous and Mental Disease* 139 (1964): 458–74. The terminal point of such regressive tendencies was the *Muselmann,* the prisoner who assumed the aspect of a "living corpse" in the course of dying from starvation and illness. Niederland emphasized in this respect the value of maintaining some aspect of ego identity, alertness, and reality-adapted functions in enhancing the chances of staying alive, even if he also reported his impression that more than any other factor survival for most prisoners depended on luck and circumstance.

[26] Understanding regression in somewhat literal terms as a return to actual infancy or childhood, Rappaport denied its existence in the camp inmate on the grounds that the captive had to stay alert at all times to utilize the smallest chance that promised survival. He then appeared to contradict himself by conceding that if captives did suffer from apathy and emotional bluntness, this could be called regression, "but it was adaptation to the environment, regression in the service of the ego" ("SG," 42), which was in fact precisely Niederland's argument.

[27] In keeping with my claim that the tension between mimesis and antimimesis in the theorizing of trauma is unresolvable, Rappaport denied that the camp victim identified with the enemy, but he did not abandon the notion of identification altogether, since he retained the vocabulary and concepts of superego and ego-ideal, both of which concepts Freud understood as precipitates of the subject's unconscious identifications with the father figure. On this basis he differentiated between the "prechanneled identification" of the inmate's precamp self and the "enforced emergency identification" for the purposes of self-preservation ("SG," 42–43).

Des Pres's approach was similar. Psychological theories of imitation or identi- fication have historically been linked to different theories of stage acting. The mimetic theory has been equated with an immersive or identificatory mode of stage acting, in which the actor is fully absorbed in his role, whereas the anti- mimetic theory has been associated with Diderot's portrayal of the ideal actor in *Le Paradoxe sur le comedien* as a cool simulator who remains completely con- scious of and detached from the imitative representations he performs on the stage.[28] These dramaturgical issues were played out in Des Pres's analysis of the camp survivor's imitation of the SS. Accusing Bettelheim of offering a "neg- ative" image of the camp inmate by claiming that the victim tended to identify with the aggressor, Des Pres insisted on the survivor's ability to act on "two lev- els," with and against the camp administration, with and against power (*TS,* 99–100). This duality of action was exemplified by those members of the *Son- derkommandos* who ran the Nazi gas chambers—but who also attempted to burn down Treblinka and Sobibor and blow up the crematoria at Auschwitz. Citing the influential memoir of Eugen Kogon, a well placed prisoner-functionary in Buchenwald who had been a key member of the resistance, Des Pres observed:

> The essential paradox of extremity is that life persists in a world ruled by death . . . [The survivor] . . . must maintain detachment; he too must preserve an identity apart from the one imposed by his environment. But since for him death is the immediate determinant of behavior, he must find a realm of separateness not in mind only but also in action. The survivor must act on two levels, be "with and against," as Eugen Kogon says. And what this means in practice is that to stay alive survivors often worked for, or even in, camp administration . . . Overtly the survivor defers to death, covertly he or she defies it. This duality of behavior, of concrete action on separate levels, is one of the principal characteristics of existence in extremity—or in any insti- tution, slavery for example, which through threat and force attempts to reduce its members to nothing but functions in the system. (*TS,* 99–100)[29]

---

[28] See Leys, *Trauma: A Genealogy* (Chicago, 2000), 50–51, 162–72.

[29] Des Pres's reference is to Eugen Kogon's *The Theory and Practice of Hell,* trans. Heinz Norden (New York, 1950), written after the latter's liberation from Buchenwald. It is worth pointing out that al- though Kogon represented the prisoner's imitation of the SS as largely a form of deception that con- cealed the latter's hostile intentions, he also described the existence of a "curious friend-enemy assimila- tion" and even "gratitude complex" that developed over time between the older prisoner-functionary and the enemy. These prevented the prisoner from seeking revenge against his enemy (*The Theory and Prac- tice of Hell,* 318–19). This gratitude complex is precisely what underlies the notion of identification with the aggressor, or Stockholm syndrome, and is held by the CIA interrogation manual of 1963 to lead to prisoner compliance with those in power.

Des Pres thus portrayed the survivor as an actor who is capable of acting duplicitously and hence of retaining control of the scene of trauma.[30] It makes sense, then, that he should have made use of the dramaturgical ideas of the sociologist Erving Goffmann, who had emphasized the performative dimension of human behavior in order to suggest that what matters in all social interactions is not whether the actor or individual actually possesses certain qualities or feelings, but how well dramatically a particular role is performed or projected. Specifically, Des Pres borrowed from Goffman's work on life in "total institutions" in order to distinguish between "primary" and "secondary" adjustments to life in the camps. Goffman had defined primary adjustments as those adjustments the individual makes when he "'cooperatively contributes required activity to an organization and under required conditions,'" thereby becoming a "'normal,' 'programmed,' or built-in member. He gives and gets in an appropriate spirit what has been systematically planned for, whether this entails much or little of himself'" (*TS*, 100).[31] Secondary adjustments were those habitual and unauthorized arrangements by which members of total institutions subvert the organization's requirements and by which, accordingly, the individual "'stands apart from the role and the self that were taken for granted for him by the institution'" (*TS*, 101). Goffman had suggested that secondary adjustments constitute what he called the "*underlife*" of the institution, to which Des Pres added: "In extremity this 'underlife' becomes the literal basis of life" (*TS*, 101). According to Des Pres, examples of secondary adjustment included all those actions, such as moving in and out of the ghetto, traveling the streets after curfew, and "organizing" food and other necessities in the camps, that were deemed illegal by the Nazis but which were necessary to life (*TS*, 101–8).

On the basis of these distinctions, Des Pres rejected Bettelheim's notion that in the camps old prisoners tended to identify with the aggressor: "The condition of life-in-death forced a terrible paradox upon survivors. They stayed alive by helping run the camps, and this fact has led to the belief that prisoners identified not with each other but with their oppressors. Survivors are often accused of imitating SS behavior. Bruno Bettelheim has argued that 'old prisoners' developed 'a

---

[30] Of course, duplicity can also be a form of corruption or lie, as in the case of Pasqualino, the central character of Lena Wertmuller's film, *The Seven Beauties,* who deceives in order to survive in ways Bettelheim deplores (*Surviving*, 300). Des Pres accepts the idea that duplicity can function in this way when he observes that, although the survivor's imperative to live on "two levels," for and against the structure of power, "opens the door to every manner of hypocrisy and lie, and therefore becomes a permanent occasion for corruption, "it cannot be avoided" (*TS*, 100).

[31] Des Pres cited Erving Goffman's *Asylums: Essays on the Social Situation of Mental Patients and Other Inmates* (1961); hereafter abbreviated *A.* Goffman included concentration camps among the "total institutions" that interested him, making use especially of Elie A. Cohen's *Human Behavior in the Concentration Camp,* and Eugen Kogon's *The Theory and Practice of Hell.*

personality structure willing and able to accept SS values and behavior as its own.'" (TS, 116). Des Pres countered Bettelheim by arguing that in order for prisoners to act like the SS they had to occupy positions of real power, such as that of a Kapo, or Block leader. But inmates occupying those positions had "almost certainly" (TS, 116) been sadists or killers before they arrived at the camps. This was certainly true at Buchenwald, Des Pres maintained, for at the time Bettelheim was there all the positions of power were held exclusively by criminals of various kinds. But the behavior of those criminals was "not a case of imitation," because these prisoners were "like their masters from the start" (TS, 117). In other words, criminal inmates had no need to imitate their oppressors because they already shared the Nazi's values. By contrast, if non-criminal camp victims imitated the SS, they did so in the mode of a deceptive camouflage:

> The assumption that survivors imitated SS behavior is misleading because it generalizes a limited phenomenon, but also because it overlooks the duality of behavior in extremity. Eugen Kogon, a member of the Buchenwald underground, points out that "the concentration camp prisoner knew a whole system of mimicry toward the SS," an "ever-present camouflage" which concealed true feelings and intentions. *Strategic* imitation of the SS was enormously important because thereby political prisoners held positions of power which would otherwise have gone to the criminals. (TS, 117)

And again: "Imitation of SS behavior was a regular feature of life in the camps, and large numbers of prisoners benefited because positions of power were secretly used in ways which assisted the general struggle for life" (TS, 118).

According to Des Pres, the behavior of every noncriminal prisoner expressed a self-conscious discipline of solidarity and collective action that at its most political took the form of organized resistance. Rather than emphasizing, as Bettelheim and others had done, that people under oppression could fall into abjection, Des Pres insisted rather that solidarity and resistance were inherent in every victim's biological drive to go on living. To speak of a resistance movement in the concentration camps was therefore to speak of a general human tendency, "*a kind of logic or potential inherent in the social foundation of survival struggle*" (TS, 123, his emphasis). It was not true that the victims did not revolt, because "to live was to resist, every day, all the time" (TS, 154). Suggesting that in camps where this tendency operated most effectively, resistance was organized and was responsible for saving thousands of lives, Des Pres described in terms that are purely Diderotian the emotional detachment required of the political operative when it became necessary to imitate the enemy. Resistance activities, he stated, citing the words of a survivor, were governed by a "'cold, unemotional, devastatingly logical approach to every problem'" (TS, 128–29).

It as if Des Pres attributed to every inmate, as epitomized in the actions of members of the organized resistance, the capacity to imitate the enemy with the calculated sang froid Diderot ascribed to the ideal theater actor, or with the dramaturgical calculation Goffman ascribed to the social actor. Indeed, although Des Pres claimed that the behavior of the survivors was covert and hence "undramatic" (*TS*, 172), it might be said that he viewed the camp inmate's imitations as a dramatic performance the actor carried out in a condition of cool self-possession and control: "Compassion was seldom possible, self pity never. Emotion only blurred judgment and undermined decisiveness, it jeopardized the life of everyone in the underground . . . The behavior of the underground was always strategic" (*TS*, 131).

Without mentioning Diderot's name, Goffman provided a similarly Diderotian account of the dramaturgy of social interaction.[32] But there is a sense in which Goffman was more nuanced than Des Pres, in that he allowed for a wider range of adjustments to total institutions, including at one extreme a "conversion" response in which the inmate appears to take over the official or staff view of himself and "tries to act out the role of the perfect inmate." Goffman cited as examples the way certain American prisoners in Chinese P.O.W. camps "fully espoused" the Communist view of the world, or the way in which, according to Bettelheim, whom he cited with approval, long-time prisoners in some concentration camps adopted the values, vocabulary, actions, and expressions of the Gestapo as their own (*A*, 63–64). Goffman thus appeared to accept the notion that in some modes of imitation the actor is so swept up in and identified with his role as to completely lose himself in it. Even here, though, the performative language in which Goffman characterized conversion behavior leaves one in doubt

[32] [W]hile the performer is ostensibly immersed and given over to the activity he is performing, and is apparently engrossed in his actions in a spontaneous, uncalculating way, he must none the less be affectively dissociated from his presentation in such a way that leaves him free to cope with dramaturgical contingencies as they arise. He must offer a show of intellectual and emotional involvement in the activity he is presenting, but must keep himself from actually being carried away by his own show lest this destroy his involvement in the task of putting on a successful performance [. . .] The disciplined performer is also someone with "self control." He can suppress his emotional response to his private problems, to his team-mates when they make mistakes, and to the audience when they induce untoward affection or hostility in him. And he can stop himself from laughing about matters which are defined as serious and from taking seriously matters defined as humorous. In other words, he can suppress his spontaneous feelings in order to give the appearance of sticking to the affective line, the expressive *status quo,* established by the team's performance . . . And the disciplined performer is someone with sufficient poise to move from private places of informality to public ones of varying degree of formality, without allowing such changes to confuse him. Erving Goffman, *The Presentation of Self in Everyday Life* (New York, 1965, 1959), 216–17.

(This book, though not this passage, was also cited by Des Pres. *TS*, 165). For a Diderotian reading of Goffman's dramaturgy, see Claude Javeau, "Diderot, Goffman et le Mensonge Social," *Revue Internationale de Philosophie* 38 (1984): 171–81. Goffman's work also relates to that of hypnosis theorist Theodore Sarbin, who proposed a similarly Diderotian account of hypnotic acting (see my *Trauma: A Genealogy,* 164–71).

as to whether he ever meant to describe the process of conversion as a fully im-mersive or mimetic phenomenon. In any case, Des Pres ignored this aspect of Goffman's analysis, in order to insist on the strategic nature of all imitations.

Another difference between the two authors is that Goffman was prepared to acknowledge the existence of a relationship between his dramaturgical, or "sym-bolic-interactionist" framework, and a more conventional "psycho-physiological" approach centered, for example, on the concept of "stress." Although he himself phrased the basic facts about the self in sociological terms, he accepted as a matter of course that a psychology was also implied, because the sociological settings for any performance of the self had to be "read" by the individual and others for the "image of himself that they imply" (A, 47). Arguing that the relation of the cognitive process to other psychological processes was inevitably variable, Goffman illustrated this point by referring to the feeling of guilt. For example, hav-ing one's head shaved is easily perceived as a curtailment of the self and is very likely to involve acute psychological stress for the individual; but for an individual sick with his world or "guilt-ridden" it may bring psychological relief: "while this mortification may enrage a mental patient, it may please a monk" (A, 48).[33] In short, Goffman acknowledged the existence of psychological processes accom-panying objectively observed behavior and the likelihood that such psychological processes do not map onto outward appearances in any simple way.

By contrast, Des Pres ruled any appeal to psychology out of court. His was not a theory of a divided ego or self, as many sympathetic commentators have claimed—misunderstanding him in this regard because they wish to salvage a place for psychology in his scheme (more on this in a moment). Eschewing all ref-erence to inner emotion or feeling, he proposed a duality of "action," not of the psyche. For him, there could be no appeal to a multiplicity of intentions, con-scious or unconscious, determining the prisoner's behavior, because in extremity no such multiplicity of intentions existed:

> To be of use, the psychoanalytic method, which is that of interpretation, must be ap-plied to actions which have more than one meaning *on the level of meaning.* But that is not the case with extremity . . . The purpose of action in extremity is to keep life going; the multiplicity of motive which gives civilized behavior its depth and complexity is lost. We have seen that life in the camps depended on a duality of behavior, but this dual-

[33] Primo Levi's explanation for the absence of suicide during incarceration is compatible with Goff-man's insight: "[I]n the majority of cases, suicide is born from a feeling of guilt that no punishment has at-tenuated; now, the harshness of imprisonment was perceived as punishment, and the feeling of guilt (if there is punishment, there must have been guilt) was relegated to the background, only to re-emerge af-ter the Liberation. In other words, there was no need to punish oneself by suicide because of a (true or presumed) guilt: one was already expiating it by one's daily suffering" (DS, 76).

ity—this layering of behavior—is very different from the kind of layering which psycho-analysis probes. In extremity, action splits into "primary" and "secondary" levels of adjustment, each of which is real and separate in itself. Precisely here the psychoanalytic approach misleads us: in its search for a second meaning on the first or primary level, it overlooks the secondary level. For psychoanalysis, covert behavior is implicit behavior. But for survivors it becomes explicit, actual, necessary in an immediate practical way. (*TS*, 155–56)

The effect of Des Pres's analysis was to deny the relevance of the unconscious: when behavior was governed by necessity there was a duality at the level of action, but there was no internal duality of the psyche in the sense of a conflict internal to the subject in which unconscious intentions might be at odds with the ego's or superego's demands, or in which the subject's identification with the aggressor might fuel the superego's chastisements. As a result, if for Des Pres there was a bonding between survivors in the struggle for life, there was no "unbonding" in the Freudian sense: there was no death drive, and no unconscious yielding to the enemy.

Curiously, though, in an account of the survivor that displaced attention from a psychoanalytic emphasis on psychology of the survivor's inner life to the determining role of the external environment, the factor that Des Pres most discounted was the actual political realities of camp life. In his book and related texts, Des Pres criticized Bettelheim for misrepresenting the role of the Austrian prisoner, Eugen Kogon, who in Buchenwald had played a central, even a crucial, role in the political resistance, especially during the hectic months leading up to the camp's liberation. Kogon was selected by the Americans to write the official report of the camp, and his book, *The Theory and Practice of Hell,* based on that report, was a key source of information for Des Pres.[34] Bettelheim had dismissively described Kogon—a non-Communist, Catholic, "Rightest" political prisoner—as a member of the privileged elite of the prisoner population, a group Bettelheim portrayed as often serving its own interests at the expense of less fortunate victims.[35] Des Pres rightly rejected this portrait of Kogon, who was by all other accounts a courageous man. But what has gone unnoticed in the generally sympathetic response to Des Pres's work is the extent to which he downplayed the power politics of camp life. In contradiction to Des Pres's claim that morality, trust, and decency survived intact in the camps, Kogon documents the extent to which the different political factions in Buchenwald were ruthlessly pitted against each other in the struggle for life and the ways in which the lowest prisoners were sacrificed by the

[34] See *The Buchenwald Report,* trans. and ed. David A. Hackett, foreword by Frederick A. Praeger (Boulder, Colo., 1995).

[35] Bruno Bettelheim, *The Informed Heart: Autonomy in a Mass Age* (New York, 1960), 184–87.

resistance so that others, including the prisoner elite, could survive.[36] This was especially true toward the very end when, on Nazi orders, the Buchenwald camp leaders colluded in several large selections of less favored prisoners for certain death in transports and death marches, in order to forestall the greater threat of general evacuation or total liquidation. The seductions of power and ethical dilemmas involved in such activities were brilliantly analyzed, for example, by the survivor David Rousset in his extraordinary, neglected novel, *Les jours de notre mort* (1947).[37] But they were completely glossed over by Des Pres in favor of a sociobiological emphasis on the "adaptation" of the prisoners to extremity and the triumph of human decency among them. The result was that he ignored the actual politics of Buchenwald in favor of what might be described as an alternative "politics," that of a protofascist "vitalism" according to which all actions and decisions in extremity are ethically justified since they serve life.

The Subject of Imitation

When in a 1976 article in the *New Yorker* Bettelheim criticized *The Survivor,* Des Pres replied, and the issues between the two men were joined.[38] Reacting to Des Pres with indignation, Bettelheim reaffirmed the decisive importance of the survivor's feeling of guilt and implicitly justified the mechanism of identification from which that feeling was held to derive (*S*, 296–97). In the ensuing controversy, Bettelheim, with all his by now well-documented intellectual and personal flaws, came to stand for everything that was held to be wrong with

[36] Kogon's account of the prisoner's mimicry of the SS as a kind of camouflage for good intentions did not prevent him from observing the ways in which positions of influence could also be used for evil. He observed in this regard that the privileges the Communist underground leadership in Buchenwald was able to wrest away from the SS mainly benefited German-speaking prisoners among the various nationality groups (*The Theory and Practice of Hell*, 265).

[37] "In a K-Z society [from the German *Konzentration Lager*] the question of survival immediately raises the question of power," says the Communist prisoner, Nicolas, in Rousset's novel, in an excerpt published as "The Days of Our Death," *Les temps modernes* (1947), 152. Des Pres quotes the British Buchenwald prisoner Christopher Burney as saying of the frantic days before the end of Buchenwald when the camp leaders were trying to stave off liquidation that " 'every moment gained saved lives' " (Des Pres, "The Bettelheim Problem," 642). What Des Pres does not say, but what Burney's memoir clearly demonstrates, is that the saving of lives depended on the sacrifice of a large number of less fortunate prisoners, mostly Jews, whom the underground decided it was too risky to fight over. "The transport of 8,000 'cretins,' as we called them, left. Few tears were shed," Burney reports of one such selection (Burney, *The Dungeon Democracy* [New York, 1946], 130).

[38] See Bettelheim, "Surviving," *New Yorker,* 2 (1977): 31–52; idem, *Surviving and Other Essays* (1979), hereafter abbreviated *S*; and Des Pres, "The Bettelheim Problem."

psychoanalytic approaches to the camp survivor.[39] Here I want briefly to review two important strands of criticism of Bettelheim, one sociological and the other psychoanalytic, in order to show their solidarity with each other and with the work of Des Pres. I shall examine the sociological critique first.

In his first report on the psychological response to extremity, based on his ten-month imprisonment in Dachau and Buchenwald in 1938–39, Bettelheim had said that the Nazis' primary goal in the camps was to break prisoners as individuals, thereby aggregating them into a docile mass from which no resistance could arise.[40] He had analyzed the different stages of adjustment through which prisoners went during the process of incarceration, from the initial psychological shock of arrest, through the phase of transportation and initiation into the camp, to the final adaptation. According to Bettelheim, whereas the main concern of the new prisoners—those who had not spent more than one year in camp—seemed to be to survive by retaining as much of their own personality as possible, old prisoners—those who had spent more than three years in camp—seemed mainly concerned with the problem of how to live as well as possible, giving the impression that they had come to accept that a fundamental change in their personality had occurred. He had suggested that surviving prisoners had reached the final stage of their adjustment when they had regressed so far into childlike submissiveness and dependency on their masters as to completely identify with them, aping their manners, dress, and brutality ("IMB," 448). By contrast, Bettelheim had presented himself as a someone who, in spite of suffering from extreme malnutrition and a deteriorated memory, had defended himself against the dangers of psychic regression by maintaining detachment and treating the behavior of his fellow inmates as scientific data to be objectively collected and assessed. As he

[39] In addition to the texts cited below I have also consulted Jacob Robinson, *Psychoanalysis in a Vacuum: Bruno Bettelheim and the Holocaust* (New York, 1970); Charles W. Smith, *A Critique of Sociological Reasoning: An Essay on Philosophical Sociology* (Towota, N.J., 1979); Ralph Tutt, "Seven Beauties and the Beast: Bettelheim, Wertmuller, and the Uses of Enchantment," *Literature Film Quarterly* 17 (1989): 193–201; Falk Pingel, "The Destruction of Human Identity in the Concentration Camps: The Contributions of the Social Sciences to an Analysis of Behavior under Extreme Conditions," *Holocaust and Genocide Studies* 6 (1991): 167–84; Paul Roazen, "The Rise and Fall of Bruno Bettelheim," *Psychohistory* 20 (1992): 221–50; Nina Sutton, *Bettelheim: A Life and a Legacy* (Boulder, Colo., 1996); Richard Pollock, *The Creation of Dr. B: A Biography of Bruno Bettelheim* (New York, 1997); Daphne Merkin, "The Mystery of Dr. B: Bruno Bettelheim and the Politics of Reputation," *New Yorker* (March 24, 1997): 76–80; Kurt Jacobsen, "Blaming Bettelheim," *Psychoanalytic Review* 87 (2000): 385–415; and Christian Fleck and Albert Muller, "Bruno Bettelheim and the Concentration Camps," *Journal of the History of the Behavioral Sciences* 33 (1997): 1–37. Immediately after his death by suicide in 1990 Bettelheim was subjected to a barrage of criticism debunking his treatment claims with the autistic children he worked with at the Orthogenic School in Chicago and more generally accusing him of charlatanism and a disastrous tendency to exaggerate and lie. The details can be followed in the materials cited here.

[40] Bruno Bettelheim, "Individual and Mass Behavior in Extreme Situations," *Journal of Abnormal and Social Psychology* 38, no. 4 (October 1943): 417–51; hereafter abbreviated as "IMB."

had defined his problem to himself in the camp, it was to *"safeguard his ego in such a way, that, if by good luck he should regain his liberty, he would be approximately the same person he was when deprived of liberty"* ("IMB," 443).

It was not difficult for critics to punch holes in Bettelheim's story. It could be pointed out that his facts were wrong or that a more sociological-political framework could explain aspects of the behavior of prisoners in different terms, especially since, according to those same critics, Bettelheim had illegitimately extended his findings about prisoner behavior in the prewar concentration camps of Dachau and Buchenwald to include the later extermination camps as well. For example, commentators could object to Bettelheim's "stage" theory of prisoner adaptation on the grounds that at Buchenwald it was from among the older prisoners, not the newer ones, that the underground leadership was eventually drawn. They could therefore emphasize that the real cleavage between prisoners in Buchenwald was not that between new and old prisoners, but between the "reds" or political prisoners on the one hand, and the "greens" or ordinary criminals on the other. The intense struggle between those two groups, as described by Kogon, Rousset and others, had been won by the politicals long after Bettelheim had left the camp. It could then be suggested that the "criminals" had had no need to identify with the SS because they already shared the latter's brutal, anti-Semitic values. As for the politicals, their objective had been to resist the Nazis by all possible means, so it made no sense to characterize them in terms of identification with the enemy.

These and related objections were raised against Bettelheim with considerable justice. What interests me, however, is what Bettelheim's sociological critics had to say about imitation. They did not deny that Bettelheim had observed imitative behavior in the camps. But they consistently refused to interpret that imitation in mimetic terms as involving the unconscious incorporation of the aggressor or indeed an unconscious process of any kind. Instead, like Des Pres, they interpreted the survivor's imitation as a strategic collaboration or simulation performed by an intact subject for the purposes of resistance. As the sociologist Norman Jackson wrote in a critique of Bettelheim twenty years before Des Pres: "the *imitation* of Gestapo behavior for the purpose of manipulation and control is not the same as the internalization of Gestapo values." For Jackson, the behavior of the German Communist prisoners could not be fully understood in terms of its overt manifestations, but had to be seen as a tactic of dissimulation designed to ensure the group's survival.[41]

A more recent work, Wolfgang Sofsky's widely admired sociological analysis, *The Order of Terror: The Concentration Camp* (1993; 1997), demonstrates the continued attraction of such an account of camp behavior. The author paints a

[41] Norman R. Jackson, "Survival in the Concentration Camp," *Human Organization* 17, no. 2 (1958): 23–26. If Jackson also acknowledged that many other inmates did appear to "internalize" Gestapo values, he restricted this process to the criminal prisoners who *already* shared the Nazi values; according to him, therefore, Bettelheim was wrong to suggest that any value changes had occurred in the prisoner popula-

much starker picture of camp life than Des Pres, whom he does not cite. He rejects the idea that a genuine communal life existed for the average prisoner who was not a member of the prisoner aristocracy or elite, suggesting instead that the exercise of absolute power in the camps destroyed the fabric of reciprocity and mutual care among the inmates. In his discussion of the "gray zone," that is to say, of the role of the prisoner-functionaries in running the camps, he is far more alert than Des Pres to the intrinsically conservative nature of collaboration and the ways in which prisoners inevitably sought to maintain their advantages and defend their privileges, often at the expense of those below them.[42]

But when he discusses imitation, Sofsky largely shares Des Pres's and Jackson's perspective by presenting the prisoner elite's modes of imitation as strategies of adaptation that presume the existence of the knowing and deceiving subject who imitates the SS in order to further the chances of survival. Recognizing "mimetic servility" (*OT*, 137) as one such strategy of adaptation, and including in it a spectrum of behaviors ranging from the "imitation of brief gestures" to "demonstrative subservience to identification with the dreaded authority and duplication of its external appearance" (*OT*, 137), Sofsky defines this servility as a "special mode of social exchange" (*OT*, 137) or "social relation" (*OT*, 138) that, pace Bettelheim and Anna Freud (*OT*, 313, n. 315), "should not be mistakenly confused with the unconscious identification of the victim with the aggressor" (*OT*, 138). Emphasizing that the master-servant relationship was an antagonistic one that was based on a very unequal distribution of power, Sofsky claims that the actions of the accomplices had a totally different meaning from those of their masters. The masters permitted the prisoners to act because the latter enhanced Nazi

---

tion through the mechanism of either imitation or internalization. I note that Jackson also used the term "identification." This process was not understood by him in psychoanalytic terms as a process of unconscious incorporation, but in terms of "reference group theory" as a mechanism that bound individuals together in group solidarity based on shared group norms and values. Jackson thus aimed to correct Bettelheim's "individualistic" approach to survival by emphasizing the survival value of group solidarity and significant reference groups. For related criticisms by the sociologist Elmer Luchterhand see "Prisoner Behavior and Social System in the Nazi Concentration Camps" (Ph.D. diss., University of Wisconsin, 1952); idem, "The Gondola-Car Transports," *International Journal of Social Psychiatry* 13 (1966–67): 28–32; idem, "Prisoner Behavior and Social System in the Nazi Concentration Camps," *International Journal of Social Psychiatry* 13 (1967): 245–64; idem, "Early and Late Effects of Imprisonment in Nazi Concentration Camps," *Social Psychiatry* 5 (1970): 102–10; idem, "Sociological Approches to Massive Stress in Natural and Man-Made Disasters," in Krystal and Niederland, *Psychic Traumatization* (1971), 29–53; idem, "Social Behavior in Concentration Camp Prisoners: Continuities and Discontinuities with Pre- and Post-Camp Life," in *Survivors, Victims, and Perpetrators,* ed. Joel Dimsdale (Washington, D.C., 1980), 261–80. Building on Jackson's work, Luchterhand criticized Bettelheim for ignoring the social system of the camps, citing especially the work of Kogon, and stressed the value for survival of "stable pairing" between inmates.

[42] Wolfgang Sofsky, *The Order of Terror: The Concentration Camp*, trans. William Templer (Princeton, 1997), 24, 312n; hereafter abbreviated *OT.*

power. But the inmates had to fear for their very existence: "They acted like their master in order to remain what they were—privileged prisoners. They followed the model in order to survive" (*OT*, 138).

Sofsky did not deny that some prisoners were as vehement in their anti-Semitism as the SS, or that, as Bettelheim had observed, they were exceptionally brutal, or that they had even attempted to conform their appearances to that of the SS by getting hold of old parts of SS uniforms and strutting around in shiny polished boots. But he argued that these prisoners' anti-Semitism was not necessarily the product of unconscious processes: "These phenomena can be rooted in an unconscious identification, though they are not necessarily so. One should not underestimate the need to set oneself off socially from those below one in the pecking order . . . [S]ervility and imitation (by no means synonymous with identification) are social relations, not mental events. Under conditions of mortal enmity, someone who wishes to escape miserable material conditions will, almost invariably, align himself or herself with those in power . . . [A]lignment with the SS was a strategy to escape the fate of the pariahs" (*OT*, 313–14).

Somewhat arbitrarily, Sofsky distinguishes "mimetic servility" from another mode of adaptation to the SS that he calls "total obedience" (*OT*, 137), and that he also presents in strategic terms. He defines mimetic servility as an "attitude" and total obedience as a "way of acting." Total obedience lacked the elements of "assimilation" and "bondage" peculiar to the believer in authority who attempted to survive by pandering to power, because total obedience was generally not based on agreement with the camp power but was founded on "self-protection, pure and simple" (*OT*, 138). Although Sofsky's language is not without certain strains, he consistently tries to use these and related words, such as "assimilation," "bondage" and "internalization" to describe the behavior of the prisoners from the "outside," that is, from the perspective of the external observer. The result is a mode of social analysis in which the prisoners are viewed as "actors" who adopted various methods for survival in a deliberately instrumental manner.[43]

---

[43] For the strains in Sofsky's language, see the passage where he is interpreting the fact, first observed by Bettelheim, that old prisoners tended to lose interest in the outside world, and to focus exclusively on camp life:

They turned aside from the world outside the camp, concentrating all their efforts on the here and now of camp life. In no sense was this displacement in thematic relevance a form of identification. It involved sealing off the field of consciousness against all events that could have posed a threat to a laboriously achieved success. In order to remain alive, the prisoners had to live in the camp. But to do that, they had to internalize its laws of survival . . . What might appear to the outsider as demoralization was the morality of a serial society, one in which every individual was superfluous. Those who wanted to escape its lethal seriality had to make sure they did not sink into the lower classes. Since they could not allow themselves to become like the majority, they sealed themselves off. The hardening of the veteran prisoners was a method of defense, survival, and social distinction. (*OT*, 148)

Something similar goes on in an earlier, also influential book by the sociologist Anna Pawelcyznska, a Polish survivor of Auschwitz and a sociologist who in the postwar years worked in Warsaw. In her introduction to the English translation of Pawelcyznska's text, Catherine S. Leach praised both Pawelcyznska's text and Des Pres's "brilliant" book for reversing society's negative view of the survivor, as exemplified by Bettelheim's theory of the prisoner's regressive identification with the aggressor. Endorsing Pawelcyznska's claim that a deeply internalized value system enabled many survivors to survive biologically and morally, that is, to resist surrender to violence, Leach stressed the idea of the prisoner's "strategic" conformity to necessity in terms that ally Pawelcyznska's views on imitation with those of Des Pres: "It is . . . an error to apply psychoanalysis to the camps where material conditions forced prisoners to make a leap out of civilization . . . Nor are crude behaviorist theories relevant to camp behavior, for they begin with the premise that the self is the victim of camp behavior . . . In thus rescuing survivors of the camps from the victim-aggressor bind, the authors enable the reader to come away with his or her own humanity—understanding, compassion, moral acuity—intact."[44] As for Pawelcyznska herself, she conceded that a genuine identification with the aggressor did occur in the case of the small number of "greens" (or criminals) who accepted the role of prisoner-functionary (*VV*, 50). But she likewise suggested that the majority of prisoners preserved an "inner freedom while outwardly accepting" Nazi rule, in terms that implied that their mimicry was only strategic: "He who under conditions of terror and coercion achieved inner freedom, at least to some extent, carried off the only form of victory possible with the existing situation. With such an attitude he disproved the doubtful theory of the need to identify with the aggressor; he expressed his solidarity with his fellow prisoners and his protest against violence" (*VV*, 142).

In this last passage, Pawelcynzska expressed a theme that can be found in the responses of virtually all of Bettelheim's opponents, namely the theme of freedom. It seems clear that Pawelcyznska and like-minded critics, such as Jackson, Sofsky, Des Pres, and numerous others, adopting the self-evidence of a com-

---

Terms such as "sealing off" and "internalize" are close to the psychoanalytic concepts of "sequestration" or "incorporation," but are not intended as psychological terms. At one point, Sofsky does in fact adopt Bettelheim's notion of regression to suggest that prisoners were forced to regress to "earlier stages of personality" and that the camps produced a condition of infantile dependency (*OT*, 91, 301, n. 20).

[44] Catherine S. Leach, Introduction to Anna Pawelcyznska, *Values and Violence in Auschwitz: A Sociological Analysis* (Berkeley, Calif., 1979), xxviii; hereafter abbreviated *VV*. Des Pres made use of Pawelcyznska's work, in his repy to Bettelheim, to support his claim that "Nowhere in Bettelheim's major statements about survivors do we find sustained attention to he fundamental form of *positive* coping, to behavior which promoted life and spiritual resistance. I am referring to the prisoners' tendency to organize and help each other, to participate for mutual support in each other's struggles" ("The Bettelheim Problem," 630).

monsense notion of freedom, espoused an ontology of the subject according to which human beings possess a unified self that is endowed with the attributes of consciousness and free will, open to direct introspection, and that can freely secure its identity. They thus express their agreement with a classical (or Kantian) idea of freedom as the self-presence and self-identity of the detached individual subject. On this basis they attribute imitation to the spontaneity of a subject who can retain a spectatorial distance from its own imitative performance. But a Freudian approach to subjectivity theorizes freedom differently, as taking place within the horizon of the subject's constitutive opacity to itself because of the existence of the unconscious. Moreover, if we accept the idea that mimetic identification centrally defines Freud's theory of unconscious, it follows that the experience of freedom cannot be understood as depending on a preexisting, self-identical, autonomous subject, but on an unconscious identification with, or incorporative binding to, the other that occurs prior to the distinction between the ego and its objects.

There is therefore a considerable distance between a Freudian approach to imitation and the sociological critiques we have been examining. We can gauge the way these issues played out in that debate over the survivor by considering the following statement by the historian of the Shoah, Helen Fein. Intervening in the controversy between Des Pres and Bettelheim, she made common cause with Eugene Genovese's powerful new Marxist history of slavery to suggest that the oppressed's behavior is always a performative or imitative mask behind which the subject hides his true identity:

> [T]he Sambo mask was donned for survival: slave responses were not infantile but cunning; deference was one of the tactics used to manipulate the master who might be paternalistic or violence-prone and to implement a rudimentary social contract to ensure their survival. Further, Genovese and others argue, slaves were not dehumanized but maintained their morale by evolving a unique Afro-American culture and maintaining as much solidarity among kin as was possible [. . .] [Camp prisoners] who survived took an active rather than a passive and dependent approach to their environment, although such self-interested activity had to be hidden from the eyes of their overseers. They also learned to dissemble . . . The drive to bear witness and hatred of their oppressors motivated the survivors to bear their sufferings rather than to succumb to grief, shock, and inertia, which soon led to death . . . Although many prisoners tended to become verbally aggressive, copying the language of the SS, the prevalence of identification with the aggressor is disputed.[45]

[45] Helen Fein, "Beyond the Heroic Ethic," *Society* 17 (1980): 52. Fein concedes that Bettelheim's observations about identification with the aggressor were plausible as regards German prisoners in Dachau and Buchenwald, "many of whom had not opposed and hoped to reintegrate themselves into a Nazified society" (52–53), but holds that Bettelheim illegitimately extended his observations to the extermination

I'm not arguing that Fein's claims are totally unwarranted. It's plausible that terrorized people do camouflage their inner feelings from their jailors. But what interests me is that in her absolutism—in her reaction against psychoanalysis—Fein seems unable to acknowledge or theorize the possibility that the master-slave relationship might also have psychic consequences for the victims and that those consequences might include an array of long-term conflictual and identificatory responses to persons in power. We are left with a picture of the victim of oppression as a completely rational, calculating subject who is always in control of his actions. By characterizing the slave, and by extension, the Nazi victim, as "not dehumanized," Fein suggests that identification with the other *is* a form of dehumanization, as if in order to identify one must first have an identity as a human being that is then demeaned or degraded by identification. Freud would be unhappy with Fein's analysis on two counts: one, because of the absence of any psychic content or consequences for the subject, even on the classic oedipal reading of Freud; and second, because Freud in the mimetic mode assumes that subjectivity is *itself* constituted by and through a mimetic relation to the other which is irreducible and constitutive.

Psychoanalytic Revisions

Paralleling the critique of Bettelheim by Des Pres and the social scientists was a line of criticism internal to psychoanalysis itself that also contributed to a general rejection or revision of the notions of identification with the aggressor and survivor guilt. In developing the idea of survivor guilt, Niederland and his colleagues were seeking to revise psychoanalysis in ways that would allow greater recognition of the influence of the external trauma on the victim than was classically acknowledged. The concept of the survivor syndrome accordingly suggested that the experience of the camps was potentially traumatic to *any* victim caught up in the system. As such, it was generally recognized as a major contribution to psychiatry.[46] But with time it came to be subjected to a variety of criticisms

---

and other camps, where they did not apply. I leave it to others more qualified than myself to decide whether Fein does justice to the complexity of Genovese's thought about imitation. I note only that the latter speaks of the ambivalent "identification with their masters" of some slaves in terms not only suggesting the bonding, dependency, and fantasmatic empowerment such an incorporation of power entailed, but also the extent to which this process was a psychological one and was not reducible to mere calculation. See Eugene Genovese, *Roll, Jordan, Roll: The World the Slaves Made* (New York, 1974), 330, 334, 342, 363–64.

[46] For positive assessments of the concept of survivor guilt see for example, *Holding on to Humanity—The Message of Holocaust Survivors: The Shamai Davidson Papers,* ed. Israel W. Charny (New York, 1992), 39; and Rafael Moses, "An Israeli Psychoanalyst Looks Back in 1983," in *Psychoanalytic Reflections on the Holocaust: Selected Essays* ed. Steven A. Luel and Paul Marcus (New York, 1984), 60.

from within the psychoanalytic field. For some, the syndrome was too rigid, be- cause it appeared to cast every survivor in a single mold. It also came to seem too "individualistic," in that treatment and recovery issues were not being placed in a generous or wide enough social context—for example, it was felt that the patient's precamp personality strengths, postliberation reception, and other experiences had been neglected. One way this criticism was expressed, fairly or not, was to accuse Niederland and the other pioneering formulators of the survivor syndrome concept of treating the survivor as a "historyless" person whose personality had been en- tirely shaped by the overwhelming event of the Holocaust.[47] In particular, there was a growing demand among psychoanalytically oriented professionals that postlibera- tion family experiences, including the experience of new or reconstituted families, be taken into account when assessing the victim's long-term adaptation. When this was done, the survivor could be seen as a person who might show symptoms con- forming to the picture of the survivor syndrome but who might also exhibit surpris- ing adaptability and strengths, indeed as a person who was not necessarily ill, or did not necessarily perceive himself or herself as ill—only different.

For some psychologists and psychoanalysts working directly with survivors in the United States and Israel, these developments did not imply the necessity of abandoning the concepts of the survivor syndrome and survivor guilt so much as revising them.[48] For others, criticism took a more radical turn, amounting in some

[47] See for example Paul Marcus and Alan Rosenberg, "A Philosophical Critique of the 'Survivor Syn- drome' and Some Implications for Treatment," in *Pychological Perspectives of the Holocaust and Its Af- termath,* ed. Randolph L. Braham (New York, 1988), 56.

[48] I am thinking especially of the work of Hillel Klein and Shamai Davidson, two influential Israeli psy- choanalysts who have sought to do justice to the more positive dimensions of the survivor experience without denying the tendency to psychopathology. (As a young man, Klein himself spent the years 1940–45 in the Polish underground and in the camps.) See especially Hillel Klein and Ilany Kogan, "Iden- tification Processes and Denial in the Shadow of Nazism," *International Journal of Psychoanalysis* 67 (1986): 45–53, where the authors attempt to distinguish a "benign" form of identification in the survivor's identifications with the dead parents or family members, identifications that are said to constitute a fan- tasmatic mode of psychic defense in the struggle for survival. The authors recognize that such identifica- tions may involve a total denial of any violent or destructive impulses toward the "idealized but disap- pointingly dead loved objects," with resulting disturbances in the handling of aggression and guilt. Cf. Hillel Klein, Julius Zellermayer, and Joel Shanan, "Former Concentration Camp Inmates on a Psychi- atric Ward," *Archives of General Psychiatry* 8 (1963): 334–42; Klein, "Problems in the Psychothera- peutic Treatment of Israeli Survivors of the Holocaust," in *Massive Psychic Trauma,* ed. Henry Krystal (New York, 1968), 233–48; idem, "Families of Holocaust Survivors in the Kibbutz: Psychological Stud- ies," in *Psychic Traumatization: Aftereffects in Individuals and Communities* (Boston, 1971), 67–92; idem, "Delayed Affects and After-Effects of Severe Traumatization," *Israel Annals of Psychiatry and Related Disciplines* 12 (1974): 293–303; idem, "Child Victims of the Holocaust," *Journal of Clinical Child Psychology* 3 (1974): 44–47; idem, "Survivors of the Holocaust," *Mental Health and Society* 5 (1978): 35–45; idem, "The Survivors Search for Meaning and Identity," in *Nazi Concentration Camps: Structure and Aims*, proceedings of the Fourth Yad Vashem International Historical Conference (Jerusalem, 1984), 543–54; and *Holding on to Humanity—The Message of Holocaust Survivors: The Shamai Davidson Papers*.

instances to a wholesale repudiation of the notions of the survivor syndrome and survivor guilt in the name of a more "sociopolitical" interpretation of survival. There developed a tendency to adopt a stark dualism of inside and outside that divested the psychic of any internal, conflictual dynamics by projecting the traumatic event wholly into the external world. "Commonsense" ideas began to replace psychoanalytic ones—for example, the claim was made that the symptoms of survivors needed no interpretation whatsoever, since the anger, depression, or sadness survivors felt were simply natural, sane, and logical responses to a horrible reality.[49] Niederland and other "pioneers" of the survivor syndrome were demonized as insensitive doctors who, having missed the war themselves, unfairly scapegoated and stigmatized survivors by projecting their own guilt onto the latter. Throughout these developments, Des Pres's work was a standard reference point.

For example, in a 1984 volume on psychoanalysis and the Holocaust, Jack Terry accused Niederland and the other architects of the survivor syndrome of expressing their contempt for survivors by blaming, exploiting, and "syndromizing" them. In response to Niederland's effort to stress the inevitability of the traumatic impact regardless of pretraumatic strengths or weaknesses, Terry sought to reindividualize the reactions of survivors to the Holocaust, which also meant emphasizing the serenity and dignity exhibited by some. "In short, not everything in everyone was damaged. The pretraumatic personality had a great influence on the individual's reaction to the trauma: the degree of libidinal and ego and superego development played a great role. An external experience cannot be independent of one's personal history if it is to have an effect."[50] Terry suggested that many important questions had been ignored in the past because of the psychiatrists' preoccupation with the victim's financial restitution, the need to prove that the survivor's symptoms were not caused by merely constitutional factors, and

[49] See for example child survivor and psychiatrist Robert Krell's condemnation of postwar psychiatrists and psychoanalysts, first for neglecting Holocaust survivors, and then for maligning and even insulting them through the use of notions of regression, identification with the aggressor, and survivor guilt. Writing from an antipsychoanalytic position, Krell condemns the work of Bettelheim, Niederland, Krystal and others for the inadequacy of their attempts to theorize the psychical impact of the camps. He suggests that the sheer scale of the trauma of the camps placed it outside the reach of any theoretical vocabulary, and that the problems of the survivor, such as depression, hatred, anxiety attacks, and psychosomatic difficulties, are justifiable feelings requiring no diagnosis or interpretation because they are simply "logical responses to a bizarre and extreme trauma" (whatever that might mean). See Robert Krell, "Survivors and Their Families: Psychiatric Consequences of the Holocaust," in Robert Krell and Marc I. Sherman, *Medical and Psychological Effects of Concentration Camps in Holocaust Survivors*, vol. 4, *Genocide: PA Critical Bibliographic Review* (New Brunswick, N.J., 1977), 24. See also Robert Krell, "Holocaust Survivors and Their Children: Comments on Psychiatric Consequences and Psychiatric Terminology," *Comprehensive Psychiatry* 25 (1984): 521–28.

[50] Jack Terry, "The Damaging Effects of the 'Survivor Syndrome,'" in *Psychoanalytic Reflections on the Holocaust: Selected Essays*, ed. Steven A. Luel and Paul Marcus (New York, 1984), 139–40; hereafter abbreviated *PR*.

above all because of the inability of the psychiatrists and psychoanalysts to overcome their emotional involvement, lack of objectivity, and countertransferences. He argued that compensation should never have been a medical matter, only a legal one between victim and victimizer, and that the patient's unconscious conflicts about receiving compensation for medical "damage" played a role in preventing recovery. He was convinced as well that the true meaning of the survivor's chronic despair, the existence of which he did not dispute, was not guilt at having survived, but the realization that so few people cared about her plight or understood her. In other words, rather like Rappaport, whose work he did not mention, Terry attributed the survivor's dejection not to the trauma of the camps itself so much as to the survivor's feeling of betrayal when confronted with the indifference of others. At the same time, and somewhat incoherently, he also ascribed the highest pathogenic potential to the survivor's inability to mourn lost loved *and* hated libidinal objects, an experience he described in terms similar to those Niederland had used to account for the origin of the very survivor guilt the idea of which Terry discredited (*PR*, 135–47).

In a discussion in the same 1984 volume, Frances Grossman went even further, suggesting that the sheer magnitude of the events of the Holocaust made questions of personal guilt meaningless. In terms that resonate with Des Pres's discussion she writes: "What is the meaning of guilt when one prisoner is forced at gunpoint to bury alive another prisoner? . . . What is the meaning of personal guilt when prisoners themselves are forced to decide which prisoners are to be sent to the gas chamber? The magnitude of these events transcends personal guilt . . . I might accept the term 'existential guilt,' but the Freudian guilt concept, which is based on a fantasy wish, is inadequate" (*PR*, 210). In answer to a question about Arendt's claims about Jewish compliance with the Nazis, Grossman again rejected all such notions of complicity as simply another version of the tendency to blame the victim of the kind so common in cases of rape or abused children: "The whole idea of blaming the victim for his own misfortunes, whether it's Jews, a woman who has been raped, an abused child, is a copout. It's just not assuming responsibility for what you've done to other people" (*PR*, 222–23). And in the same vein, Grossman elsewhere sided with Des Pres in attacking Bettelheim's ideas about identification with the aggressor and survivor guilt: "Anyone who dares to attempt to breathe life or human dignity into this image [of the alienated, regressive survivor] is immediately attacked."[51]

Grossman treated trauma as a purely external cause that came to the already constituted subject from the outside to shatter the ego's integrity. In this way she forestalled the possibility of scapegoating the survivor by denying that the victim

---

[51] Frances Grossman, "Blaming the Victim: Bettelheim's Theories on the Holocaust," *Israel Horizons* 32 (May/June 1984): 25.

colluded or participated in a fantasmatic or other way with the scene of abjection. The weakness of her approach, of course, is that by abandoning the difficulties of the unconscious in favor of a simple polarity between an external violence and a pregiven subject, she supports a view of the location of violence that not only renders unthinkable or incoherent any idea of the unconscious—of a conflictual, divided subjectivity caught up in the register of fantasy and with a compulsion to repeat—but inevitably ends up grounding explanation in a commonsense appeal to the empirical realities of the external situation without considering the questions of individual appraisal or personal history that critics of the survivor syndrome were ostensibly calling for. Nevertheless, her approach proved irresistible to some researchers, as is evidenced by the fact that her criticisms of the concept of survivor guilt were immediately taken up by Paul Marcus, the editor of the volume in which Grossman's remarks appeared, and Irene Wineman, who would go on to write about Bettelheim, Des Pres, and related topics.[52]

Marcus and Wineman cited two empirical studies in support of their position, both of which deserve scrutiny because they have come to enjoy an important status in the field. One was a study by Gloria Leon and others claiming to be the first investigation of survivors to use control groups.[53] Niederland and his colleagues had developed the concept of the survivor syndrome largely on the basis of psychiatric interviews with a self-selected group of survivors seeking help with reparation claims, a procedure that Terry and others criticized on various groungs, including the lack of controls. Leon and colleagues sought to rectify this by comparing two groups of people, one comprising a sample of survivors and their children, the other comprising a "normal" sample of nonsurvivors and their children, of similar ethnic and cultural background, in order to test for differences

[52] Paul Marcus and Irene Wineman, "Psychoanalysis Encountering the Holocaust," *Psychoanalytic Inquiry* 5, no. 1 (1985): 85–98; hereafter abbreviated "PEH." The authors echo Grossman's claims:

[W]hat is the meaning of personal guilt when one prisoner is forced at gunpoint to bury alive another prisoner (Grossman, 1984)? The conventional psychoanalytic notion of neurotic guilt (i.e., guilt experienced when there has been no violation of the individual's conscious values) has too often been applied to the survivor. One might speculate that the earlier emphasis on guilt as a central feature of the survivor may be related to the unacknowledged guilt on the part of analysts who were often personally affected by the event. However, the magnitude and context of these Holocaust events often transcended personal guilt (Grossman, 1984). The question, 'Why was I allowed to survive?' may not necessarily evoke the response of guilt (which is an inadequate word) but of responsibility (cf. Des Pres). This sense of responsibility is not motivated by personal guilt but by a feeling of relatedness to the dead—a feeling of affiliation to the Jewish people in a life-affirming way, and/or a way of bonding the survivor to his children, a bonding related, in part, to the survivor's viewing his children as symbols of rebirth and continuity. ("PEH," 91)

[53] Gloria R. Leon, James N. Butcher, Max Kleinman, Alan Goldberg, and Moshe Almagor, "Survivors of the Holocaust and Their Children: Current Status and Adjustment," *Journal of Personality and Social Psychology* 41, no. 3 (1981): 503–16; hereafter abbreviated "SHC."

in adjustment between survivors and their offspring. The survivor syndrome concept assumed a high degree of psychopathology in survivors, based on notions of regression, identification with the aggressor, and survivor guilt. But noting that Des Pres had questioned these psychoanalytic assumptions, Leon and her coauthors produced evidence, derived from self-administered questionnaires, personality evaluations, and other empirical tests, that the psychological adjustment of both groups of adult and children was in the normal range and that there were no significant differences between the two groups. Where nonsignificant differences did occur—for example, there was an elevated preoccupation with health issues among survivors—the authors explained the finding as a realistic response to health problems begun in the camps.

Leon and her associates used a similar approach to the problem of survivor guilt. It is important to emphasize, though, that the authors did not in fact evaluate survivor guilt: "The concept of pervasive survivor guilt as an extremely influential psychodynamic factor in concentration camp survivors, although not specifically assessed, did not seem evident in the findings of this investigation" ("SHC," 514). What they offered, instead, was an "equally plausible hypothesis" ("SHC," 515) to explain the phenomenon, namely, that many of the survivors had indeed been depressed after liberation from their prolonged and unspeakably harsh traumatic experiences, and since the symptoms of depression included self-blame and feelings of worthlessness, it was understandable that the content of these self-evaluations would focus on the trauma that had been experienced. (But what kind of explanation is this? Why does it rule out feelings of guilt or remorse?) Moreover, the authors went on to argue that an extreme and continuous effort was necessary to survive under such prolonged and harsh conditions of deprivation: "This effort, along with a belief that survival was not only a matter of luck and the help of God and others, but of using one's own resources, does not seem consonant with a universal syndrome of pervasive and intense survivor guilt" ("SHC," 515). What this says is that although the authors did not actually measure survivor guilt, they were convinced guilt could not be an important issue for survivors because the efforts to stay alive in the camps were simply incompatible with it.

Something similarly short of knockdown proof occurs in another study cited by Marcus and Wineman that reported the results of the psychiatric examinations of one hundred camp survivors in America twenty years after their liberation.[54] The author, Werner Tuteur, stated that although the survivors all displayed pronounced depression, anxiety, and repetitive nightmares, and although many of them suffered from survivor guilt (pace Leon et al.), the latter symptom, consid-

---

[54] Werner Tuteur, "One Hundred Concentration Camp Survivors. Twenty Years Later," *Israel Annals of Psychiatry and Related Disciplines* 4, no. 1 (1966): 78–90; hereafter abbreviated "OHC."

89

ered to be the dynamic driving force behind most depressions, was not as frequently elicited as might have been expected. Of the one hundred survivors, sixty-seven survivors admitted guilt along with severe depressions, while thirty-three expressed no survival guilt on the conscious level; among these were the psychotics. They gave such statements as "'I did everything I could to save my parents,' or, 'There was nothing I could do'" ("OHC," 86). Marcus and Wiseman interpreted Tuteur's observations to mean that survivor guilt was not necessarily a factor in the survivor's depression and was therefore "inapplicable to many survivors" ("PEH," 91). But this did not fully represent Tuteur's position, for he had gone on to warn apropos of the survivors' remarks: "Such statements, of course, must not be taken as the absolute truth, and a special study of such denial seems indicated, since all of the nonpsychotics who deny it continue at this time to suffer from nightmares the contents of which deal with their perished close relatives" ("OHC,"86). Marcus and Wineman chose to ignore this caveat.

I have stressed some of the problems of these research studies and of the use made of them by psychoanalysts and others bent on revising the interpretation of the survivor, to suggest that, although post–Des Pres critics of the survivor syndrome and the notion of survivor guilt sought to buttress their reinterpretations by an appeal to the empirical evidence, it appears they were motivated by extraempirical considerations amounting to a paradigm shift so basic that it was almost invisible to its adherents. This is borne out by the fact that the lack of solid evidence regarding the prevalence of survivor guilt apparently did not really matter to Marcus and others, since he and his colleagues did not actually deny the existence of survivor guilt but instead sought to revise its interpretation in order to understand it more "positively." Thus although Marcus and his coauthors continued to bring forward evidence purportedly challenging claims about the importance of survivor guilt, they also used the alternative tactic of conceding the presence of guilt in survivors but explaining it differently.

For example, in a 1988 critique Marcus and Rosenberg repeated many of the criticisms that had already been leveled by themselves and others against the concepts of the survivor syndrome and survivor guilt. On the one hand, they suggested that the symptoms of the survivor syndrome might be an "iatrogenic" consequence of the unconscious collaboration between physician and victim during the reparation process. They also cited again the papers of Leon and colleagues and Tuteur to show that the role of survivor guilt had been exaggerated. On the other hand, they accepted the existence of survivor guilt in many cases, and even conceded that it could have "deeply negative psychological consequences" for the survivor, while also attempting to counter the Freudian interpretation of it. Recognizing against Bettelheim and with Des Pres and others a "communal dimension" to camp life that they believed transformed the meaning of survival, they ascribed to guilt a positive role in recovery: "Following Lifton we believe that the creative aspect of guilt has been ignored in most post-Freudian thought as well as survivor syndrome literature. Guilt can not only lead us to see our shortcomings but can also contribute to our making ourselves more caring persons. It need not only be a pathological response to massive psychic trauma."[55] In effect, Marcus and Rosenberg rejected the Freudian notion of the unconscious identification of the victim with the aggressor that, as they recognized, underpinned the concept of survivor guilt ("PC," 58–59) by equating survivor guilt with the notion of "responsibility." The argument, which had already been made by Lifton and Des Pres, meant trading in the unconscious, conflictual, and compulsive dynamic of survivor guilt for a more traditional, quasireligious notion of guilt as moral conscience and ethical judgment from which all notion of conflict has been erased: "'Moral guilt involves a judgment of wrongdoing, based upon ethical principles and made by an individual (whether or not the transgressor himself), group or community,' and 'psychological guilt is an individual sense of badness or evil, with a fear of expectation of punishment' . . . Niederland and Krystal . . . elect to look at guilt only from the psychological side. This does not permit them to see that guilt can play an important role in recovery" ("PC," 68).

But this meant in turn that the concept of identification with the aggressor would also need to be revised. Given the claim that the survivor was a person who had displayed resources and strengths in the camps that had been overlooked by those who had invented the concept of the survivor syndrome, it is not surprising that the revision has taken the form of interpreting the ego's imitations as a deliberate strategic performance. This revision can be found in the work of psychoanalyst Anna Ornstein, a former survivor and analyst, to whom Marcus and Rosenberg acknowledge a major debt ("PC," 77, n. 55). In a critique of the concept of the survivor syndrome as too narrow and rigid, Ornstein grafted a neo-Freudian or Kohutian account of disavowal and psychical splitting onto Des Pres's ideas about the survivor's duality of behavior in the camps in order to interpret the survivor's compliance with the Nazis as a strategic ruse. "Survivors were helpless and passive only to those who judged them in terms of their *manifest behavior* and from 'a distance,' that is, from the observer's own perspective," she observed. "To survive physically, inmates had to follow orders without protest and resistance; their behavior had to be passive in relation to the SS and their Jewish supervisors. But survival was not possible in a passive state of mind. Survival required a great deal of activity and resistance in all aspects of camp life."[56] Equating disavowal not with the psychotic disowning of the actual perception of reality,

---

[55] Paul Marcus and Alan Rosenberg, "A Philosophical Critique of the 'Survivor Syndrome' and Some Implications for Treatment," in *The Psychological Perspectives of the Holocaust and Its Aftermath*, ed. Randolph L. Braham (New York, 1988), 68; hereafter abbreviated "PC."

[56] Anna Ornstein, "Survival and Recovery," *Psychoanalytic Inquiry* 5, no.1 (1985): 113; hereafter abbreviated "SR."

as Freud had done, but with the relatively common nonpsychotic tendency to disavow the meaning of what is actually perceived from entering consciousness so that the ego becomes divided or split, Ornstein proposed:

> This depth-psychological explanation that the mechanism of disavowal offers in relation to adaptation can be supported by the empirical findings of Des Pres, who interviewed 180 concentration camp survivors and found a regularly occurring contradiction in their stories. The contradictions indicated that survivors lived on two distinctly separate psychological levels, that they had lived a double existence: they were directed toward the outside, remaining compliant and conforming and—at the same time—they were directed toward the inside, toward the preservation of the core of the self. What needs to be remembered in this context is that there is a difference between absolute conformity to necessity and strategic conformity to necessity; an important consideration when survivors are described as "passive victims" or "tools of terror." It was the mechanism of disavowal that made it possible to attend to the details of camp life with the utmost clarity of thinking while preserving a vision of life and the future that was in keeping with one's deeply internalized value system. ("SR," 114)[57]

It is hard to know what to make of this. No doubt, Des Pres would have rejected as illegitimate Ornstein's fusion of his ideas about the duality of action in the camps with her ideas about psychological dividedness, since he rejected the value of psychology as a means of explaining camp behavior. In any case, what is clear is that by grafting Des Pres's sociological interpretation of the survivor to her own Kohutian one, Ornstein converted unconscious traumatic identification with the enemy into a tactical imitation on the part of the ego or self that deliberately performs its divided strategem like an actor who, with perfect lucidity ("with the utmost clarity of thinking"), observes from a distance, or represents to himself, the imitations he performs on the stage.

Something similar happens in Marcus's engagement with the problem of identification. In a paper on Bettelheim, Marcus and Rosenberg rebuked Bettelheim for failing to modify a psychoanalytic approach that treated the victim as an isolated individual and neglected the victim's social environment. Praising Des Pres for his trenchant criticisms of Bettelheim, they used Des Pres's dramaturgical ideas about the prisoner's duality of action to convert the theory of the victim's unconscious identification with the aggressor into a theory about the victim's calculated and strategic imitations:

> Bettelheim's classical psychoanalytic perspective, with its emphasis on the discrete individual devoid of his social context, also led him not to take into account what Des Pres calls the "duality of action in extremity" . . . For example, inmates on the "primary" level

---

[57] As I pointed out in this chapter, n. 3, Ornstein was mistaken in saying that Des Pres had interviewed survivors.

may have appeared to have acted "childishly" or "regressively" when forced to by their overlords, they may have imitated certain SS behavior and complied with SS demands, and may have altogether looked as if they had been broken as persons by the Nazi assault. However, on the "secondary" level, and often at the same time and in other contexts, inmates were resisting camp controls and trying to fend off the Nazi assault. In other words, for the sake of survival they made strategic accommodations to their ordeal in certain contexts that looked as if they had been completely broken, while in other ways they were resisting their Nazi overlords.[58]

For Marcus and Rosenberg, "acting child-like" and "being 'regressed'" are not the same thing, for the acting is one of appearance only, an "ego-driven act of strategic accommodation in the service of survival" ("RBB," 554). We find the same approach in Marcus's later book on Bettelheim, which is presented as a defense of the complexity and subtlety of the latter's psychoanalytic approach to the survivor but which also redresses the apparent neglect of the social context inherent in that approach by drastically reducing the role of unconscious factors.[59]

My review of the sociological and psychoanalytic literature of the survivor has been intended to show the extent and degree of the consensus about the survivor that emerged in the wake of Des Pres's work, to the point that the psychoanalytic notion of identification with the aggressor gave way to ideas about strategic imitation, and the notion of survivor guilt was revised and reinterpreted in such a way as to displace it from its previous position of importance. The overall effect of these developments was to establish a post-Freudian or neo-Freudian account of the survivor from which all classical psychoanalytic notions of the unconscious and mimesis had been purged. The time was ripe for survivor guilt to disappear altogether.

---

[58] Paul Marcus and Alan Rosenberg, "Reevaluating Bruno Bettelheim's Work on the Nazi Concentration Camps: The Limits of His Psychoanalytic Approach," *Psychoanalytic Review* 81, no. 3 (Fall 1994): 553–54; hereafter "RBB."

[59] Paul Marcus, *Autonomy in the Extreme Condition: Bruno Bettelheim, the Nazi Concentration Camps, and the Mass Society* (Westport, Conn., 1999).

Image and Trauma

Imagery and PTSD

IN 1985, two physicians, Elizabeth Brett and Robert Ostroff, published a paper on the centrality of the image to the conceptualization of posttraumatic stress disorder, or PTSD. Their article had a polemical intent. They claimed that researchers had failed properly to appreciate the significance of imagery in the diagnosis and treatment of PTSD and that what they characterized as the "diagnostic and clinical confusion" marring the field of posttraumatic stress could be remedied only by reconceptualizing the official criteria for PTSD in terms of the image.[1] They were not alone in emphasizing the role of the image in trauma. Starting in the 1980s, in books and articles by Cathy Caruth, Bessel van der Kolk, and others, the notion of the traumatic image, conceived as an "iconic" memory that haunts the victim in the form of flashbacks, dreams, and other intrusive repetitions, has come to dominate American (and to some extent also, European) discussions of trauma.[2] One result of this has been the coalescence of the question of violence and trauma around the notion of the image in ways that reinforce our sense, as Samuel Weber has put it, that we can rely on the image to tell us what violence is.[3]

---

[1] Elizabeth A. Brett and Robert Ostroff, "Imagery and Posttraumatic Stress Disorder: An Overview," *American Journal of Psychiatry* 142, no. 4 (April 1985): 417–24; hereafter abbreviated "IP."

[2] A development discussed in my *Trauma: A Genealogy* (Chicago, 2000), especially chap. 7.

[3] Samuel Weber, "Wartime," in *Violence, Identity, and Self-Determination*, ed. Hent de Vries and Samuel Weber (Stanford, Calif., 1997), 81–82. What is interesting about this development is that it disavows the fact that the digital-televisual-video media permit a postproduction manipulation of images in ways that undermine their veridical or indexical status.

What is at stake in the recent emphasis on the traumatic image? In 1980, largely as a result of agitation by the anti–Vietnam War movement, PTSD was introduced into the third edition of the *Diagnostic and Statistical Manual of Mental Disorders* (*DSM-III*), the official classification manual of the American Psychiatric Association. The new diagnostic category was welcomed by many in the field of trauma studies because it gave official recognition to signs and symptoms of a disorder that had long been observed in victims of trauma. *DSM-III* represented a fundamental shift away from the Freudian tradition that had previously dominated American psychiatry to a more ostensibly "objective" approach to mental illness.[4] From the start, however, it was evident that the new diagnostic scheme for PTSD was far from complete. In its initial formulation PTSD was defined as an anxiety disorder with four diagnostic criteria: (A) the traumatic event; (B) reexperiences of the event; (C) numbing phenomena; and (D) miscellaneous symptoms, a group that included survivor guilt as an optional criterion. The traumatic event itself was defined as an event that involved a "recognizable stressor that would evoke significant symptoms of distress in almost everyone."[5]

There were several ambiguities in those criteria and definitions. The invention of PTSD had been propelled by the widespread desire to obtain formal acknowledgment of the idea that severely traumatic events could have prolonged psychological consequences in anyone, regardless of the individual's prior history or personality. In this regard, the invention of PTSD necessitated a shift away from the previous approach to trauma, which concentrated on the ways in which stressful life events were "mediated" by the subjective interpretation of the victim. As Brett and her colleagues noted, the PTSD "revolution" meant that investigators now had to identify the relevant environmental stressors "regardless of the coping styles or resources of the individuals exposed to the events."[6] This meant that the previous, largely psychoanalytic emphasis on the role played in the traumatic reaction by the subject's earlier experiences, especially his or her early libidinal history, was replaced by a focus on the role of the external environment. The fact that PTSD was one of the few disorders in *DSM-III* to focus on etiology also strengthened the new tendency of researchers to highlight the causal role of the external event, since the symptoms associated with trauma *without* the presence of the highly stressful event were not held to constitute the disorder.[7]

[4] On this point see Allan Young, *The Harmony of Illusions: The Invention of Post-Traumatic Stress Disorder* (Princeton, 1995); and Wilbur J. Scott, "PTSD in *DSM-III*: A Case in the Politics of Diagnosis and Disease," *Social Problems* 37 (1990): 294–310.

[5] *The Diagnostic and Statistical Manual of Mental Disorders* (3d ed., *DSM-III*), (American Psychiatric Association, 1980), 236, 238.

[6] Robert S. Laufer, Elizabeth A. Brett, and M. S. Gallops, "Post-Traumatic Stress Disorder (PTSD) Reconsidered: PTSD among Vietnam Veterans," in *Post-Traumatic Stress Disorder: Psychological and Biological Sequelae*, ed. Bessel van der Kolk (Washington, D.C., 1984), 61.

[7] Bonnie L. Green, Jacob D. Lindy, and Mary C. Grace, "Posttraumatic Stress Disorder: Toward *DSM-IV*," *Journal of Nervous and Mental Disease* 173 (1985): 407.

Yet from the start what was lacking was a clear definition of what constituted a recognizable stressor, as well as methods to operationalize and objectify the traumatic experience. In this context, the aim of Brett and Ostroff's paper was to reformulate PTSD in terms of the image so that the task of operationalizing and objectifying the disorder could proceed more effectively. Brett had served on the subcommittee assigned to help formulate PTSD for *DSM-III*, and this was her chance to propose further clarification. The authors began by defining the image: "Images are mental contents that possess sensory qualities. They are distinguished from mental activity that is purely verbal or abstract. While images can have qualities associated with any of the sensory modalities, visual imagery is believed to be the most common ("IP," 417). The definition came from Mardi J. Horowitz, who for many years had been simulating stress responses in the laboratory by studying the impact of stressful films on experimental subjects. Horowitz had also been associated with the working groups that had helped formulate PTSD for *DSM-III*.[8] The distinction Brett and Ostroff made in their article between the image on the one hand and speech or abstract mental activity on the other echoed the more general distinction that had been adopted by Horowitz between the image (or icon) and lexical representation. His idea was that the image was one fundamental mode by which perceptions, memories, ideas, and feelings were represented in the mind, and that images could be distinguished from lexical or verbal forms of mental representation.

Images, as internal psychic representations, were also said by Horowitz to be different from perceptions in that, unlike the latter, they were not simple replicas of an external stimulus, but complex amalgams of memory fragments, reconstructions, and fantasies whose formation could be influenced at any time by the subject's emotional states, proneness to experimental compliance, suggestibility, and other factors.[9] Yet there was a tendency, inherent in Horowitz's information-processing approach to cognition as well as in his experimental protocols, to collapse the image into perception, itself defined as a simple copy of the traumatic stimulus. One consequence was his readiness to treat images as if they were faithful replicas of the external world. This is a crucial issue to which I shall return, because what was lost in Horowitz's collapse of the image into perception was his own psychodynamic understanding of the potentially identificatory-mimetic or fantasmatic nature of the mental image. As a result, not only was the mental image abstracted from the human relationships that from a "mimetic" point of view might be considered to produce it and give it meaning, it also came to be understood antimimetically in indexical terms as if it were the causal outcome or literal imprint of the external

---

[8] Young, *The Harmony of Illusions*, 110.

[9] Mardi J. Horowitz, *Image Formation and Cognition* (New York, 1970), 4.

trauma.[10] In 1985, in an article on the many problems left unresolved by the new diagnosis of PTSD, Green and her colleagues observed that although the exact form of the intrusive images or experiences thought to define PTSD was not specified in *DSM-III*, the manual implied that those images and experiences were a "direct recapitulation of the event." Green and her group cautioned against endorsing that assumption without further study of the content of dreams, on the grounds that they had seen dreams that were directly linked to the traumatic event, as determined by later associations, presenting in a "partially disguised form."[11] But it was an assumption that was already becoming normative in the field. In short, Brett and Ostroff's paper on imagery exemplified the antimimetic tendency in American psychiatry to treat the image as an externally produced mental content uncontaminated by any mimetic-fantasmatic-suggestive dimension.

Against this background, one of the striking things about Brett and Ostroff's paper was its claim to originality—its contention that, five years after the invention of PTSD, the fundamental importance of imagery had yet to be fully acknowledged. The authors stated that, with two important exceptions, all the major figures who had worked on trauma had failed to maintain a focus on imagery or to conceptualize its role in PTSD. In their view, either imagery had been mentioned only anecdotally, without being given a systematic or prominent place in the theoretical model of trauma (this was true, they said, of Abraham Kardiner, William Niederland, Henry Krystal, and others who had done work on patients with war neuroses or concentration camp syndrome); or the range of imagery had been "overly restricted" in that the authors in question had only mentioned the images involved in traumatic nightmares and had failed to realize the importance of images in the awake state (this criticism applied to Freud, Kardiner, and others); or the many ways in which imagery could be manifested had not been explicitly described; or contradictory views about imagery had been offered, as when authors R. K. Grinker and John Spiegel in their work on combat stress in World War II designated traumatic nightmares as part of the traumatic neurosis but also stated that such nightmares were not primarily about combat trauma but about other conflicts ("IP," 420). According to Brett and Ostroff, these various failures meant

[10] See Leys, *Trauma: A Genealogy*, 250, where I suggest that Peirce's notion of the "index" comes far closer to Bessel van der Kolk's contemporary hypostatization of the literalness of the traumatic image than his notion of the "icon." Verbal testimony in Lanzmann's *Shoah* has recently been conceptualized in explicitly Peircian-indexical terms by suggesting that testimony as index has a referential force "that exists prior to any interpretive response" and that its meaning is produced not by interpretation but by "the event that produced it." In this view, testimony or representation is collapsed into the event. See Robert Brinkley and Steven Youra, "Tracing *Shoah*," *Proceedings of the Modern Language Association* 111 (1996): 108–27; and Paul Berger, *After the End: Representations of Post-Acopalypse* (Minneapolis, 1999), 73. In *Trauma: A Genealogy* I criticize such literalist readings of trauma.

[11] Green, Lindy, and Grace, "Posttraumatic Stress Disorder: Toward *DSM-IV*," 409.

that the concept of the image had to be extracted from the previous literature if it was to be given the kind of prominence they sought for it.

They were helped in their project especially by the work of Horowitz, who had focused on the relationship between imagery and stress disorders through more than two decades of experimental-theoretical-therapeutic inquiry. Their proposals for the reorganization of PTSD in terms of the image represented an application of Horowitz's theories ("IP," 421). According to their summary of Horowitz's views, the traumatic event was considered stressful because it lay outside the realm of the individual's ordinary experience. The victim was unable to process the meaning of the traumatic information because it could not be assimilated into existing cognitive schematas. Instead, "untamed" images of the trauma remained stuck in a hypothetical image storage system, from which they repeatedly pressed for revisualization and assimilation in the form of peremptory flashbacks and imagistic intrusion. Horowitz posited that the amnesia, constriction of thought processes, and emotional deadening or numbing held to be characteristic of the trauma victim were forms of denial by which the subject attempted to defend against the intrusive images and to reduce the anxiety associated with them. He believed that the intrusion and denial states alternated according to various intrapsychic trends and gradually decreased in severity and frequency as the affects were worked through and a new equilibrium was achieved.[12] Horowitz's significance for Brett and Ostroff was not just that he had studied the formal properties of the image in experimental settings or had developed interview protocols designed to assess objectively the role of imagery in actual patients. It was also that he had decisively expanded the role of the image in the stress disorders by arguing that images regularly occurred not only in dreams, to which earlier workers had tended to restrict them, but also in the awake state, where they had not been generally or systematically noticed ("IP," 419). On the basis of Horowitz's approach, Brett and Ostroff proposed to organize the symptoms of stress around two "dimensions." The first dimension involved *repetitions or reexperiencings of the trauma in the form of unbidden and intrusive images*, images that were accompanied by affective states and actions. The second dimension involved *defensive efforts to deny the trauma*, including emotional numbing, amnesia, and other attempts to suppress or avoid the trauma. They went on to argue that all the theorists whose work they had briefly reviewed could now be placed in one of two distinct groups, depending on whether or not the author's ideas conformed to the proposed two-dimensional framework. Freud, Horowitz, Lifton, and others could all be seen to share the same two-dimensional model, because each held that trauma-linked imagery, thoughts, or perceptions led to painful affects that in turn produced defensive re-

---

[12] See especially Mardi J. Horowitz, *Stress Response Syndromes* (New York, 1976); hereafter abbreviated *SRS*.

actions. Freud's suggestion that the ego was overwhelmed in trauma because of an extensive breach in the mind's protective shield against stimuli, with a consequent unleashing of the repetition compulsion and tendency of the victim to reexperience the trauma in nightmares, was held to be comparable to Horowitz's assumptions about the liability of the trauma victim to experience unbidden recurrent images. The only discrepancy between the two thinkers from this point of view was that Freud had failed to appreciate the importance of waking imagery. Freud's ideas about the patient's defensive efforts to control the repetition were assimilated to the denial or numbing phase of the two-dimensional model.[13]

From a "genealogical" perspective, Brett and Ostroff's groupings of previous workers on trauma appear artificial and contrived. But they served the purpose of demonstrating how the ideas of certain major theorists of trauma, notably Freud, could be viewed as essentially conforming to the two-dimensional framework they were advocating, thereby reinforcing its seeming validity and plausibility. The elegance and economy of the new model lay in part in its self-vindicating character. In fact, it was irrefutable.[14] Either traumatized subjects experienced intrusive images or they did not. If they did, the images were held to be an expression of the repetition compulsion, as the unassimilated traumatic experience repeatedly pressed for expression and processing in the form of daytime flashbacks, sleeping nightmares, and other images. If the victims did not experience such images, the explanation was that they were in the denial or numbing phase of the traumatic syndrome. In other words, the absence of reported images did not mean that such images did not exist. As Brett and Ostroff explained: "[A]n absence of imagery can be conceptualized as the result of defensive activity rather than as evidence of its nonexistence or irrelevance for stress disorder" ("IP," 421). For example, in a statement held by Ostroff and Brett to indicate Freud's lack of awareness of the pervasiveness of traumatic imagery in the awake state, he had famously remarked of victims of shellshock, railway accidents, and other traumas that although they suffered from nightmares they were not much occupied with memories of the event in their waking lives. "Perhaps," he had said, "they are more concerned with *not* thinking of it."[15] Horowitz had cited the same remark of Freud's when commenting

---

[13] Two influential theorists of trauma, Abram Kardiner and Henry Krystal, were the only authors who did not fit the two-dimensional framework of trauma, primarily, Brett and Ostroff said, because each made massive adaptive failure the central problem and therefore were unable to account adequately for the symptoms peculiar to PTSD—the repetitive images, memories, and affects and the resulting defensive or numbing defenses. For another discussion of these issues see Elizabeth Brett, "Psychoanalytic Contributions to a Theory of Traumatic Stress," in the *International Handbook of Traumatic Stress Syndromes*, ed. John P. Wilson and Beverley Raphael (New York, 1993), 61–68. Brett and Ostroff conceded, though, that the Kardiner-Krystal model might provide a better description of the severe stress response, in which the defensive functioning was so extensive that the dimension of repetition or reexperiencing was obscured or obliterated ("IP," 420–21).

[14] As Allan Young observes in *The Harmony of Illusions,* 141.

[15] Sigmund Freud, *Beyond the Pleasure Principle* (1920) in *The Standard Edition of the Complete Psychological Works of Sigmund Freud*, trans. and ed. James Strachey (London, 1953–74), 18:13.

on the failure of earlier theorists to mention intrusive images among the frequent symptoms of the combat neuroses. He had attributed that failure not only to theoretical presuppositions but more generally to the fact that

> thought experience is, in general, harder to report than physical sensation. Many persons, unless they are specifically asked, do not express such qualities of thought as intrusive entry into awareness or unusual intensity of imagery. If asked, they avoid discussion of such experiences as part of a general defensive effort. Thus, intrusive and repetitive conscious experiences would be indicated within [the] categories of startle reactions, difficulty of concentrating, preoccupation with combat, nightmares, and irrational fears or phobias. In addition, the menace of such unpleasant intrusions probably contributes to the behavioral signs of restlessness, irritability, and insomnia. (*SRS*, 37)

In short, Horowitz made the case for the centrality of intrusive imagery in the stress disorders by arguing that traumatic images only appeared to be absent owing to the patient's defensive efforts to suppress them, and by recasting other symptoms not previously associated with images as signs of intrusive visual contents and experiences.[16]

Miscellaneous Symptoms

Among the consequences that flowed from the new emphasis on the image in trauma was a tendency to encourage researchers to find imagery where it had not previously been detected, by suggesting that the patient's defensive maneuvers to suppress imagery had led to serious underreporting of its occurrence.[17] The result was that after the mid-1980s the concept of the trau-

---

[16] Niederland had mentioned hypermnesia, or "overly sharp, distinct, and virtually indelible memories," as one of several symptoms of camp survivors. Brett and Ostroff acknowledged Niederland's observations in this regard, while noting that he did not articulate the role of imagery in a more "formal" sense ("IP," 419). For his part, Horowitz cited Niederland's observations on hypermnesia as proof that recurrent, unbidden images in the awake state were a "striking occurrence" after stressful events (*SRS*, 17).

[17] As more than one author observed, in the *DSM-III* formulation of PTSD it was not clear whether it should be left to the patients to make the link between the traumatic event and their symptoms or whether it was the clinician's ability to link the two that was important. Some methods that were being developed to assess the incidence of PTSD required patients to make the connection between the numbing symptoms and the stressful experience. But on the two-dimensional model proposed by Brett and Ostroff, numbing or denial rendered victims incapable of associating their experiences to the traumatic event. The two-dimensional model thus suggested that posttraumatic stress disorder might be seriously underreported, with the consequence that if the new model were to prevail, and researchers rather than patients were to assume responsibility for coupling the symptoms and the image, a considerable increase in the reported incidence of PTSD could be anticipated. See Green, Lindy, and Grace, "Posttraumatic Stress Disorder: Toward *DSM-IV*," 409; Susan D. Solomon and Gloriosa J. Canino, "Appropriateness of DSM-IIIR Criteria for Posttraumatic Stress Disorder," 232; and Robert S. Laufer, Elizabeth A. Brett, and M. S. Gallops, "Posttraumatic Stress Disorder (PTSD) Reconsidered: PTSD among Vietnam Veterans," all in van der Kolk, *Post-Traumatic Stress Disorder*, 60–79.

matic image came to dominate American research on PTSD. But the consequence I want to pursue here concerns the status of the concept of survivor guilt.
From the perspective of the new model of PTSD, the original symptom criteria
proposed for the disorder contained considerable redundancy, or overlap. In particular, the fourth or "Miscellaneous Symptoms" category contained a heteroge-
neous group of symptoms most of which could now be incorporated without difficulty into the two dimensions of reexperiencing or numbing. The symptoms of
hyperalertness or exaggerated startle response, sleep disturbances, and the intensification of symptoms by exposure to events that symbolized or resembled
the traumatic event—all originally listed in the "Miscellaneous Symptoms" category—could now be regarded as forms of reexperiencing and their relocation to
that dimension could be seen as a conceptual clarification. Similarly, the memory
impairment and avoidance symptoms, also originally listed in the "Miscellaneous
Symptoms" category, could now be reclassified as aspects of denial or numbing,
yielding a similar conceptual advance.

That left one item in the "Miscellaneous Symptoms" category unaccounted for,
namely, survivor guilt—a symptom that, since the earliest postwar psychiatric discussions of the Holocaust survivor had been widely regarded as one of the most
characteristic signs of posttraumatic stress. In their article on imagery, Brett and
Ostroff expressed some uncertainty as to where to place survivor guilt in their revised model of PTSD. At first they suggested that it belonged to the dimension of
reexperiencing. As they wrote: "The startle response, sleep disturbance, survivor
guilt, and intensification of symptoms after exposure to reminders of the stressor,
are all forms of or accompaniments to imagic and affective re-experiencing phenomena" ("IP," 422). But that solution was only temporary. When in 1987 the diagnostic criteria for PTSD were revised along the lines of Brett and Ostroff's two-
dimensional model, survivor guilt suffered a demotion. In fact, it was dropped as
an optional diagnostic criterion and reduced instead to merely an "associated"
feature of the disorder.

The change did not occur without debate. "There was controversy over
whether to include the survivor guilt item from *DSM-III* . . . as an aspect of reexperiencing," Brett, Spitzer, and Williams wrote in their capacity as members of
the subcommittee charged with responsibility for the revisions, "but it was finally
eliminated because it was not clear that survivor guilt is present in all cases of
PTSD. It was agreed that survivor guilt is a prominent symptom of certain kinds of
PTSD, and it was listed as an associated feature of the disorder. The diagnostic
criteria are intended to be parsimonious, and the subcommittee believed that the
removal of the guilt item from the criteria would not result in false negative diagnoses."[18] In other words, according to Brett and her colleagues, the dimensions

[18] Elizabeth A. Brett, Robert L. Spitzer, and Janet B. W. Williams, "*DSM-III-R* Criteria for Posttraumatic Stress Disorder," *American Journal of Psychiatry* 145 (1988): 1233.

of intrusion or denial were capable of capturing PTSD so adequately that the omission of survivor guilt did not matter diagnostically. Thereafter, survivor guilt could be safely omitted from the checklists and other instruments used to assess the nature and incidence of posttraumatic stress.

We can measure the effect of dispensing with survivor guilt as one of the diagnostic criteria for PTSD by noting that in a subsequent collection of papers that arose from the revision process for the *next* edition of the *Diagnostic and Statistical Manual of Mental Disorders*, *DSM-IV* (1994) only one article referred to the topic. In a discussion of natural disasters and PTSD, Bonnie Green observed that survivor guilt, as measured by the Disaster Interview Schedule, "does seem infrequent and its removal from the DSM-III-R criteria does seem justified." She reported that even in the case of the Buffalo Creek flood, a famous disaster in which many people had died, more recent follow-up studies that attempted to operationalize the concept of survivor guilt, by asking in a structured clinical interview whether the person wondered about surviving when others did not and about any of his or her behaviors during the event that were worrisome, found that feelings of guilt were still "quite infrequent"—if survivor guilt was ranked, it would have tied for last place.[19] (I note in passing that operationalizing the concept of survivor guilt meant assessing its presence or absence on the basis of the survivor's replies to a questionnaire, a research approach that ruled out of limits the notion of unconscious guilt as an affect revealed by latent dream constructions, transference phenomena, and so on.)[20]

Green's reference to the flood in Buffalo Creek is an interesting marker of the shift in attitude toward the centrality of the experience of guilt to the survivor experience. For the Buffalo Creek disaster of 1972 had been the topic of a well-known paper by psychiatrist Robert J. Lifton, in which the guilt of the survivor had been a prominent theme. Equally striking is the fact that in Lifton's study the question of survivor guilt was inextricable from that of the traumatic image. A brief examination of his paper will allow me to start raising some critical questions about the status of the image in PTSD.

In their paper on imagery, Brett and Ostroff had praised Lifton as one of the few researchers, along with Horowitz, who had managed to sustain a focus on imagery in work on trauma. Lifton had begun one of his books with the sentence "We live on images,"[21] and in his studies of survivors of Hiroshima and the Viet-

[19] Bonnie L. Green, "Disasters and Posttraumatic Stress Disorder," in *Posttraumatic Stress Disorder: DSM-IV and Beyond*, ed. Jonathan R. J. Davidson and Edna B. Foa (Washington, D.C., 1992), 92. Interestingly, in the Diagnostic Interview Schedule that was used in several studies discussed by Green, survivor guilt was operationalized by asking a question about a horrifying experience that made the subject feel "ashamed of still being alive" (79), so that in those studies the key term was in fact shame, not guilt.

[20] See in this regard Harvey J. Schwartz, "Conscious and Unconscious Guilt in Patients with Traumatic Neuroses," *American Journal of Psychiatry* 141, no. 12 (1984): 1638–39, who objects to a recent article on the absence of guilt in survivors of Cambodian camps, on the grounds that the report depended exclusively on the victims' conscious responses.

[21] Robert Jay Lifton, *The Broken Connection: On Death and the Continuity of Life* (New York, 1983), 3.

nam veteran he had repeatedly emphasized the importance of death images in the traumatic response. According to Lifton, as summarized by Brett and Ostroff and discussed by me in chapter 2, trauma disrupted the normal symbolic processes by which the individual made sense of the world. Meaning was shattered, and the individual experienced a "death imprint" consisting of vivid memories and images of death and destruction that were associated with extreme fear and anxiety. The victim was haunted not only by such images but also by an "image of ultimate horror" that encapsulated or stood for all the scenes in which he felt he might have saved others. The traumatic image was therefore connected to a feeling of guilt at having survived when others had died. Lifton had also emphasized the role of psychic numbing in trauma, that is, the survivor's loss of the ability to feel and be involved with the world, a symptom he had suggested was produced by the survivor's strong identification with the dead. Finally, he had stressed the existence of impaired human relationships after trauma, drawing attention to the patients's search for meaning and symbolization as he attempted to work through the disaster ("IP," 418–19).

Nevertheless, despite Lifton's interest in the traumatic image, there are aspects of his thought that did not fit easily into Brett and Ostroff's framework. In particular, there is the issue of the part played by identification in the production of the traumatic image. For Brett and Ostroff, the traumatic experience, as manifested in the intrusive image, was a formal entity that ought to be assessed independently of the question of unconscious-symbolic or subjective meaning. To the objection that they thereby isolated the image from the individual doing the imaging and hence from what the image meant to the victim, they replied: "We disagree that the form of the stress response is essentially a function of what the traumatic event meant. Psychodynamic understandings of meaning do not explain the form of the symptoms. While it is critically important in a psychodynamic treatment to examine why a particular event is overwhelming, this does not explain why being overwhelmed results in intrusive thoughts as opposed to another kind of symptom. Freud developed the notion of the repetition compulsion in order to explain the form of traumatic symptoms. The psychodynamic understanding of meanings is a secondary step."[22] Their emphasis on the *form* of the traumatic response allowed them to consider the role of imagery in PTSD without regard to the subject's relations to others, the role of expectation, suggestion, or other identificatory-mimetic factors. By contrast, as we saw in chapter 1, for Lifton the death image was the product of the survivor's highly charged, fantasmatic identifications with those who had died. His concept of survivor guilt also depended on the idea

---

[22] See Ann Pollinger Haas and Herbert Hendin's letter to the editor, "What Is the Role of Traumatic Imagery?" and "Drs. Brett and Ostroff Reply," in *American Journal of Psychiatry* 143 (January 1986): 124–25. See also Brett, ""Psychoanalytic Contributions to a Theory of Traumatic Stress," in Wilson and Raphael, *International Handbook of Traumatic Stress Syndromes*, 65.

that the survivor of trauma identifies with the dead. In short, Lifton's ideas about the traumatic image could only be squared with Brett and Ostroff's by downplaying the identificatory aspects of his thought.

The Buffalo Creek disaster had occurred when coal waste, negligently dumped into a mountain stream by the Buffalo Mining Company in West Virginia, created an artificial dam that then gave way, causing a massive "tide" of coal waste water to flood and devastate the mining hamlets in the valley. One hundred twenty-five people had been killed, and nearly five thousand made homeless. Lifton and a junior colleague, Eric Olson, had been hired as consultants to assess the psychic impairment of the survivors by the lawyers for the claimants in a lawsuit against the mining company. (The claimants eventually received $13.5 million in an out-of-court settlement.) In summarizing their findings, Lifton and Olson had described three fundamental survivor symptoms, each of which was connected to the other and to the theme of the traumatic image.

Consonant with my remarks in chapter 1 concerning Lifton's focus on death in the traumatic experience, the first symptom listed was the *death imprint*, consisting of "memories and images of the disaster." These images, still "indelible" thirty months afterward, often appeared in terrifying, recurrent dreams. Here is Lifton and Olson's report of one survivor's account of such a dream:

> "I've never been to no funerals except the ones right after the flood . . . In the dream there is a big crowd at the funeral—the whole family is watching. I'm being buried. I'm scared to death. I'm trying to tell them I'm alive but they don't pay no attention. They act like I'm completely dead but I'm trying to holler to them that I'm alive. They cover me up and lower me down, but I can see the dirt on me. I'm panicked and scared. I become violent trying to push my way through the dirt . . . I think I'll suffocate if I don't fight my way out. I feel like I'm trying to shout that I'm alive."[23]

Lifton and Olson had observed that the dream reflected the state of being "as-if dead" ("HM," 3), a state they held to be characteristic of the most severe kinds of survivor experience. In other words, the dream images were identificatory or mimetic in nature, in that in the dream the survivor imagined that he had suffered the same fate as his dead relatives and had put himself in their place. Or perhaps it would be more accurate to say that the dream images were at once mimetic and antimimetic in character, as the survivor mimetically merged with the dead *and* antimimetically distanced himself from the scene of death, by describing himself as someone who could *see* and represent the scene of entombment to himself and hence could register his protest at the dirt being thrown over his corpse.

The second symptom of trauma Lifton and Olson had mentioned was *survivor*

---

[23] Robert J. Lifton and Eric Olson, "The Human Meaning of Total Disaster," *Psychiatry* 39 (1976): 3; hereafter abbreviated "HM," The ellipses in the quoted passage are in the original.

guilt, the survivor's feeling of remorse at his survival, and his belief that he had somehow survived at the expense of those who had perished. Lifton and Olson had stated that survivor guilt was found especially in recurrent dreams, in which a single image exemplified the entire disaster experience with its combination of fear, pity, and guilt. They wrote:

> People who have gone through this kind of experience are never quite able to forgive themselves for having survived. Another side of them, however, experiences relief and gratitude that it was *they* who had the good fortune to survive in contrast to the fate of those who died—a universal and all-too-human survivor reaction that in turn intensifies their guilt. Since the emotion is so painful, the sense of guilt may be suppressed and covered over by other emotions or patterns, such as rage or apathy.
>
> But whether or not suppressed, that guilt continues to create in Buffalo Creek survivors a sense of a burden that will not lift. They feel themselves still bound to the dead, living a half-life devoid of pleasure and with limited vitality. ("HM," 5)

Finally, it was precisely the feeling of limited vitality, depression, or *psychic numbing* that Lifton and Olson had characterized as the third major symptom of trauma. Calling numbing the essence of the "disaster syndrome," they had described it as simultaneously a product of a melancholic, ambivalent, and hence guilty identification with the dead and a defense against that same identification:

> Numbing . . . is an aspect of persistent grief; of the "half-life" defined by loss, guilt, and close at times to an almost literal identification with the dead. As one of the plaintiffs put it: "I feel dead now. I have no energy. I sit down and I feel numb" [. . .]. Numbing is closely related to the psychological defense of denial . . . Numbing and denial are sustained because of the survivor's inability to confront or work through the disaster experience. He is thus left psychologically imprisoned in death- and guilt-related conflicts that can neither be dealt with nor eliminated. ("HM," 5–6)[24]

Lifton's language of the "literal" (or "almost literal") here to characterize the survivor's fantasmatic identification with the dead might make it seem as if he adhered to the kind of literalism found in the work of Caruth and van der Kolk, where the traumatic image or "icon" is theorized as a literal memory or replay of the traumatic event that is considered to be aporetically severed from all knowledge and representation. In a recent interview with Lifton, Caruth can be seen trying to push him in that literalizing direction, and there are moments when he seems to accede to her formulations. For example, when speaking of the new "knowledge

---

[24] "The indelible image is always associated with guilt," Lifton observes in "Survivor Experience and the Traumatic Syndrome," in *The Broken Connection: On Death and the Continuity of Life* (New York, 1983), 172.

of death and therefore a knowledge of life" that the survivor brings back from his immersion in death, Lifton says that the survivor has in that sense "lived out the mythology of the hero, but not quite." Caruth picks up on that "not quite" aspect of the survivor's experience, in order to suggest that the survivor doesn't bring back simply a mastered knowledge of death but something else: a confrontation with death that has "that anticipatory quality of not being fully assimilated or known but projected into a future." "That's right," Lifton replies, apparently accepting Caruth's ideas about the "deathlike break," interruption of representation, and the literal that she associates with the traumatic experience.[25]

But in seeming to agree with Caruth here, Lifton ignores or occludes the mimetico-identificatory dimension of the image inherent in his own descriptions of the death encounter. For if, according to Lifton and Olson's report of the Buffalo Creek disaster, the survivor's unconscious identification with the dead is so great that it is as if the survivor himself is dead, by the same token the traumatic image or memory cannot be a literal replay of the scene. This is because in the survivor's report of his dream, as cited above, the dreamer does not represent the traumatic scene literally, as a scene of the death of others, but fantasmatically as a scene of identification in which he himself occupies the place of the dead.

Moreover, it is not clear that the concept of survivor guilt *can* be coherently retained once the image has been purged of its identificatory-imitative dimensions in the ways Brett and Ostroff wish. Rather, a history of the concept of survivor guilt shows that the latter has been inseparable from the notion of identification. A mimetic concept of the traumatic experience and the concept of survivor guilt have gone hand in hand. Conversely, an antimimetic concept of the traumatic image, defined by Brett and Ostroff and numerous others as a faithful replica of the external event stripped of any mimetic dynamic, and the repudiation of the notion of survivor guilt have likewise gone together. So it is therefore not at all surprising that recent definitions of PTSD simultaneously thematize the idea of the purely external traumatic image and eliminate the notion of survivor guilt. It is as if the notion of survivor guilt was itself a kind of "psychoanalytic" survivor in the post-Freudian world of *DSM-III* and was incoherent within a new paradigm that wanted nothing to do with the notion of unconscious identification and related ideas.

This does not mean that survivor guilt has disappeared from the lexicon of trauma. It continues to have currency—for example, it has frequently been mentioned as one of the aftereffects of September 11. But in the official world of trauma studies it has lost its previous position of importance as well as its theoretical rationale. The net effect has been to foreground the role of imagery in

[25] Cathy Caruth, "An Interview with Robert Jay Lifton," in *Trauma: Explorations in Memory*, ed. Cathy Caruth (Baltimore, 1995), 135–36.

PTSD in ways that suppress consideration of what I have been calling mimesis, and to encourage instead a tendency to treat the external stressor and its correlative, the traumatic image, as purely external and objective phenomena.

Stress Films

The work of Mardi J. Horowitz exemplifies these developments or tendencies in a particularly interesting way, and because his ideas have proven so influential, they are worth examining in more detail. Horowitz had started to develop his ideas about the image in the 1960s when, after a long period of neglect, the topic of imagery experienced a dramatic revival. He had contributed to that revival in 1970 with his first book, *Image Formation and Cognition.*[26] From the start, it was understood that there were many different types of images, including quasiperceptual images, memory-images, imagination-images, hypnagogic images (images of the kind experienced in the drowsy state or in hypnosis), eidetic images ("projected images," usually visual, so vivid as to seem to the waking subject like a perception), and so on. But there were abundant taxonomic, phenomenological, and theoretical problems in defining the image, and many controversies.

Horowitz had begun *Image Formation and Cognition* by distinguishing the image from perception, reserving the word "image" for mental representations formed within the psychic system and using the term "perceive" for images derived directly from an external visual stimulus. According to him, the word "image" was problematic because its root meaning signified "replica," or "copy," whereas images were not "merely imitations" but memory fragments, reconstructions, reinterpretations, and symbols that stood for objects, feelings, or ideas (*IFC*, 4). For him, then, the word "image" did not refer to "external replicas" but only to mental representations defined in this way.

During the 1950s the Canadian neurologist William Penfield had begun publishing his enormously influential studies of the intrusive visual images that he had produced by stimulating with electrodes the exposed cortex of humans suffering from epilepsy. He had claimed that the images reported by his patients were ex-

[26] For the 1960s revival of interest in the image see Mardi J. Horowitz, *Image Formation and Cognition* (1970), chap. 4 (hereafter abbreviated *IFC*); and Robert Holt, "Imagery: The Return of the Ostracized," *American Psychologist* 19 (1964): 254–64, which cites among the factors contributing to the resurgence of interest in the image: the firsthand accounts of concentration camp prisoners, one important recurrent theme of which was what one former captive called "the 'famous' cinema of prisoners"; the experience of "pseudo-hallucinatory imagery" brought on by prolonged isolation, sleep deprivation, and other pressures, or by forcible indoctrination or thought reform; LSD research; the work of Piaget, Penfield, and others on the image; and the rise of cognitive science.

act "flashbacks of their past lives" or literal "reruns" of perceptual memories stored in putative "engrams" or memory neurones in the brain.[27] But in one of his earliest papers Horowitz had expressed reservations about Penfield's views, arguing that, since some of Penfield's patients *saw themselves* in the visual images, the images must represent reconstructions of various perceptions as "imaginative images." He had compared the images constructed in this way to the hallucinatory visual experiences (or "flashbacks") (*IFC*, 15) produced in subjects who had taken LSD and other drugs. His own experiments on brain stimulation lent support to this view, for his patients had reported experiencing images that seemed to involve outright fantasies or mixtures of perceptions and primary process mental activity.[28] At that same moment, in texts cited by Horowitz, the cognitive psychologist Theodore Sarbin had argued against the general tendency to reify mental images by treating them as "literal" imitations or copies of external objects, a tendency he criticized as mechanical. Instead, he had emphasized the "nonliteral" and role-playing character of human imagery. Sarbin had applied these insights to the field of hypnosis by conceptualizing the hypnotic rapport between hypnotist and subject in similar role-playing terms, with the result that human imagery was treated by him as essentially an imaginative, mimetic-suggestive phenomenon.[29]

[27] See W. Penfield and T. Rasmussen, *The Cerebral Cortex of Man* (New York, 1950); W. Penfield and H. Jasper, *Epilepsy and the Functional Anatomy of the Human Brain* (Boston, 1954); W. Penfield and P. Perot, "Hallucinations of Past Experience and Experimental Responses to Stimulation of Temporal Cortex," *Transactions of the American Neurological Association* 85 (1960): 80–84. W. Penfield, "Speech Perception and the Uncommitted Cortex," in J. C. Eccles, ed., *Brain and Conscious Experience* (New York, 1966): 217–37.

[28] Mardi J. Horowitz, John E. Adams, and Burton B. Rutkin, "Visual Imagery on Brain Stimulation," *Archives of General Psychiatry* 19 (October 1968): 469–86. Horowitz objected that the visual images experienced by Penfield's patients must have been reconstructions because the patients saw *themselves* in the scene, whereas in the actual scene they were simply caught up in it and could not have been spectators of themselves. This is exactly the same argument Freud used in his essay on screen memories, those childhood memories that are characterized by their unusual sharpness and the apparent insignificance of their content and whose analysis, Freud suggested, leads back to indelible childhood experiences. Freud noted that in the majority of such screen memories the subject sees himself in the recollection as a child, but he sees this child as an observer from outside the scene would see him, suggesting that such a picture cannot be an exact repetition of the impression that was originally perceived, for the subject "was then in the middle of the situation and was attending not to himself but to the external world" (Freud, "Screen Memories" [1899], in *The Standard Edition*, 3:321). More recently, Richard A. Bryant has expressed doubt about the historical accuracy of visual intrusions in patients diagnosed with PTSD after experiencing brain trauma, questioning current cognitive and information-processing ideas inherent in recent ideas about traumatic imagery ("Posttraumatic Stress Disorder: Flashbacks, and Pseudomemories in Closed Head Injury," *Journal of Traumatic Stress* 9 [1996]: 621–30).

[29] See especially Theodore R. Sarbin, "The Concept of Hallucination," *Journal of Personality* 35 (1967): 359–80, cited by Horowitz in support of the idea that the image is not a mere copy or imitation of the model or external event; and idem, "Toward a Theory of Imagination," *Journal of Personality* 38

This leads me to a second point, Horowitz's understanding of the part played by suggestion in the formation of images. In his response to Penfield and in other early writings, Horowitz had emphasized the role played in the construction of visual images by the subject's perceptual expectations, as those were determined by factors such as unconscious wishes, fears, and memories.[30] That those expectations might involve the factor of suggestibility had also been noted by him. He had pointed out that people in certain situations were led to fabricate events in order to please, that they omitted to report events that had occurred in order to escape (real or imagined) censure, or that they distorted or altered their reports with changes in the interpersonal environment (*IFC*, 4–5). For Horowitz, the interpersonal environment included the effects of unconscious suggestion. He had cited the well-known study by hypnosis expert Martin Orne, of the role played by the unconscious demand characteristics of the experimenter in influencing the experimental results, as proof that images were susceptible to the suggestive demands of the experimental situation (*IFC*, 42). In short, for Horowitz images were nonlexical modes of thought shaped by various unconscious influences that constructed condensed and symbolic visual representations of various experiences and emotional trends. He had cautioned that the tendency of patients to confabulation posed difficulties of experimental design and control for those who wished to operationalize research on images by studying them in the laboratory, since it made the patient's subjective reports of image experiences—the only primary source of information—"quite fragile" (*IFC*, 4), as he put it. It was not clear how this obstacle was to be overcome (*IFC*, 43).

The case was no different when it came to traumatic images. For example, in the case of a young woman who suffered from unbidden or intrusive images of her mother's scowling face while having sex with her husband, Horowitz had considered three different theories to explain the images, without choosing between them. First, viewed as sequels to psychic trauma, he had mentioned the fact that the woman had once had a traumatic perceptual experience when her scowling mother caught her masturbating; he had suggested that sexual arousal might have reminded her of the earlier event, reactivated the vivid shock memory, and released the associated images into awareness. Second, the images might be interpreted as the expression of repressed mental contents, in which

---

(1970): 52–76. For Sarbin's theory of hypnosis as role-playing see "The Concept of Role-Taking," *Sociometry* 7 (1943): 273–85; idem, "Contributions to Role-Taking Theory: I. Hypnotic Behavior," *Psychological Review* 57 (1950): 255–70; William Coe and Theodore R. Sarbin, "An Experimental Demonstration of Hypnosis as Role Enactment," *Journal of Abnormal Psychology* 71 (1966): 400–406; Theodore R. Sarbin and William Coe, *Hypnosis: A Social Psychological Analysis* (New York, 1972).

[30] Horowitz, Adams, and Ratkin, "Visual Imagery on Brain Stimulation," 469–86; Mardi J. Horowitz, "Visual Images in Psychotherapy," *American Journal of Psychotherapy* 22 (1968): 55–59.

case it was the patient's repressed incestuous feelings toward her father that got released in sexual excitement and with it the accompanying prohibition of her mother's angry face. Third, considered as a means for transforming feeling states, the images of the angry face of her mother might have served as a vehicle to change the woman's sexual pleasure into fear and disgust, while perhaps also satisfying various exhibitionist trends. Compatible with the second and third theories was the idea that the traumatic images might have functioned as a partial screen for ideas and feelings that were currently dangerous or anxiety provoking (*IFC*, 123–24).

Likewise, in the case of Ned, a schizophrenic patient who experienced recurrent intrusive images of his father beating his mother, Horowitz had treated the images as possibly memories of traumatic perceptions. But he had also observed that, although it was known that violence sometimes occurred in the man's family, there was no verification of the specific incident other than Ned's memory, "which could have confused fantasy with reality" (*IFC*, 145). And he concluded his discussion of these and similar cases by remarking that "content derived from a 'traumatic' perception is depicted in the intrusive images. The images are not, however, simply repetitions of the trauma. They are revived again and again as a vehicle and screen for the expression and concealment of other ideas and feelings" (*IFC*, 150). For Horowitz, then, peremptory images could not necessarily be taken at face value as literal revivals or reexperiences of the traumatic scene, since they might serve as a defense against important emotional trends. These included identificatory-mimetic trends, as when he recognized in the intrusive images various complex sexual-aggressive-mimetic identifications with parental and other figures.

Even when he made use of the familiar concept of dissociation, so central to the work of Janet and other turn-of-the-century theorists of trauma as well as current researchers, to characterize the split between a patient's good and bad images of herself, Horowitz did not treat the traumatic image in the literalist terms found in the more recent work of Brett, Ostroff, Caruth, and others. Of one patient, Mary, who fell seriously ill after an unwanted pregnancy and childbirth and suffered from images of an earthquake, Horowitz had focused not so much on the possibility that the images might be traced back to her much earlier experience of an earthquake in San Francisco as on the overall meaning of the situation for the patient, especially the way the images served the purposes of denial and defense. "She describes her unbidden images as alien symptoms and denies to herself their implications," he had written. "She does not translate their full meaning into words. Thus, she encapsulates the dreaded ideas and feelings as 'foreign' images" (*IFC*, 167). The patient's defensive dissociations and splittings, not the traumatic perceptions per se, gave the images their tremendous sense of perceptual reality: "[T]he loss of the sense of self-willed control over the course of

thought lends images a quality of quasi-reality: the images are not clearly demar-
cated from perceptions" (*IFC*, 168).

Horowitz had observed in this connection that unbidden images could feel like
external perceptions to the subject, and hence could easily be regarded as
"some unpleasant aspect of the outer world rather than a dangerous part of the
inner world" (*IFC*, 168). He had also stated that traumatic memories, with their
"propensity for formation of vivid images" were especially useful for defense, because they invoked intense fear and a sense of danger. "Dormant traumas may
be revived for this purpose," he had remarked, "or contemporary traumas may
remain unresolved, because they both trigger and screen internal conflict. Images
that generate feelings such as fear, guilt, and hate, albeit for defensive purposes,
will be regarded by the reflective self as unbidden and unwelcome" (*IFC*, 170).
Horowitz had objected to the use then being made of "image therapy" to treat
traumatized patients because, he argued, rather than producing insight, request-
ing patients to visualize images could encourage them to shore up defenses by
producing images in compliance with the therapist's suggestions. "I suspect that
many forms of image therapy are veiled modes of offering suggestion and support to patients," he had written (*IFC*, 305). In sum, Horowitz's concept of the image in 1970 appeared remote from the antimimetic, literalist ideas about the image that would mark Brett and Ostroff's later approach, since according to him
images might well be mimetic-suggestive and confabulatory in nature. In numerous scattered statements, he characterized intrusive images as frequently symbolic or fantasmatic representations of the traumatic experience rather than exact
replicas of the past.

Nevertheless, there were aspects of Horowitz's theoretical approach and experimental protocols that undeniably tended toward the literal. In particular, as I
noted earlier, Horowitz tended to collapse the traumatic *image* into traumatic *perception*, defined as an exact replica of the traumatic event or stimulus. As a result, in spite of his insistence on the need to distinguish the mental image from
perception, and in spite also of his perceptive remarks about the identificatory-
mimetic-suggestive character of the image, when it came to traumatic images
the distinction he otherwise insisted on between image and perception was more
or less systematically elided. "Clinical studies suggest that traumatic visual perceptions have a tendency to return to awareness as unbidden visual images and
that various defensive or controlling measures may be activated in response to
this tendency," he wrote.[31] In this formulation, traumatic perceptions are equated
with the traumatic image: reality enters the psychic apparatus in the form of
veridical perceptions that, because they are so terrifying and new, persist in the

[31] Mardi J. Horowitz, "Psychic Trauma: Return of Images after a Stress Film," *Archives of General Psychiatry* 20 (1969): 559; hereafter abbreviated "PT."

form of visual images or replicas that are only subsequently distorted or modified by unconscious influences of various kinds.

Horowitz's information-processing approach to cognition—his desire to revise psychoanalytic concepts by operationalizing them in information-processing terms—led him in the same literalizing direction, as the external stimulus was conceptualized as "information" or a "percept" that, held in a special or "active" memory system, haunted the victim in the form of intrusive images until these could be assimilated and mastered. Freud's theory of the repetition compulsion, according to which in the traumatic neuroses the hypothetical "protective shield" against stimuli is breached with a consequent unleashing of the death drive, was interpreted in the same cognitive, information-processing way. Horowitz ignored the mimetic dimension of Freud's concept of "breaching" and instead interpreted the traumatic situation as involving the strictly external imposition of stimuli that lodged in the mind as "untamed memories" or peremptory images ("PT," 552).[32]

Horowitz's experimental approach to trauma, using stress films, also tended toward the antimimetic and the literal. Several investigators before him, especially emotion theorist Richard Lazarus, had shown that witnessing unpleasant films could produce pronounced emotional and physiological effects. Others had demonstrated the impact of such films on subsequent hypnagogic reverie and dreams. In an effort to control and objectify the stressor, Horowitz in his own experiments typically exposed college students or other experimental subjects to a stressful or traumatic film and to a nonstressful or so-called neutral film, in order to determine whether the traumatic film caused the return of more involuntary and intrusive visual images than the latter. He introduced several research design safeguards to control for the effects due to the order of presentation of the films and other factors. The results of his first experiment showed that "visual imagery, film references, and intrusive thoughts were reported with significantly greater frequency . . . during posttraumatic periods than during postneutral periods" ("PT," 556). Throughout his discussion, Horowitz treated the intrusive images as if they were directly derived from the traumatic film, so that what was intrusively repeated were unmastered perceptions or repetitions of the traumatic stimulus. The *image*, previously conceptualized by him not as strict imitations or copies of reality but as reconstructions and reinterpretations, was now collapsed into a *perception,* defined as a strictly iterative process, as when, in a summary of his findings, he wrote that "traumatic perceptions have a tendency to return to awareness as vivid and potentially intrusive images" and, more generally, that "psychic trauma tends to be re-enacted" ("PT," 559).[33]

[32] See also Mardi J. Horowitz and Nancy Wilmer, "Stress Films, Emotion, and Cognitive Response," *Archives of General Psychiatry* 30 (1976): 1339–44. For a discussion of Freud's concept of breaching see Leys, *Trauma: A Genealogy,* chapter 1.

[33] For a similar formulation see Mardi J. Horowitz, "Cognitive Response to Stress and Experimental Demand," *Archives of General Psychiatry* 25 (1971): 419–28. Horowitz summarizes the history of his

Horowitz's experimental protocols also encouraged the idea that mental images were exact reruns of traumatic scenes. Before and after viewing each film, students in a typical experiment had to engage in a tone-matching task whose object was to identify whether each preceding organlike tone was higher, lower, or the same as the immediate one. The task was interrupted at intervals and the subjects were asked to record all the contents of their awareness, such as thoughts, feelings, sensations, memories, or "flashes," experienced during the preceding period. Only after they had completed the third period of tone matching following the second film were the subjects informed that visual imagery was a focus of interest. They were then encouraged to reconsider their subjective experiences and to write down on a separate sheet of paper all clear instances of visual imagery, amplifying their previous reports when necessary. For Horowitz the purpose of the tone-matching tests was to make the students direct their attention "outwards rather than inwards," as he put it. The tests also helped disguise from them the true purpose of the experiment and hence helped control for reporting bias or the problem of suggestive confabulation. For as Horowitz observed, subjects might report more visual imagery if they believed that this would please the investigator, or if they shared his predictions, thus posing a mimetic dilemma that Horowitz tried to solve, as we shall see.

But these same procedures, by focusing the subject's attention on the external stimulus, also promoted the student's tendency to project the mental images outward, as if any images that they experienced were perceptions directly derived from the external stimulus. That tendency was further encouraged by the way in which students were asked to report on the contents of their mental experiences. For instance, they were asked to assess their mental images not only for intrusiveness but also for intensity, by rating twelve significant scenes from the film according to the vividness of the imagery on recalling those scenes. The task inevitably tied the images to specific scenes, as if they were an exact replica of them. The content analysis of the students' reports continued the trend, as independent analysts were asked to tally the students' self-reports about intrusive imagery in ways that connected those reports directly to the film contents.[34]

---

work on unbidden images as follows: "What is important here is the conviction, based on observations, that the contents of unbidden images are quite frequently based upon previous perceptual realities. This conviction was startling because I expected, given the patient populations selected and my training in theory, that these contents would emerge mainly as fantasy elaborations based on current intrapsychic conflicts. The contents did, of course, contain fantasy elaborations and served various impulsive and defensive purposes, but the frequency of contents repeating a traumatic perception of a serious life event that had actually occurred was impressive" ("Stress Response Syndromes and Their Treatment," in *Handbook of Stress: Theoretical and Clinical Aspects*, ed. Leo Goldberger [New York, 1982], 711–12).

[34] Thus the manual of content analysis gave operational definitions for "Film Reference," as follows: "Any reference to either film, including references made before seeing either test film"; or for "Intrusive Thought": "any thought of a film during the tone task which was described by the subject as intrusive" ("PT," 556).

Earlier, in 1964, Lazarus had criticized much of the work then being carried out using stress films on the grounds that researchers assumed that a stimulus, such as a film, was either threatening or not, without regard to the subject's own assessment. He had pointed out that the interest in stress and related issues, such as threat, emotion, and anxiety, had arisen from the observation of the behavior of people in real-life situations, such as their behavior after bereavement or the effects of concentration camps, military combat, and other examples. To be valuable, laboratory experiments had to be effective analogues of the postulated processes in the naturalistic phenomena of stress. It had seemed to him, however, that very little of the recent experimental work on the problem of stress served to advance understanding, sometimes because of the "painful absence of clear conception" and sometimes because of the failure of adequate design. In particular, he had argued that one could not assume that the threat was simply "out there as an attribute of the stimulus," because its threat value depended on the appraisal process, which in turn depended on the "person's beliefs about what the stimulus meant for the thwarting of motives of importance to him." Thus the same stimulus could be threatening or not, depending upon the "interpretation the person makes concerning its future personal significance."[35] Lazarus's complaint had something in common with contemporaneous critiques of ego-psychology and information-processing approaches to the concept of reality, approaches in which, as one commentator put it, "the 'environment' becomes essentially a matter of demands and noxious impingements that one ought to be rid of, that is to say, become 'autonomous form.' "[36]

Lazarus in the same article had gone on to demonstrate the role of the appraisal process by showing to various groups a film, *Subincision* (the same film Horowitz would later use in his own experiments), varying the sound track in ways designed to minimize, or alternatively, to enhance the threatening content. That film, a short, black and white, silent film, showed naked Aborigines in the Australian bush undergoing puberty initiation rites involving scenes of extensive penile cutting with sharp stones, bleeding wounds, and adolescents repeatedly wincing and writhing in pain. The boys appeared to volunteer for the procedure, which was conducted by older men.[37] Lazarus had demonstrated on college students and midlevel airline executives that the degree of stress from viewing the

[35] Richard Lazarus, "A Laboratory Approach to the Dynamics of Psychological Stress," *American Psychologist* 19 (1964): 404; hereafter abbreviated "LA."

[36] George S. Klein, "The Ego in Psychoanalysis: A Concept in Search of Identity," 56 (1969–70): 522. For a related discussion of ego-psychology and adaptational theories of reality, as pregiven, unvaryingly fixed, and objectively "out there," see Robert S. Wallerstein, "Psychoanalytic Perspectives on the Problem of Reality," *Journal of the American Psychoanalytic Association* 21 (1973): 5–33; and Heinz Hartmann, "Notes on the Reality Principle" (1956), in *Essays on Ego Psychology* (New York, 1964), 241–67.

[37] As Lazarus noted, the film, made by the anthropologist G. Roheim in the 1940s, had first been used for research when A. Aas and B. J. Schwartz used it to experimentally study mutilation and castration

film was a function of the context, and that the viewer's response could be influenced by the "suggestive" character of the sound track. If *Subincision* was accompanied by a soundtrack that took a distant, intellectual, and detached anthropological view of the proceedings, or one using an official-sounding travel-oguelike voice that took a denying attitude toward the pain being depicted (as if everything was a happy experience for the boys), the threat of the film, as measured by various psychophysiological tests, was reduced in both groups of subjects. But a third "trauma" soundtrack emphasizing the horror of the situation, the dread of the boys, and the harmful consequences that would befall some of the participants, increased the stressful response.[38] Drawing on these results, Lazarus had proposed that threat depended on the manner in which stimuli were appraised and interpreted. More generally, he indicated that the responses of individual subjects to stressful stimuli were a function of their respective personalities and defensive-coping styles, as measured by various measurement scales, as well as their degree of identification with the actors or persons in the film ("LA," 409).[39] For Lazarus, the stress reaction was therefore mediated psychologically by various factors, including identificatory ones.

In a subsequent paper Lazarus had emphasized the complexity of responses to the film *Subincision*, owing to its ambiguous content. He had noted in this regard that different subjects were stressed by different aspects of the scenes; that some showed no signs of stress whatsoever; that responsiveness to the film content was in part a function of personality variables, in part a function of the order of presentation of the various scenes, but that those interactions were complex; that the threats in the *Subincision* film could not be entirely explained on the basis of the theme of castration or mutilation; that unusual features of the past experi-

---

fantasies. See A. Aas, *Mutilation Fantasies and Autonomic Response* (Oslo, 1958); and B. J. Schwarz, "An Empirical Test of Two Freudian Hypotheses concerning Castration Anxiety," *Journal of Personality* 24 (1956): 318–37.

[38] Lazarus also presented the original silent film undoctored in any way. A related study produced even more dramatic results. This time there was no soundtrack at all, only a prior orientation session, and the subjects could then view the silent film with equanimity once they had been led to interpret the events in a benign way. The details are in R. S. Lazarus and Elizabeth Alfert, "Short-Circuiting of Threat by Experimentally Altering Cognitive Appraisal," *Journal of Abnormal Psychology* 69 (1964): 195–205.

[39] See also Richard S. Lazarus and Edward M. Opton, Jr., "A Study of Psychological Stress: A Summary of Theoretical Formulations and Experimental Findings," in *Anxiety and Behavior*, ed. Charles D. Spielberger (New York, 1966), 225–62 (hereafter abbreviated "SPS") for a useful overview of the theoretical issues in stress studies and of the limitations of film research. The authors observe: "We have assumed from the beginning that *identification* with the film characters was the key process involved. But our data have not yet given firm support to this assumption. We apparently still have much to learn about the processes of identification and vicarious threat" (226, their emphasis). For Lazarus's general theory of psychological stress and the appraisal process see his *Psychological Stress and the Coping Process* (New York, 1966).

ence of some of the subjects accounted for strong reactions; and that homosexual fantasies in some subjects might be stimulated by observing the physical intimacy between the Aborigines during the ritual. "The methodological problems inherent in separating the various types of threat content from a complex film of this sort make it unsuited to an effective attack on the issue of threat content," he cautioned ("SPS," 240–41). On the basis of these and related considerations, Lazarus would go on to take a prominent role in the still-continuing debate over the nature of the emotions, siding with those on the "cognitivist" side who believe in the role of appraisal, meaning, and interpretation in emotional reactions to traumatic or other events—a topic that will return in chapter 4.

Horowitz largely disregarded Lazarus's concerns. It is true that, as we have seen, he was bothered by the possibility that the subjects' reports of images might be influenced by the suggestive context. For example, in his first paper on film stress he mentioned as one source of concern in interpreting the results the "possibility of a bias toward compliance in the subjects." Acknowledging that "subjects and assistants may consciously and unconsciously comply with the wishes of the investigator," Horowitz conceded that his own experiment had "only partially controlled for such bias" by gradually increasing the explicitness of the instructions and comparing data from each phase of the experiment. In other words, Horowitz had only progressively made it clear to the students that their mental imagery was the specific focus of the experimental inquiry. He noted in this regard that the data on visual imagery during the period of general instructions did show a similar distribution to that of the later period of more specific instructions, when the students were asked to concentrate on their visual images. The similarity in distribution implied that there was no distortion due to bias. But he also recognized that the subjects in his experiment could have surmised the experimenter's expectations during the period of general instructions. As he put it, only replication with alteration of demand characteristics and personnel could fully control for this "hazard of compliance" ("PT," 558–59).

Although no such replication was attempted in this particular experiment, in subsequent film studies Horowitz again expressed worries about the influence of "suggestion effects" on the production of images, and tried to control for this in different ways, such as varying the content and order of instructions to the experimental subjects, comparing different groups according to sex or profession, and so on. It does not seem to me that the problem of compliance was or could be fully solved or met by these means.[40] Nevertheless, Horowitz proceeded on the

[40] See for example Mardi J. Horowitz and Stephanie S. Becker, "Cognitive Response to Stress and Experimental Demand," *Journal of Abnormal Psychology* 78 (1971): 86–92; idem, "The Compulsion to Repeat Trauma: Experimental Study of Intrusive Thinking after Stress," *Journal of Nervous and Mental Disease* 153 (1971): 32–40; Mardi J. Horowitz, Stephanie S. Becker, and Maurice L. Moskowitz, "Intrusive and Repetitive Thought after Stress: A Replication Study," *Psychological Reports* 29 (1971): 763–67.

assumption that it *had* been solved, to such an extent that after the publication of his book, *Stress Response Syndromes* (1976), where in an important chapter he discussed the problem of compliance, the topic disappeared from his work. The result was that from then on he tended to treat the threat of trauma as if it was indeed simply "out there" as an objective property of the traumatic film or traumatic event, and to disregard the role-playing, contextual-mimetic dimension of the imagery experience. His commitment to operationalizing psychoanalysis meant that the exploration of the meaning the images might have for the individual, or the problem of mimetic-suggestive compliance, gave way to reliance on questionnaires and other modes of evaluation designed to externalize and objectivize the mental image. In particular, his development of measurement scales, such as the now widely used "Impact of Event Scale," provided researchers and clinicians with a metric for assessing traumatic "intrusion" experiences (intrusively experienced ideas, images, feelings or bad dreams) and "avoidance" responses (consciously recognized avoidance of certain ideas, feelings, or situations) in terms that eliminated any consideration of subjective meaning.[41]

In his influential book, *Stress Response Syndromes* (1976), Horowitz anticipated *DSM-III* by making the case for including a distinct "stress response entity" in the new manual, to be organized around the phenomena of intrusive images and their denial. Indeed, at a time when official psychiatry was still claiming that the problem of stress or combat neurosis had been solved in Vietnam, he predicted the delayed appearance of symptoms of stress in Vietnam veterans.[42] Horowitz acknowledged that stress responses combined both internal and external elements and that the complex of ideas and feelings, including intrusions, aroused in a patient after stress were activated not only by the trauma itself but by personal conflicts that existed prior to the traumatic incident. Moreover, in recognizing Freud's contribution to the theory of stress or trauma, he also acknowledged the significance of Freud's earlier discovery that claims to the reality of the traumatic scene or seduction were not always true, so that, in Horowitz's words, "The 'traumatic event' did not always represent an external stress but also involved internal components" (*SRS*, 19). In this context, he directly addressed the dilemma faced by all those who dealt with stress, namely, that the more thor-

---

[41] See Mardi J. Horowitz, Nancy Wilner, and William Alvarez, "Impact of Event Scale: A Measure of Subjective Stress," *Psychosomatic Medicine* 413 (May 1970): 209–18; and Nathan J. Zilberg, Daniel S. Weiss, and Mardi J. Horowitz, "Impact of Event Scale: A Cross-Validation Study and Some Empirical Evidence Supporting a Conceptual Model of Stress Response Syndromes," *Journal of Consulting and Clinical Psychology* 50 (1982): 407–14. The significance of Horowitz's Impact of the Event Scale was thus that it transformed the "reexperiences" category for PTSD from a source of possible mimetic phenomena into an antimimetic one (a metric, with no content).

[42] Mardi J. Horowitz and George F. Solomon, "A Prediction of Delayed Stress Response Syndromes in Vietnam Veterans," *Journal of Social Issues* 31 (1975): 67–80.

oughly the stress response was studied in a single individual, the more it seemed to lose its connection with an immediate stress event and gained connections to conflicts and character traits present before the actual event (*SRS*, 27). Nor did he himself doubt that every stress syndrome was "composed of both sources of influence" (*SRS*, 28) or that the stress event complex was an "amalgam of internal and external components of meaning" (*SRS*, 57). Even when he presented the results of his film experiments, he observed that the intrusive repetitions often occurred in "covert forms" (*SRS*, 63). Later in the book, when discussing psychotherapy and working through, he stated that memories of trauma might be regarded as having "some psychological, but not necessarily historical, reality" and that memories arising early on in treatment could be "organizers as well as 'screens' that both filter out and filter in elements of the objective event" (*SRS*, 117–18).

Nevertheless, the aim of *Stress Response Syndromes* was to make the case for a distinct stress response syndrome marshaled around the external stressor and the states of traumatic intrusion and denial, and it did so in terms that tended to eliminate concern for subjective meaning and to highlight instead questions about the traumatic image. Horowitz's model of trauma was based on the entry of "information" from external stress events; as such, it sought to redress the tendency in psychoanalysis to accentuate the role of the endogenous drives and internal conflicts in the stress response by focusing instead on the cognitive dimension and the role of the external stressor. When the drives did enter his model, they appeared as yet another source of "information" for the psychic system to process, playing a role very different from that envisaged by Freud, where the unconscious produces that indistinction between reality and fantasy that is the hallmark of the primary process. In sum, the net effect of Horowitz's overall approach to trauma was to foreground the role of the external stressor and imagery in ways that tended to isolate the traumatic event from the question of meaning and mimesis and to encourage the tendency to treat the stressor and its correlative, the traumatic image, antimimetically as a purely objective phenomenon. In this way he set the stage for Brett and Ostroff's subsequent reformulations of PTSD.[43]

---

[43] Horowitz later expressed some uneasiness about too-rigid adherence to the official diagnosis of PTSD. For example, in the 1986 edition of *Stress Response Syndromes*, he observed that "[e]xclusive adherence to official diagnostic labels may inhibit individualized case formulations" (49). It is worth noting that in recent years the intrusive image has been downplayed by those scientists who, in the spirit of the antimimetic tendencies of contemporary American psychiatry, emphasize hormonal measures and brain anatomy in their research on PTSD. At the same time, in the work on posttraumatic stress of Bessel van der Kolk and his colleagues, the imagistic or specular dimension persists in the claim that traumatic experiences are encoded as "iconic" memories or imprints considered to be absolutely true to the traumatic event (for a discussion and critique of these ideas see Leys, *Trauma: A Genealogy*, 245–54).

PTSD and Shame

As I have said, what particularly interests me about these developments is the way in which, simultaneously with the elevation in importance of the notion of the image, the concept of survivor guilt has been eliminated from the diagnostic criteria for posttraumatic stress. More precisely, the notion of survivor guilt and with it the notion of mimesis have not been eliminated so much as suppressed. Indeed I argue in *Trauma* that the mimetic pole of the mimetic-antimimetic oscillation that has characterized the history of the concept of trauma cannot simply be made to disappear but that, according to the logic that has shaped the conceptualization of trauma from the start, *both* mimesis and antimimesis are internal to the traumatic experience. This suggests that all attempts to resolve that oscillation between mimesis and antimimesis in favor of one pole or the other are destined to fail. And in fact the "PTSD revolution" remains incomplete and present formulations continue to be highly unstable. Even the role of the stressor has become a source of contention because of the felt need to include the "appraisal process" or subjective meaning in evaluations of PTSD, especially now that since *DSM-IV* the emphasis has shifted from the external event to a mixture of exposure to trauma coupled with the patient's reaction or vulnerability to it. An argument has even made to remove the stressor criterion, so central to Horowitz, Brett, and Ostroff, from the requirements of PTSD and to view the disorder as a symptom complex without a specific cause. In any case, as it now stands the stressor criterion has been greatly broadened in *DSM-IV*, in order to allow for the inclusion of those patients who develop extreme reactions to minor incidents as well as those "secondary victims" who experience trauma indirectly by being confronted with trauma in others. The result is that, as one critic has recently put it, for a vulnerable subpopulation of patients "the 'perception' of threat or trauma is almost as essential an element to the stressor's impact and the production of symptoms as the objective severity of the stressor itself."[44] But this places precisely the sort of emphasis on contextual meaning that Brett in her work on imagery had hoped to avoid. Can the problem of mimesis be far behind?

In fact, if we refuse to treat the instabilities inherent in current formulations of PTSD as indicating merely that more research needs to be done, and instead regard them as symptomatic of the inevitable strains in *any* attempt to definitively resolve the mimetic-antimimetic antithesis, a number of pertinent issues arise. For example, since PTSD was officially recognized in 1980 it has been classified as an anxiety disorder. But there have been recurrent doubts about the wisdom and validity of that classification, with the result that at various times proposals have

[44] J. S. March, "What Constitutes a Stressor? The 'Criterion A' Issue," in *Post-Traumatic Stress Disorder: DSMIV and Beyond,* 37–54. Cf. David A. Tomb, "The Phenomenology of Post-Traumatic Stress Disorder," *Psychiatric Clinics of North America* 17 (June 1994): 238.

been made to reclassify PTSD. Indeed, when in 1985 the criteria for PTSD were being reorganized around the intrusive image and its denial, the topic that aroused most controversy was the proposal that it should be reclassified as a dissociative disorder. The proposal rested on the claim that the reexperiencing and numbing symptoms of PTSD were mild forms of dissociation of the kind seen in multiple personality disorder and related conditions, so that the PTSD and the dissociative disorders could be viewed on a continuum. Historically, too, the proposal made sense, since dissociation was the concept Janet, Freud, and other theorists deployed when trauma was first discussed at the end of the nineteenth century; the concept of dissociation is still employed today by most theorists of PTSD. Flashbacks could thus be seen as dissociative episodes and reexperiencings as mild forms of the return of personalities, while the symptoms of numbing, such as amnesia, restricted affect, and estrangement from others, could likewise be seen as modes of dissociation.[45]

In 1987, Brett and her associates resisted the proposed change and the reclassification was rejected. But the topic did not go away, and the issue had to be dealt with again during the next round of revisions for *DSM-IV*, published in 1994. It was not that Brett herself was completely opposed to reclassifying PTSD. As she has acknowledged, even though anxiety is one of the conditions that, along with depression and substance abuse, is most frequently found to co-occur in patients with PTSD, the relationship between PTSD and anxiety is not clear. In particular, she has argued that nothing is known about the etiology of anxiety, whereas in PTSD it is possible to provide an etiological explanation based on the role of the external stressor. Since, according to Brett, in the hierarchy of descriptions in medicine etiological explanation takes priority, she thinks it makes sense to consider PTSD a disorder distinct from anxiety. But her emphasis on the causal role of the external stressor then makes her refusal to reclassify PTSD as a dissociative disorder somewhat incoherent, since patients with PTSD and the dissociative disorders do appear to share a traumatic etiology. (For example, Multiple Personality Disorder, now known as Dissociative Identity Disorder, is widely held to be caused by the trauma of childhood sexual abuse.) Moreover, as Brett has also acknowledged, patients suffering from both PTSD and the dissociative disorders not only share a traumatic etiology but are alike in another way—they are all highly hypnotizable or suggestible, as measured by their high visual imagery scores.[46] In fact, in a research study cited by Brett, dissociation at the mo-

[45] Brett, Spitzer, and Williams, "*DSMIII-R* Criteria for Post-Traumatic Stress Disorder," 1234–45; Elizabeth A. Brett, "Classifications of Posttraumatic Stress Disorder in *DSM-IV*; Anxiety Disorder, Dissociative Disorder, or Stress Disorder," in *Posttraumatic Stress Disorder: DSM-IV and Beyond*, ed. Jonathan R. T. Davidson and Edna B. Fox (Washington, D.C., 1993), 196.

[46] Brett, "Classifications of Posttraumatic Stress Disorder in *DSM-IV*," 191–205; Randall K. Stutman and Eugene L. Bliss, "Posttraumatic Stress Disorder, Hypnotizability, and Imagery," *American Journal of Psychiatry* 142 (June 1985): 741–43

ment of trauma appeared to be more predictive of PTSD than the objective character of the stressor. But once it is recognized that PTSD patients are highly suggestible, the question of the role of hypnotic-mimetic identification or confabulation in the production of the traumatic image inevitably resurfaces, and Brett's insistence on the purely external or literal character of the traumatic image begins to seem untenable.

The same question of mimesis recurs in yet another proposal to rethink the classification of PTSD, namely, the effort by well-known theorist of trauma, Judith Herman, to establish a broad stress category in order to make room for a new diagnosis, called by her "Disorders of Extreme Stress Not Otherwise Specified" (or DESNOS, for short). According to Herman, this disorder is found in a variety of populations that have suffered from very severe, prolonged, or repeated trauma, such as victims of concentration camps, torture, genocidal violence, prolonged sexual abuse, and severe family violence. DESNOS is thus a more complex form of PTSD characterized by a multiplicity of symptoms, including depression, general and phobic anxiety, paranoia, dissociative symptoms, sexual dysfunction, tendency to suicide, and numerous other emotional disturbances. In effect, Herman has sought to expand the concept of PTSD in order to do justice to the "protean" symptoms traditionally associated with prolonged victimization but lost sight of in the official definition of the stress disorders.[47]

Now from the perspective of the issues I have been considering in this chapter, what is interesting about Herman's discussion of DESNOS is that mimetic identification is basic to it. This is clear in the emphasis she places on the tendency of victims of prolonged trauma, such as victims of torture, to become adept at dissociation and trance, in other words, their tendency to experience classically mimetic phenomena ("SPRT," 217–18). It is evident, too, in the importance she attaches to the trauma victim's experience of a guilty suicidal depression that, as she states, has long been reported to be the most common finding in virtually all clinical studies of chronically traumatized people. As she writes: "The debased self-image of chronic trauma fuels the guilty ruminations of depression, and the loss of faith suffered in chronic trauma merges with the hopelessness of depression" ("SPRT," 218). But once depression is moved to the forefront of PTSD, and with it the patient's characteristic feelings of guilt, then the problem of the victim's unconscious-mimetic identification with the aggressor or scene of violence takes on renewed importance. As a matter of fact, Herman does attribute the profound alterations of personality characteristic of the depressive, guilty victim of prolonged or severe trauma to the patient's coerced incorporation of the perpetra-

---

[47] Judith Herman, "Sequelae of Prolonged and Repeated Trauma: Evidence for a Complex Posttraumatic Syndrome (DESNOS)," in Davidson and Foss, *Posttraumatic Stress Disorder: DSMIV and Beyond*, 213–28; hereafter abbreviated "SPRT."

tor's attitudes and beliefs—even though, in her refusal to engage with the question of mimesis, she is unable to give a plausible account of the origin of survivor guilt. In Herman's words: "As the victim is isolated, he or she becomes increasingly dependent upon the perpetrator, not only for survival and basic bodily needs but also for information and even for emotional sustenance. Prolonged confinement in fear of death and in isolation reliably produces a bond of identification between captor and victim" ("SPRT," 220).

She adds: "This is the 'traumatic bonding' that occurs in hostages who come to view their captors as their saviors and to fear and hate their rescuers. . . . Symonds . . . describes this process as an enforced regression to 'psychological infantalism' that 'compels victims to cling to the very person who is endangering their life.' The same traumatic bonding may occur between a battered woman and her abuser . . . Similar experiences are also reported by people who have been inducted into totalitarian religious cults" ("SPRT," 220).[48] Furthermore, Herman is quite aware that this is the same bond of identification between victim and aggressor that Freud, Ferenczi, Niederland, Bettelheim and numerous others viewed as a central feature of the extreme traumatic situation. A repudiated, guilt-inducing identification with the aggressor thus returns to haunt Herman's new category of stress disorder. In doing so, it subverts the efforts of all those, such as Brett, Ostroff, and Herman herself, who seek to eliminate the mimetico-identificatory dimension of the traumatic experience by defining trauma antimimetically in terms of a purely external event, or image.

This has not prevented theorists from continuing to seek antimimetic solutions to the problem of stress. One sign of that tendency is that, now that survivor guilt has been dropped as one of the diagnostic criteria for PTSD, shame has come to take its place as the emotion that most defines the traumatic state. This has meant recasting the theory of the identification with the aggressor into a hypothesis that links trauma to shame. Thus in her extraordinary account of her work with victims of racial violence in South Africa, psychologist Pumla Gobodo-Madikizela observes: "Current psychological discourse has recast the theory of identification with the aggressor into the shame hypothesis, which holds that experiences of helplessness, powerlessness, and trauma in early childhood are inextricably interwoven with a violent lifestyle in adulthood."[49] Other theorists have privileged the role of shame in PTSD by turning to the work of Silvan Tomkins

[48] Herman's reference is to Martin Symonds, who gave the name "Stockholm Syndrome" to the tendency of victims to identify with the aggressor. See Martin Symonds, "Victim Responses to Terror: Understanding and Treatment," in *Victims of Terrorism*, ed. F. M. Ochberg and D. A. Soskis (Boulder, Colo., 1982), 94–103. See also Thomas Strenz, "The Stockholm Syndrome: Law Enforcement Policy and Hostage Behavior," ibid., 149–63.

[49] Pumla Gobodo-Madikizela, *A Human Being Died That Night: A South African Story of Forgiveness* (Boston and New York, 2003), 157, n. 3.

and his followers, such as Paul Ekman, who have defined the affects in anticognitivist or antiintentionalist terms as a finite set or constellation of inherited "central and peripheral physiological events."[50] It is to such recent theories of shame that I now turn.

[50] Andrew M. Stone, "The Role of Shame in Post-Traumatic Stress Disorder," *Journal of Orthopsychiatry* 62 (1992): 131. In a rapidly expanding literature on shame and posttraumatic stress see also: Bernice Andrews, Chris R. Brewin, Suzanna Rose, and Marilyn Kirk, "Predicting PTSD Symptoms in Victims of Violent Crime: The Role of Shame, Anger, and Childhood Abuse," *Journal of Abnormal Psychology* 109 (2000): 69–73; Deborah A. Lee and Peter Scragg, "The Role of Shame and Guilt in Traumatic Events: A Clinical Model of Shame-Based and Guilt-Based PTSD," *British Journal of Medical Psychology* 74 (2001): 451–66; Amy Street and Ileana Arias, "Psychological Abuse and Posttraumatic Stress Disorder in Battered Women: Examining the Role of Shame and Guilt," *Violence and Victims* 16 (2001): 65–78; Jennie Leskela, Michael Dieperink, and Paul Thuras, "Shame and Posttraumatic Stress Disorder," *Journal of Traumatic Stress* 15 (June 2002): 223–26; Candice Fearing, Lynn Taska, and Kevin Chen, "Trying to Understand Why Horrible Things Happen: Attribution, Shame, and Symptom Development following Sexual Abuse," *Child Maltreatment* 7 (February 2002): 26–41.

CHAPTER **FOUR**

Shame Now

Shame's Revival

SHAME'S RISE to prominence in the United States is a relatively recent phenomenon. To be sure, the emotion of shame figures importantly in numerous philosophical, literary, critical and other writings extending all the way back to the ancient Greeks. But from the start of the twentieth century until the early 1960s, shame was rarely differentiated from guilt, appearing instead as a minor variant of the latter. The subordination of shame to guilt reflected the dominance of psycho-analysis and the significance Freud attached to guilt (or anxiety) as the decisive psychic affect.[1] And it can be found as well in Ruth Benedict's *The Chrysanthe-mum and the Sword: Patterns of Japanese Culture* (1947), in which she distinguished between guilt and shame cultures, and E. R. Dodds's brilliant *The Greeks and the Irrational* (1951), in which Benedict's ideas are applied to the ancient Greeks.[2] But starting with the 1953 work of Gerhart Piers and Milton B. Singer, who operated within a revised psychoanalytic framework, and the 1962–63 work of Silvan Tomkins, who rejected Freud's assumptions in favor of a neo-Darwinian,

---

[1] The absence of any discussion of shame in Jean Laplanche and J.-B. Pontalis's *The Language of Psychoanalysis* (New York, 1973) is indicative of the lack of interest in the topic among French psycho-analysts as late as the 1970s.

[2] Ruth Benedict, *The Chrysanthemum and the Sword: Patterns of Japanese Culture* (Boston, 1947); E. R. Dodds, *The Greeks and the Irrational* (Berkeley, 1951). Benedict emphasized the public dimension of shame, its dependence on external rather than internal (or internalized) sanctions, and the absence of confession and atonement in shame cultures (223).

systems-theory approach to the affects, a radical reconsideration of shame has taken place.[3] Moreover, before the 1950s shame was considered, along with guilt, anxiety, anger, fear, grief, and humiliation, to be an essentially negative emotion. But a reevaluation of shame has now been going on for some time, a reevaluation that casts shame as at least potentially a positive, not a destructive emotion. Offering a variety of hypotheses about postwar changes in American society that might be thought to explain the new importance of shame, writers now make guilt shame's "other," the carrier of bad, negative, and destructive implications, while identifying shame as more productive, even possibly healing, in its very nature. More precisely, although shame is often characterized in terms of inadequacy, lack, or failure in relation to some personal ideal or standard, it is also widely perceived to contain a positive component.[4] For some theorists, indeed, shame serves at the limit as a site of resistance to cultural norms of identity.

There are two principal reasons for such a profound and sweeping revaluation of shame. First, shame is now considered more productive than guilt because it is thought that, whereas the actual or fantasmatic acts that produce guilty feelings are in principle irreversible, or at least inexpungeable, feelings of shame concern aspects of selfhood that are imagined to be amenable to correction or change (more on this below). Second and more broadly, many theorists find shame a better affect than guilt to think with. Donald Nathanson believes you can do better self theory with shame than with guilt; Bernard Williams believes you can do better moral theory with shame than with guilt; Eve Sedgwick believes that, using Tomkins's theories, you can do better queer theory with shame than with guilt; Giorgio Agamben believes you can do better survivor testimony theory with shame than with guilt; Elspeth Probyn thinks you can do better gender and cultural studies with shame rather than guilt; psychiatrists and therapists think you can do better trauma theory with shame than with guilt; and so on. The result is that shame has emerged in recent years as a privileged operator not only for various psychological-psychotherapeutic projects, but also for diverse kinds of theoretical-interpretive undertakings.

[3] Gerhart Piers and Milton B. Singer, *Shame and Guilt: A Psychoanalytic and a Cultural Study* (New York, 1953); Silvan S. Tomkins, *Affect Imagery Consciousness*, vols. 1 and 2 (New York, 1962–63), hereafter abbreviated *AIC*. Other relevant writings on shame in the early postwar period include texts by Camus and Erving Goffman. For Camus's work see E. L. Constable, "Shame," *MLN* 112 (1997): 641–65; and for Goffman see his *Stigma: Notes on the Management of Spoiled Identity* (New York, 1963).

[4] For example, Barber and Clark have observed that in Eve Sedgwick's hands, shame is "a uniquely productive affect that vivifies and consolidates the subject in a moment of wincing isolation," noting in this regard Sedgwick's acknowledgment that Silvan Tomkins's treatment of shame as the affective ground for the psyche is "one of the very few available theoretical models that allow for its positivity." Stephen M. Barber and David L. Clark, *Regarding Sedgwick: Essays on Queer Culture and Critical Theory* (New York, 2002), 26–27; hereafter abbreviated *RS*.

My project in this and the following chapter is to examine modern shame theory by singling out certain key motifs for discussion. Not every shame theorist I shall discuss adopts each of the motifs I shall be considering, and I shall do my best to indicate this. A few more preliminary remarks are in order. First, the preceding chapters have been intimately concerned with trauma, whereas in this chapter the link to trauma is less perspicuous. On the one hand, as I mentioned at the end of the last chapter, shame has now taken the place previously occupied by survivor guilt in theorizations of PTSD. Whereas researchers in the past tended to claim that trauma survivors experienced guilt for surviving, or made little distinction between guilt and shame, an emerging consensus now asserts that shame is the relevant emotion in posttraumatic stress. So in the case of recent studies of stress there is the same close association between trauma and shame as there used to be between trauma and guilt. On the other hand, the theorist to whom many PTSD researchers have turned for ideas about shame is the American psychologist Silvan S. Tomkins, whose work—to be discussed in the present chapter—has little to do with trauma as such but rather engages with the more general question of the emotions. Similarly, literary critic Eve Kosofsky Sedgwick—whose work on shame looks to Tomkins as a shining example—is focused on questions of queer identity, not trauma. Furthermore, Giorgio Agamben's ideas about the shame of Auschwitz, which I analyze in the chapter after this one, are cast in post-Heideggerian, Levinasian terms that may appear remote from questions of trauma as these have been formulated in recent American psychiatry.

However, there are several important cross-linkages. For example, Paul Ekman, Tomkins's most influential disciple working in the emotion field today, whose research I also examine in these pages, has deployed some of the same films to experimentally confirm Tomkins's ideas about the affects that trauma theorist Mardi Horowitz made use of in his work on posttraumatic stress. Sedgwick for her part stages one of her discussions of shame and identity in terms of the trauma of 9/11. And Agamben in his ruminations on the ethical consequences of Auschwitz refers to the work of current trauma theorists, such as Shoshana Felman.

Second, in engaging with the topic of shame in this chapter I am inevitably drawn into the debate that has dominated the general field of the study of emotions for more than fifty years, namely, the debate over whether the affects ought to be understood in intentionalist or cognitive terms, or whether they can be understood as antiintentionalist or anticognitive in nature. Guilt has traditionally belonged to the intentionalist pole of that debate, since guilt has been understood as involving the subject's conscious or unconscious intentions toward some person or object. In the work of Tomkins and his followers, however, the emotions generally, and shame in particular, are theorized in antiintentionalist terms as automatic, reflex-like corporeal and facial responses. The claim is that the averted, downcast eyes of the shamed individual and accompanying bodily sensations are the product of built-in, inherited physiological systems of reaction or "affect programs" that are inherently independent of any intentional object. With few exceptions all the shame theorists I shall discuss in this and the subsequent chapter endorse the antiintentionalist position on the emotions. In the course of my analysis of their work, in a manner rarely pursued by those who support the intentionalist position on the emotions, I shall undertake to critically assess the empirical-experimental evidence used to support the new materialist approach to the affects. My purpose here will be to show that the antiintentionalist, anticognitive position embraced by the shame theorists who interest me cannot be sustained not only because it is theoretically incoherent but also because the empirical-experimental evidence for it is flawed.

Shame and Specularity

In a recent essay Jacques Derrida writes of his feeling of unease at the moment when,

> caught naked, in silence, by the gaze of an animal, for example the eyes of a cat, I have trouble, yes, a bad time overcoming my embarrassment. Whence this malaise? I have trouble repressing a reflex dictated by immodesty. Trouble keeping silent within me a protest against the indecency. Against the impropriety that comes of finding oneself naked, one's sex exposed, stark naked before a cat that looks at you without moving, just to see . . . It is as if I were ashamed, therefore, naked in front of this cat, but also ashamed for being ashamed. A reflected shame, the mirror of a shame ashamed of itself, a shame that is at the same time specular, unjustifiable, and unable to be admitted to. At the optical center of this reflection would appear this thing—and in my eyes the focus of this incomparable experience—that is called nudity.[5]

Although it is rare for someone to declare that he experiences shame when exposed to the gaze of a cat rather than that of another human being, Derrida's statement is otherwise unexceptional in its assumption that shame is an emotion that is *routed through the eyes* and that the logic of shame is a *scene of exposure* (this is true even if the scene is only an imagined one and the observer is not an external spectator but an internalized other).

"'Shame lives on the eyelids,' according to an old Greek proverb," Anne Carson observes in her wonderful recreation of Euripides's several descriptions of Phaedra's shame. "I guess this means it makes you cast your eyes down."[6]

---

[5] Jacques Derrida, "The Animal That Therefore I Am (More to Follow)," *Critical Inquiry* 28 (Winter 2002): 372–73. For Derrida, the question of our shame is connected to that of a passivity, or suffering, or vulnerability that we share with animals in relation to death.

[6] Anne Carson, "Euripides to the Audience," *London Review of Books*, September 5, 2003, 24.

Charles Darwin in the modern period likewise defined shame in terms of a desire for concealment from the gaze of another.[7] Freud expressed the same motif when, in an astonishing footnote in *Civilization and its Discontents* (1930), he suggested that the feeling of shame had its origin in primitive man's assumption of an upright gait. "This made his genitals, which were previously concealed, visible and in need of protection, and so provoked shame in him," he wrote.[8] For Sartre, too, shame is a specular emotion: "I am ashamed of myself as I appear to the other," he writes.[9] Carroll Izard and Silvan Tomkins also link shame to the theme of sight and exposure when they characterize the shame response as an act that reduces facial communication: "By dropping his eyelids, head, and sometimes the whole upper part of his body, the individual calls a halt to looking at another person, particularly the other person's face, and to the other person's looking at him, particularly at his face. In self-confrontation the head may also be hung in shame symbolically, lest one part of the self be seen by another part and become alienated from it."[10] "Shame requires an audience," Jacqueline Rose likewise remarks: "Unlike guilt, which can fester quietly inside you, shame only arises when someone knows, or fears, they have been seen. Shame relies on the art of exposure, even if exposure is what it hates most, and most militantly struggles against."[11] The philosopher Bernard Williams writes from an anti-Kantian perspective remote from Rose's psychoanalytic stance, but he too emphasizes the spectatorial dimension of shame. "In my experience of shame," he writes, "the other sees all of me and all through me, even if the occasion of shame is on my surface—for instance, in my appearance; and the expression of shame, in gen-

---

[7] "Under a keen sense of shame there is a strong desire for concealment," Darwin observes. "We turn away the whole body, more especially the face, which we endeavour in some manner to hide. An ashamed person can hardly endure to meet the gaze of those present, so that he almost invariably casts down his eyes or looks askant." Charles Darwin, *The Expression of the Emotions in Man and Animals*, 3d ed., with an introduction, afterword and commentaries by Paul Ekman (Oxford, 1998), 319–20.

[8] Sigmund Freud, *Civilization and its Discontent* (1930), in *The Standard Edition of the Complete Psychological Works of Sigmund Freud*, trans. and ed. James Strachey, 24 vols. (London, 1953–74), 21:53, n. 1.

[9] J.-P. Sartre, *Being and Nothingness: An Essay on Phenomenological Ontology*, trans. Hazel E. Barnes (New York, 1956), 221, 261–302. Jacques Lacan objects to Sartre's placing shame exclusively in the register of sight, remarking that in the original scene of shame described by Sartre, in which he is surprised by the gaze of another while looking through a keyhole, a crucial part is played by the sound of a footstep in the corridor, a sound Sartre compares to the rustling of leaves. Jacques Lacan, *The Four Fundamental Concepts of Psycho-Analysis*, ed. Jacques-Alain Miller, trans. Alan Sheridan (New York, 1978), 84.

[10] Carroll E. Izard and Silvan S. Tomkins, "Affect and Behavior: Anxiety as a Negative Affect," in *Anxiety and Behavior*, ed. Charles D. Spiegelberger (New York and London, 1966), 117–18; hereafter abbreviated "AB."

[11] Jacqueline Rose, *On Not Being Able to Sleep: Psychoanalysis and the Modern World* (London, 2003), 1.

eral as well as in the particular form of it that is embarrassment, is not just the desire to hide, or to hide my face, but the desire to disappear, not to be there."[12]

I could multiply quotations but they would all make the same point, namely, that shame has been consistently theorized as a *specular affect that has the fantasy of visibility and disclosure built right into it.* The feeling of guilt does not have this spectatorial dimension. According to shame theorist Helen Lewis: "In contrast to the wordless shame experience, in which the whole self is the object of the 'other's' disapproving look, the experience of the self in guilt is neutralized."[13] Or as Williams puts it: "The most primitive experiences of shame are connected with sight and being seen, but it has been . . . suggested that guilt is rooted in hearing, the sound in oneself of the voice of judgement."[14] Whatever we might think of Williams's distinction between seeing and hearing, it seems clear that according to shame theory you could go to your grave with a guilty secret but, since shame is identical to exposure, the feeling of shame is one of *already having been exposed* to the gaze of some real or fantasized other.

The spectatorial dimension of shame aligns it with the antimimetic, dramaturgical pole of trauma theory as the latter is analyzed in *Trauma: A Genealogy.* The subject of shame is imagined as an actor who changes from a person unselfconsciously immersed in herself (in her life, her world) into someone who feels ashamed because she becomes suddenly aware of herself as an actor performing in front of an audience. "Shame requires a sophisticated type of self-consciousness," Gabriele Taylor remarks. "A person feeling shame will exercise her capacity for self-awareness, and she will do so dramatically: from being just an actor absorbed in what she is doing she will suddenly become self-aware and self-critical. It is plainly a state of self-consciousness which centrally relies on the concept of another, for the thought of being seen by another is a catalyst for the emotion."[15] Sedgwick also expresses shame theory's commitment to the dramaturgical when she observes:

> [W]henever the actor, or the performance artist, or, I could add, the activist in an identity politics, proffers the spectacle of her or his "infantile" narcissism to a spectating eye, the stage is set (so to speak) for either a newly dramatized flooding of the subject by the shame of refused return, or the successful pulsation of the mirroring regard through a narcissistic circuit rendered elliptical (which is to say: necessarily distorted) by the hyperbole of its original cast. As best described by Tomkins, shame effaces itself; shame points and projects; shame turns itself skin side out; shame and pride, shame and dig-

---

[12] Bernard Williams, *Shame and Necessity* (Berkeley, 1993), 89, see also his endnote 1, "Mechanisms of Shame and Guilt," 219–23.

[13] Helen B. Lewis, *Shame and Guilt in Neurosis* (New York, 1971), 253.

[14] Williams, *Shame and Necessity*, 89.

[15] Gabriele Taylor, *Pride, Shame, and Guilt* (Oxford, 1985), 67.

nity, shame and self-display, shame and exhibitionism are different interlinings of the same glove. Shame, it might finally be said, transformational shame, *is performance.* I mean theatrical performance.[16]

This is a more complex set of remarks than the others just cited, but for Sedgwick, the subject of shame is a self-conscious actor through and through.[17]

Shame and the Self

But what is it that is spectatorially and dramatically exposed in shame? For Derrida and Freud, echoing a theme that goes back to the story of Genesis, what is exposed in shame is the naked body, specifically the sexed naked body. But most of today's shame theorists, moving away from any exclusive emphasis on the exposure of nudity and sexual difference, believe that one can be ashamed of virtually any aspect of the self—indeed that it is *the self as such*, with all its attributes, that is put in question in shame. In Izard's and Tomkins's formulation: "The shame response is literally an ambivalent turning of the eyes away from the object and toward the face, toward the self" ("AB," 118). In contrast to the other affects, Tomkins writes, shame is an experience "of the self by the self . . . Why is shame so close to the experienced self? It is because the self lives in the face, and within the face the self burns brightest in the eyes. Shame turns the attention of the self and others away from other objects to this most visible residence of self, increases its visibility and thereby generates the torment of self-consciousness" (*AIC*, 2:133).

Various developments have shaped the rise of a psychology of shame centered on notions of the self. They include theoretical shifts within psychoanalysis, a renewed focus on the question of narcissism, the rise of Otto Kohut's self psychology, and many other factors.[18] Of considerable influence in recent years has been the theory of shame first proposed by Tomkins, who traces the origin of the

[16] Eve Kosofsky Sedgwick, *Touching Feeling: Affect, Pedagogy, Performativity* (Durham, N.C., and London, 2003), 38; hereafter abbreviated *TF*.

[17] Sedgwick's ideas resonate with Erving Goffman's dramaturgical ideas about the role-playing character of the emotional performance. She writes: "There's a strong sense, I think, in which the subtitle of any truly queer (perhaps as opposed to gay?) politics will be the same as the one Erving Goffman gave to his book *Stigma: Notes on the Management of Spoiled Identity.* But more than its management, its experimental, creative, performative force." Eve Kosofsky Sedgwick, "Queer Performativity: Henry James's *The Art of the Novel*," *GLQ* 1 (1993): 4; hereafter abbreviated "QP."

[18] See especially Frances J. Broucek, "Shame and Its Relationship to Early Narcissistic Developments," *International Journal of Psychoanalysis* 63 (1982): 369–78; Warren Kingston, "A Theoretical Context for Shame," *International Journal of Psychoanalysis* 64 (1983): 213–26; and Andrew P. Morrison, *Shame: The Underside of Narcissism* (Hillsdale, N.J., 1989).

shame experience to a very early developmental moment, between three and seven months of age, when the infant's natural interest in the world, especially in the mother's face, as expressed by the infant's desire to look and see, is barred by the counter gaze of a "stranger" (which could be the gaze of the same loving mother who is now distracted, angry, or otherwise suddenly "strange"). The effect is to reduce, without completely annihilating, the child's interest in the world. Tomkins explains: "The innate activator of shame is the incomplete reduction of interest or joy. Hence, any barrier to further exploration which partially reduces interest or the smile of enjoyment will activate the lowering of the head and eyes in shame and reduce further exploration or self-exposure" ("AB," 118). In Sedgwick's summary of his ideas: "Shame floods into being as a moment, a disruptive moment, in a circuit of identity-constituting identificatory communication. Indeed, like a stigma, shame is itself a form of communication. Blazons of shame, the 'fallen face' with eyes down and head averted—and, to a lesser extent, the blush—are semaphores of trouble and at the same time of a desire to reconstitute the interpersonal bridge. But in interrupting identification, shame, too, makes identity" (*TF*, 36).[19] It is precisely because of its identity-forming potential that shame interests Sedgwick. "[A]t least for certain ('queer') people," she writes, "shame is simply the first, and remains a permanent, structuring fact of identity" (*TF*, 64).

The idea that what is exposed in shame is some aspect of the self or personal identity sets up the basic opposition in current theory between shame and guilt, according to which shame concerns *the self*, or who you are, whereas guilt concerns *your actions*, or what you do. Sedgwick usefully sums up the by now conventional wisdom on this topic when she observes that "shame attaches to and sharpens the sense of what one is, whereas guilt attaches to what one does" (*TF*, 37). She notes that although Tomkins is less interested than anthropologists, moralists, and popular psychologists in distinguishing between the two affects, the implication remains that "one *is something* in experiencing shame, though one may or may not have secure hypotheses about what. In the developmental process, shame is now often considered the affect that most defines the space wherein a sense of self will develop . . . Which I take to mean, not at all that it is the place where identity is most securely attached to essences, but rather that it is the place where the *question* of identity arises most originarily and relationally" (*TF*, 37). The same point is repeatedly made by others. As Donald Nathanson, Tomkins's most influential disciple in the psychotherapeutic professions, observes: "What is exposed in the moment of shame is something deeply personal, some particularly intimate, sensitive and vulnerable aspect of the self. Unlike guilt,

---

[19] For a description of shame along similar lines see for example Carroll E. Izard, *Human Emotions* (New York and London, 1977), chap. 15.

the complex emotion released when we have violated some rule or done harm to another person, shame monitors our sense of self."[20]

All this suggests that what is crucially at stake in the current tendency to replace guilt with shame is an impulse to displace questions about our moral responsibility for what we *do* in favor of more ethically neutral or different questions about our personal attributes. Normally we cannot be held responsible for who we are in the same way we can be held responsible for what we do—or what *we imagine we have done*, for according to Freud we can feel guilty for entirely fantasmatic events because, unable to distinguish between the virtual and the actual, the unconscious equates the intention or wish with the deed itself. The concept of survivor guilt conforms to this Freudian logic: as psychoanalysts treating survivors of the concentration camps understood all too well, the survivor's feeling of responsibility for the death of others is not necessarily based on reality but may be of an unconscious, magical kind. By defensively identifying with the aggressor, the survivor fantasmatically participates in the violence directed against others and consequently suffers from self-reproach. The real or imagined instrumentality involved in guilt makes notions of responsibility and reparation relevant to it.[21] That this can include feeling responsible for one's actions (or one's failures to act) in situations where one is objectively innocent is, as we have seen, attested to by Primo Levi when he observes that the fact of being a victim is not contradicted by the survivor's feeling of guilt.

But shame theory displaces the focus of attention from action to the self by insisting that even if shame can be connected to action, it does not have to be, since shame is an attribute of personhood before the subject has done anything, or because he is incapable of acting meaningfully. Take the case of someone who has experienced the degradation of a brutal prison environment, such as a concentration camp. The prisoner has done nothing grossly inhumane during his incarceration. But he has witnessed cruelty to others, and afterward torments himself for numerous minor acts he has performed or irrepressible thoughts he has entertained while in prison. Psychologist Sue Miller, one of the few shame theorists to refer to the literature of the Nazi camps before Agamben made shame central to his discussion of the survivor, indicates that in such a case the victim

---

[20] Donald Nathanson, "Understanding What Is Hidden: Shame in Sexual Abuse," *Psychiatric Clinics of North America* 12, no. 2 (1989): 381. Bernard Williams echoes the psychologists' emphasis on the self when he writes: "Shame might be thought to be in its very nature a more narcissistic emotion than guilt. The viewer's gaze draws the subject's attention not to the viewer, but to the subject himself; the victim's anger [in the case of guilt], on the other hand, draws attention to the victim" (Williams, *Shame and Necessity*, 222).

[21] I have already elaborated this point in chapter 1. For an interesting discussion of the case of a car driver whose instrumentality in accidentally knocking down and killing a child whom he could not have seen or avoided leads to feelings of guilt and remorse, see Taylor, *Pride, Shame, and Guilt*, 91.

experiences a mix of both guilt and shame, according to whether he focuses on guilty recollections of what he did or imagines he did, or on the moral shame he feels for being a weak or inferior person.[22] Miller's discussion could be used to resolve Levi's apparent inability to distinguish between guilt and shame, for which Agamben reproaches him, by suggesting that Levi was correct to refer to the shame he felt when in a crowd of terrified and apathetic prisoners he was forced to witness the public hanging of a courageous man who had participated in a failed attempt to blow up the crematoria at Auschwitz. The condemned man cried out, "'Comrades, I am the last one!'" just before the trapdoor opened. "I wish I could say that from the midst of us, an abject flock, a voice rose, a murmur, a sign of assent," Levi writes. "But nothing happened. We remained standing, bent and gray, our heads dropped . . . To destroy a man is difficult, almost as difficult as to create one: it has not been easy, nor quick, but you Germans have succeeded. Here we are, docile under your gaze . . . Alberto and I went back to the hut, and we could not look each other in the face. That man must have been tough, he must have been made of another metal than us if this condition of ours, which has broken us, could not bend him. Because we are also broken, conquered . . . and now we are oppressed by shame."[23] Levi here reproaches himself not so much for a guilty action, or a failure to act, as for a personal failing, for being *the kind of person* who lacks the attributes of courage so conspicuously displayed by the doomed man.

In a comparable scene, the pale-skinned black writer James Weldon Johnson, author of *The Autobiography of an Ex-Colored Man* (1927), is an appalled witness to the lynching, by burning alive, of a black man. "I was fixed to the spot where I stood," Johnson writes, "powerless to take my eyes from what I did not want to see. It was over before I realized that time had passed . . . I walked a short distance away and sat down in order to clear my dazed mind. A great wave of humiliation and shame swept over me. Shame that I belonged to a race that could be so dealt with."[24] Like Levi, Johnson—who could have intervened only at the cost of being victimized himself—experiences shame not for anything he has done, but for who he is. We might say that in such situations shame begins where guilt leaves off, because of the impossibility of action, or the subject's enforced passivity. It is not surprising, then, that shame is viewed today as the affect of disempowerment, the chief emotional consequence of social injustice and inequality.[25]

[22] Sue Miller, *The Shame Experience* (New York, 1985), 41–42.

[23] Primo Levi, *Survival in Auschwitz,* trans. Stuart Woolf (New York, 1996), 149–50.

[24] James Weldon Johnson, *The Autobiography of an Ex-Colored Man* (1927; New York, 1979), 187.

[25] Tomkins thus characterizes shame as the affect of mortifying powerlessness and loss of face that guarantees a "perpetual sensitivity to any violation of the dignity of man" (Eve Kosofsky Sedgwick and Adam Frank, eds., *Shame and Its Sisters: A Silvan Tomkins Reader* [Durham, N.C., 1995], 136).

At first sight, it appears that Sedgwick for one doesn't want to strip the affect of shame of all traits of agency. She explicitly advocates Tomkins's affect theory—his great challenge to psychoanalysis, in her view—because she feels it allows her to address those "middle ranges of agency" (*TF*, 13) that are ignored in postmodernist accounts that according to her too easily reduce agency to an extreme binarism of voluntary or compulsion. And in her own highly original analyses of the circuits of shame between self and other in writings by Henry James and other authors, she emphasizes the active, performative dimension of the subject's shame experience. Nevertheless, action in the sense of intentional agency is precisely what is missing in Sedgwick's and Tomkins's work, because for them and many others today *the affects are not intentional states but can be autotelic.* What this means is the subject of my next section.

Autotelism

In her writings, Sedgwick gives salience to a feature of Tomkins's affect theory that plays an important role in the success of his ideas, namely, that unlike the drives, the affects are only contingently related to objects—they have a freedom with respect to objects that the drives do not possess. From this it follows that the affects have the potential to be autotelic, by which she means that they can be discharged in a self-rewarding or self-punishing fashion independently of any object whatsoever.

Tomkins's work is based on the claim that psychologists had misunderstood the centrality of the affects to human motivation by conceptualizing them as subordinate to, or derivative of, the drives. This was an error, Tomkins argued, because the drives are too narrowly constrained in their aims, time relations, and above all their object relations to make them a suitable basis for human motivation, which requires a much higher degree of flexibility or freedom. As Sedgwick observes of the need for air and water: "[O]nly a tiny subset of gases satisfy my need to breathe or of liquids my need to drink" (*TF*, 18). According to Tomkins, this objection applies to the sexual drives as well. For anyone familiar with the work of Jean Laplanche and J.-B. Pontalis, who argue that for Freud desire has extraordinary freedom with respect to objects precisely because it has no predetermined objects of its own, it comes as a surprise to learn from Tomkins that sexuality is constrained in its object-orientation in much the same way that hunger is.[26] As a matter of fact, Tomkins conceded that sexuality is the most flex-

---

[26] Jean Laplanche and J.-B. Pontalis, "Fantasy and the Origin of Sexuality," *International Journal of Psycho-Analysis* 49 (1968): 1–17. Cf. Jean Laplanche, *Life and Death in Psychoanalysis*, trans. Jeffrey Mehlman (Baltimore, 1976).

ible and hence the most affectlike of the drives in terms of the range of objects which can instigate it (*AIC*, 1:126–27, 140). Nevertheless, for Tomkins what makes even the sexual drive an inadequate basis for human motivation is a trait it shares with the other drives, its immediate *instrumentality*, its "defining orientation toward a specified aim and end different from itself" (*TF*, 19). The affects do not have this instrumental character. As Tomkins puts it: "[I]t is the gap between [the emotional] responses and instrumental responses which is necessary if the affective response is to function like a human motivational response. There must be introduced into the machine a critical gap between the conditions which instigate the self-rewarding or self-punishing responses, which maintain them, which turn them off, and the 'knowledge' of these conditions, and the further response to the knowledge of these conditions. The machine initially would know only that it liked some of its own responses and disliked some of its own responses but not that they might be turned on, or off, and not how to turn them on, or off, or up, or down in intensity."[27]

It is because of its instrumental character, the fact that like the other drives sexual desire is structured by lack and oriented toward an aim different from itself, that Tomkins demotes sexuality in his account of human motivation. This move is repeated by Sedgwick in her critique of the psychoanalytic and poststructuralist emphasis on libido as the ultimate source of human behavior. In Sedgwick's case, the demotion of sexuality is also related to her quarrel with what she regards as the routine moralism of much poststructuralist theorizing; it represents her attempt to step outside Freud's "repressive hypothesis" to "forms of thought that would not be structured by the question of prohibition" (*TF*, 12). Tomkins's claim that the shame response makes its appearance by the time a baby is about seven months old provides Sedgwick with empirical evidence for the assertion that shame makes its appearance before the oedipus complex, and before the child can have any concept of taboo or prohibition (*TF*, 98).[28]

In contrast to the drives, Tomkins held that affects have far greater freedom with respect to objects. As Sedgwick writes, quoting and paraphrasing Tomkins: " '[A]ny affect may have any "object." This is the basic source of complexity of human motivation and behavior.' The object of affects such as anger, enjoyment,

---

[27] Silvan S. Tomkins, "Simulation of a Personality: The Interrelationships between Affect, Memory, Thinking, Perception, and Action," in *Computer Simulation of Personality: Frontier of Psychological Theory*, ed. Silvan S. Tomkins and Samuel Messick (New York, 1963), 18–19.

[28] For a discussion of the evidence linking shame to the earliest experiences of the child see Donald L. Nathanson, ed., *The Many Faces of Shame* (New York, 1987), chap. 1. What in the seven- or eight-month-old child's response to strangers (as manifested by lowering of the eyes, hiding of the face, weeping, screaming, or refusal of contact) had been interpreted as an early manifestation of anxiety by earlier researchers into child development, is now reinterpreted as an anticipatory shame reaction.

excitement, or shame is not proper to the affects in the same way that air is the object proper to respiration. 'There is literally no kind of object which has not historically been linked to one or another of the affects' . . . Affects can be, and are, attached to things, people, ideas, sensations, relations, activities, ambitions, institutions, and any number of other things, including other affects. Thus, one can be excited by anger, disgusted by shame, or surprised by joy" (*TF*, 19). But in a questionable interpretive move, Tomkins, Sedgwick, and others in their camp then go on to argue that because affects are not tied to any one object but can be contingently attached to a vast range of objects, *they are intrinsically independent of all objects.* Thus Sedgwick asserts that the multiplicity of objects of the affects implies that they are in principle objectless and hence can be satisfied without regard to the means-end logic or instrumentalism that defines the drives. The freedom of affects in regard to objects, Sedgwick writes, "gives them a structural potential not enjoyed by the drive system: in contrast to the instrumentality of drives and their direct orientation toward an aim different from themselves, the affects can be autotelic" (*TF*, 19).

I consider this a mistake: it doesn't follow that because the affects can have a multiplicity—even a vast multiplicity—of objects they are inherently without any relation to objects whatsoever. The mistake, in other words, is thinking that having multiple objects undoes objectality altogether. Sedgwick extends the same questionable logic to sexuality when she claims that "even though sexual desire is usually oriented toward an aim and object other than itself, it is much more malleable in its aims and objects than are the other drives, and also has the potential of being autotelic"(*TF*, 20). In short, *for Tomkins and Sedgwick the affects are nonintentional states.*[29] (This is not the position of Bernard Williams, who turns to the structure of shame in ancient Greece because he thinks it provides a superior account of action and ethics than Kantian or neo-Kantian accounts of

---

[29] Thus in a section of *Affect, Imagery, Consciousness* entitled "Independence of images (purposes) and affects," Tomkins writes:

> We conceive of the human being as governed by a feedback system in which a predetermined state is achieved by utilizing information about the difference between the achieved state at the moment and the predetermined state to reduce this difference to zero. Our argument . . . is that because the human affect system is independent of the human feedback system, the latter may have 'aims' independent of affects, and the affects may come and go without recourse to or dependence on the feedback system . . . The purpose of an individual is a centrally emitted blueprint which we call the *Image* . . . Despite the fact that there may be intense affect preceding and following the achievement of any Image, there may yet be a high degree of phenomenological independence between what is intended and the preceding, accompanying and consequent affect . . . The Image is a blueprint for the feedback mechanism: as such it is purposive and directive. Affect we conceive of as a motive, by which we mean immediately rewarding or punishing experience mediated by receptors activated by the individual's own responses. Motives may or may not actualize themselves in purposes. (*AIC*, 1:121–22).

guilt.[30] Nor is it the position of critic Jacqueline Rose, who mentions Tomkins's work but stays largely within the psychoanalytic paradigm when discussing shame and accordingly links shame to unconscious intentional states.)

The idea that one or other emotion can be autotelic implies that the way to understand joy or happiness is that they are elicited or "triggered" by what we call the object, but the object is nothing more than a stimulus or tripwire for an inbuilt behavioral-physiological response. We might put it that in this account the object of the emotion is turned into the trigger or "releaser"of the reaction, with the result that the response is purged of instrumentality.[31] Tomkins adopts just such a trigger theory of the emotions. In his words:

> If the affects are our primary motives, what are they and where are they? Affects are sets of muscle, vascular, and glandular responses located in the face and also widely distributed through the body, which generate sensory feedback which is inherently either "acceptable" or "unacceptable." These organized sets of responses are triggered at subcortical centers where specific "programs" for each distinct affect are stored. These programs are innately endowed and have been genetically inherited. They are capable, when activated, of simultaneously capturing such widely distributed organs as the face, the heart, and the endocrines and imposing on them a specific pattern of correlated responses. One does not learn to be afraid or to cry or to be startled, any more than one learns to feel pain or gasp for air.
>
> Most contemporary investigators have pursued the inner bodily responses after the James-Lange theory had focused attention on their significance. Important as they undoubtedly are, I regard them as of secondary importance to the expression of emotion through the face [. . .] If we are happy when we smile and sad when we cry, why are we reluctant to agree that smiling or crying is primarily what it means to be happy or sad?[32]

---

[30] Williams's shame theory overlaps in certain regards with that of Tomkins and Sedgwick. Like them, he defines shame in spectatorial terms as an emotion that concerns the self. Like them, he privileges shame over guilt because he thinks shame can understand guilt, but guilt cannot understand shame: for Williams, guilt can only tell us what harms we have done voluntarily or involuntarily to others, but it cannot tell us what kinds of failings and inadequacies in the self are the source of those harms—only shame can do this. And like them, he thinks shame has a more positive aspect than guilt, because it can help us rebuild the self that has done harmful things (thus the interest of ancient Greek shame culture, he thinks, is that it provides us with a model for a richer, more realistic, and more truthful account of ethics). But there are obvious points of difference between Williams and contemporary shame theorists. In particular, Williams is not interested in the kinds of biological accounts of shame that interest Tomkins, Sedgwick, and others. His project is intended as a philosophical challenge to Kantian accounts of ethics which he regards as too rationalistic and abstract. In particular, he reproaches Kantians for forgetting the origin of guilt feelings and guilty actions in the emotion of anger against an internalized other—an account of the origin of guilt that recalls Freud, whom Williams does not mention.

[31] For the relationship between Tomkins's views on the innate activators of the affects and Konrad Lorenz's ideas about the role of "releasers" in animal behavior see *AIC*, 1:249–71.

[32] Silvan Tomkins, "Affect as the Primary Motivational System," *Loyola Symposium on Feelings and Emotions, 1968* (New York, 1970), 105–6.

This passage brings out Tomkins's commitment to the idea that there exists a limited number of discrete primary emotions defined as pancultural or universal, inherited, and adaptive responses of the organism, an idea that in Tomkins' version treats the emotions as distinct affect "programs" or "assemblies" that can and do combine in "central assemblies" with the purposive cognitive and other systems but from which they are in principle independent. As hardwired, reflexlike, subcortical and hence noncognitive, species-typical genetic programs, behaviors, and physiological reactions, the affects have activators or triggers that are innate and hence independent of learning, although he held that they can also be stimulated by the learned activators of memory, imagination, and thinking (*AIC*, 1:248). He thus argued for a "radical dichotomy between the 'real' causes of affects and the individual's own interpretations of these causes" and claimed that "it is the latter which is ultimately responsible for transforming motives [affects] into governing Images" (*AIC*, 1:248). At first, Tomkins thought there were eight different primary affects, including shame, but later decided there were nine.[33]

Tomkins thus proposes a noncognitive, or nonintentionalist, account of the affects. The debate between those who support some version of his theory, which denies that the basic emotions depend on cognitive appraisals, and those who think that the affects are linked to beliefs about or cognitive appraisals of the external and internal world has been going on for more than forty years. In her work on Tomkins, Sedgwick dismisses the cognitivist position as part of the "'commonsense' consensus of current theory" (*TF*, 112). But although it is fair to say that most philosophers support some version of the cognitivist position, within the psychological sciences the opposite is true: the antiintentionalist, anticognitivist, affect program theory dominates American psychology textbooks today and enjoys widespread acceptance in the emotions field.[34] The success of the affect program theory depends in part on its claim to be rooted in the life sciences, especially the science of evolution, and to be empirically well supported. But is it well founded? Can Tomkins's affect theory be coherently sustained? An examination of the key experiments that have been adduced in its favor suggest that it cannot.

The Evidence

The controversy began in the early 1960s when the cognitivists Stanley E. Schachter and J. E. Singer, on the one hand, and Tomkins on

[33] Tomkins's eight primary or innate affects were: interest, surprise, joy, anger, fear, distress, disgust, and shame. Later he added contempt (or what he called "dissmell").

[34] An examination of any recent textbook of psychology would demonstrate this. For one critical assessment of the current situation, see *The Psychology of Facial Expression*, ed., James R. Russell and Jose Miguel Fernandez-Dols (Cambridge, 1997), 10–11.

the other, simultaneously established their opposed arguments.[35] In a famous study published in 1962, Schachter and Singer injected experimental subjects with what the latter were told was a special vitamin capable of improving eyesight, but was in fact adrenaline, in order to induce physiological arousal under controlled conditions. The researchers then manipulated the subjects' environment in various ways so as to induce different emotional states as reflected in the subjects' observed behavior and in their self-reports. The conclusion was that emotions are context-sensitive responses that depend on the interpretation of environmental cues and the intensity of diffuse physiological arousal rather than on the specific quality of the subjects' accompanying bodily state. The experiment thus appeared to lend decisive support to the cognitivist position. Richard Lazarus's experimental investigations of the role of appraisal in stress, some of which were briefly discussed in chapter 3, also appeared to validate the cognitivist position by emphasizing the role of cognition in the appraisal of threat.[36]

At the same moment, 1962–63, Tomkins published the first two volumes of what would eventually become a four-volume study of personality and emotion in which he laid out his affect program theory and emphasized the importance of facial expression.[37] He was keen to put his ideas to an empirical test and encour-

[35] Rather than burden the reader with extensive footnotes at this juncture, which would make reading the text more difficult, I have chosen to add a guide to the literature on the affect program theory in a brief appendix. In another book in progress, I plan to assess the history of experimental and theoretical work on the emotions from the 1960s to the present.

[36] S. Schachter and J. E. Singer, "Cognitive, Social, and Physiological Determinants of Emotional State," *Psychological Review* 69 (1962): 379–99. Schachter and Singer's experiments were taken to refute the James-Lange "feeling" theory of the emotions, according to which emotions are the feeling of the bodily changes that occur directly on the perception of some exciting cause. Although critics have pointed out that the Schachter-Singer experiments were not decisive in this regard, lacked adequate controls, and have in any case been difficult to replicate, they have been widely cited in support of the cognitivist position (see appendix). For Tomkins's criticisms of the Schachter-Singer experiment and appraisal theory see his "The Quest for Primary Motives: Biography and Autobiography of an Idea," *Journal of Personality and Social Psychology* 41 (1981): 306–29; hereafter "QPM." In this paper Tomkins defends the idea that there are distinct emotions each one of which is physiologically differentiated and that feelings precede cognition and can therefore occur without any "object" or reason. He praises as "brilliant" (316) in this regard the work of R. B. Zajonc, who claimed that feeling and cognition are under the control of two separate and partially independent systems or mechanisms and that emotional reactions can occur without any extensive perceptual or cognitive coding. Nussbaum is not the only person to point out, however, that Zajonc's continued use of intentional and cognitive terms, such as "affective judgements," to characterize the emotions undermines his claim that the affects are precognitive (Martha C. Nussbaum, *Upheavals of Thought: The Intelligence of Emotions* [Cambridge, 2001], 113).

[37] Silvan S. Tomkins, *Affect Imagery Consciousness,* 4 vols. (New York, 1962–92). See also Silvan S. Tomkins and Robert McCarter, "What Are the Primary Affects?" (1964), reprinted in *Exploring Affect: The Selected Writings of Silvan S. Tomkins*, ed. Virginia Demos (Cambridge, Mass., 1995), 217–62, a paper reporting the results of experiments designed to test the ability of observers to recognize facial expressions in selected posed photographs. This paper served as a blueprint for Ekman's and Izard's subsequent experimental research.

aged two younger researchers, Paul Ekman and Carroll Izard, to carry out this work.[38] Ekman and Izard developed separate research projects designed to demonstrate the existence of basic, universal emotions through the experimental study of human facial expression. Their fundamental assumption, based on what turns out to have been a misreading of Charles Darwin's work on facial expression, was that distinct facial movements are directly linked to a discrete number of subcortically controlled, innate emotions that form a part of our evolutionary heritage. Following Tomkins, Ekman argued that activation of each emotion, defined in terms of innate neural programs associated with distinct physiological responses, initiates an affect program that controls the movements of the face. According to Ekman, socialization might determine the range of elicitors that can trigger the affect programs and can moderate facial movements according to conventional "display rules," but the underlying emotions may nevertheless leak out. Ekman therefore attempted to separate out the involuntary, intentionless, biologically determined facial movements from those that are governed by so-called display rules. In a series of influential cross-cultural judgment studies, he and his colleagues claimed to show that facial movements, as manifested in posed or spontaneous photographs of the human face, are universally recognized by literate and isolated, illiterate people alike as expressing the basic emotions. Ekman originally focused on six basic affect programs—fear, anger, happiness, sadness, surprise, and disgust—but now claims there are fifteen, including shame and guilt.[39]

In addition, in a canonical experiment first reported in 1972, Ekman and his collaborator, Wallace Friesen, secretly videotaped the spontaneous facial movements of American and Japanese students while each student was watching neutral and stress-inducing films when alone in the viewing room. The experiments built on Lazarus's work on stress and used some of the same stressful films. Ekman and Friesen stated on the basis of a facial movement scoring system they had devised that the negative facial responses of the Americans and Japanese to the stress films were very similar. However, when an "authority figure" from the student's own culture (actually a research assistant dressed in a

[38] Paul Ekman, "Afterword: Universality of Emotional Expression? A Personal History of the Dispute," in Charles Darwin, *The Expression of the Emotions in Man and Animals*, 363–93, 445–48.

[39] Ekman is committed to the idea that the basic emotions share a list of characteristics that includes distinctive universal signs, distinctive physiology, automatic appraisal (the emotion occurs involuntarily, without intention), and so on. He admits that the evidence is not available for all the emotions, such as shame and guilt, but expects the issue to be resolved by future research. See for example Paul Ekman, "Basic Emotions," in *Handbook of Cognition and Emotion*, ed., T. Dalgleish and M. Power (Sussex, U.K., 1999), chap. 3. On the same topic, Izard has observed that the precise mechanisms in the neural activation of shame have not been determined (*Human Emotions*, 393); nor, as he acknowledges, has shame yet to be associated with a particular facial pattern (Carroll E. Izard, "Emotions and Facial Expressions: A Perspective from Differential Emotions Theory," in Russell and Fernandez-Dols, *The Psychology of Facial Expression*, 60).

white coat) was introduced into the room and interviewed that student about his feelings while the latter was viewing additional stress material, the facial behavior of the American and Japanese students diverged. The authors reported that the Japanese masked their negative feelings about the stress films more than the Americans by producing polite smiles when in the presence of the authority figure. Slow-motion videotape analysis, it was claimed, demonstrated at a microlevel the occurrence of the Japanese students' characteristic negative emotional expressions before these were replaced by polite smiles. The experiment therefore purported to demonstrate the "leakage" of the Japanese students' basic negative emotions prior to the covering over of those emotions by the Japanese cultural display rule controlling for polite, smiling faces. Ekman and Friesen therefore seemed to prove that the universal, biologically based emotions remained intact behind the culturally determined behavior, and hence to demonstrate the validity of the affect program theory.[40]

In his recent, highly regarded book, *What Emotions Really Are* (1997), Paul Griffiths criticizes the cognitivists, or what he prefers to call the "propositional attitude" theorists, among whom he includes most philosophers who have recently written on the emotions, for relying on conceptual analysis and ignoring the life sciences. He advocates instead as empirically well-grounded the Tomkins-Izard-Ekman affect program theory, as least as regards the so-called basic emotions.[41] But reproaching philosophers for armchair theorizing and for ignoring the empirical evidence serves in this case to distract attention from the inadequacies of the

[40] The original sources are: Paul Ekman, "Universals and Cultural Differences in Facial Expressions of Emotion," in *Nebraska Symposium on Motivation*, 4th ed., ed. J. K. Cole (Lincoln, 1971), 207–83; Wallace V. Friesen, "Cultural Differences in Facial Expression in a Social Situation: An Experimental Test of the Concept of Display Rules" (Ph.D. diss., University of California, San Francisco: Microfilm Archives, 1972). See also Paul Ekman and Wallace V. Friesen, *Unmasking the Face* (Englewood Cliffs, N.J., 1975), 24. For Tomkins's endorsement of Ekman and Izard's cross-cultural results, see Tomkins, "The Quest for Primary Motives: Biography and Autobiography of an Idea," 325. The Tomkins-Ekman view that facial expressions are hardwired to the brain lends itself to the idea that owing to culture individuals can put on a false face, but that even practiced liars cannot always control the facial "leakage" of their true feelings, a view that in the wake of 9/11 has been of interest to military intelligence. For a recent popular discussion of the work of Ekman and others on terrorist surveillance and lie detection, see Robin Marantz Henig, "Looking for the Lie," *New York Times Magazine,* February 5, 2006.

[41] Paul E. Griffiths, *What Emotions Really Are: The Problem of Psychological Categories* (Chicago and London, 1997); hereafter abbreviated *WERA*. In this influential book Griffiths distinguishes between the primary or basic emotions, of which he thinks there are only six or seven (surprise, fear, anger, disgust, sadness, joy, and perhaps contempt) and to which he thinks the affect program theory applies, and the higher, cognitive emotions (such as guilt, envy, jealousy, love, and for him also, shame) for which he thinks a quite different neural system is involved. His problem is then to explain how the modular, informationally encapsulated primary emotions are connected to the higher emotions.

scientific evidence on offer.[42] Two important publications in particular have recently shown that the experiments used to support the affect program theory are fundamentally flawed. In 1994, in a masterly assessment of the cross-cultural facial judgment or recognition experiments reported by Ekman and his colleagues, James A. Russell demonstrated that the results were artifactual, depending on a forced-choice response format and other problematic methods that begged the questions to be proved in ways that radically undermined Ekman's claims for the universal nature of the emotions.[43] In an equally impressive critique published the same year, Alan Fridlund showed that the description given by Ekman and Friesen over the years of their famous Japanese-American study was inaccurate, and their interpretation of the results in terms of the opposition between authentic emotional expressions versus display rules was unsupportable.[44] The net result of Russell's and Fridlund's assessments was to dramatically challenge the empirical and theoretical validity of the by now well-entrenched Tomkins-Izard-Ekman affect program theory of the emotions.

[42] It is true that philosophers are often ignorant of the recent scientific literature on the emotions. But as I try to show in these pages, much of that literature is itself flawed, empirically and conceptually. This does not mean we are forced into an either/or situation, having to choose between a philosophical-cognitivist approach toward the emotions that lacks any sense of the body's implication in the affects, or a scientific, anticognitivist, "affect program" type of approach that valorizes the role of corporeal processes but strips the organism of intentionality. Emotions appear to be at once intentional and corporeal behaviors involving the organism's embodied disposition to act toward the objects in its world, and an adequate account of them will need to do justice to this.

[43] James A. Russell, "Is There Universal Recognition of Emotion from Facial Expression? A Review of the Cross-Cultural Studies," *Psychological Bulletin* 115 (1994): 102–41. Ekman replied to Russell's critique in "Strong Evidence for Universals in Facial Expressions: Reply to Russell's Mistaken Critique," *Psychological Bulletin* 115 (1994): 268–87; and Russell replied in turn in "Facial Expressions of Emotion: What Lies beyond Minimal Universality?" *Psychological Bulletin* 118 (1995): 379–91. See also Russell and Fernandez-Dols, *The Psychology of Facial Expression*, for a useful history of the theory linking facial expression to emotion, a statement of the theory's fundamental assumptions, and an assessment of the debate with Ekman. In 1976 Ekman and Friesen made the photographs they had used in their judgment studies available in slide form in *Pictures of Facial Affect*, and in 1978 they published a coding scheme for measuring facial movements based on those images in *The Facial Action Coding System*, or FACS for short. In spite of the apparently irrefutable criticisms by Russell and Fridlund of the basic experiments on which it is based, FACS has been used ever since as a standard benchmark in experiments on the relationship between the emotions and facial expression.

[44] Alan J. Fridlund, *Human Facial Expression: An Evolutionary View* (Cambridge, 1997), 286–93; hereafter abbreviated *HFE*. Cf. Alan J. Fridlund, "The New Ethology of Human Facial Expression," in Russell and Fernandez-Dols, *The Psychology of Facial Expression,* 103–29. For Ekman's replies to Fridlund see appendix. For a valuable recent assessment of the Ekman-Fridlund debate that finds very little evidence for the emotion-facial expression link presumed by Ekman, see Brian Parkinson, "Do Facial Movements Express Emotions or Communicate Motives?" *Personality and Social Psychology Review* 9, no. 4 (2005): 278–311. I thank the author for allowing me to see a preprint of his paper and for a helpful exchange of communications.

Fridlund and Russell went on to propose instead that facial movements or displays should be viewed not as expressions of unintentional, hardwired, discrete internal states leaking out into the external world, but as evolved, meaningful behaviors designed to communicate motives in an ongoing interpersonal context or transaction. As Fridlund has put it: "Displays are specific to intent and context, rather than derivatives or blends of a small set of fundamental emotional displays . . . Instead of there being six or seven displays of 'fundamental emotions' (e.g., anger), there may be one dozen or one hundred 'about to aggress' displays appropriate to the identities and relationships of the interactants, and the context in which the interaction occurs" (*HFE*, 128). From this perspective, humans and other animals produce facial movements or displays when it is strategically advantageous for them to do so and not at other times, because facial behaviors are relational or communicative signals that take into account the presence (real or imagined) of other organisms. Deception is thus regarded as omnipresent in nature and potentially highly advantageous for the displayer, not something that covers over the hidden truth of authentic feeling (*HFE*, 137–39). Studies of "audience effects," showing, for example, that Olympic Gold Medalists produce many facial expressions during the medal ceremony but smile almost exclusively when interacting with the audience and officials, have been held to confirm the transactional character of facial movements.[45] Fridlund characterizes his position as a "paralanguage" theory of facial expression in order to emphasize that in humans the role of facial movements is not to express inner emotions but to accompany and supplement speech.

Griffiths in *What Emotions Really Are* made no reference to Fridlund and Russell's 1994 criticisms of Ekman's experiments. More recently, however, he has acknowledged their work. Indeed, he now characterizes the paralanguage theory of facial expression as the main contemporary alternative to the affect program theory. But it is a sign of the allure of the Tomkins-Izard-Ekman position that Griffiths not only continues to cite without critical comment the disputed Ekman-Friesen Japanese-American study, but still defends the validity of the affect program approach by arguing on theoretical grounds that some veridical facial signs that have evolved in nature provide what he characterizes as "*hard to fake*" signals of underlying emotions. In other words, he assumes, as the affect-program people do, that there is a "state" inside the individual that, in the natural course of things, will show itself on the outside, especially the face, and that when it does it is a

---

[45] See especially in this regard J. M. Fernandez-Dols and M. Ruiz-Belda, "Spontaneous Facial Behavior during Intense Emotional Episodes: Artistic Truth and Optical Truth," in Russell and Fernandez-Dols, *The Psychology of Facial Expression*, 255–94. Fridlund appeals to the notion of "implicit sociality" to explain why subjects who are alone may produce emotional signals, the idea being that even when we are alone we are often engaged in imaginary social interactions of various kinds.

true exhibition of the emotion—precisely the point at issue in Fridlund and Russell's critiques.[46]

One of the latest entries in the field of emotion studies is Jesse Prinz's *Gut Reactions: A Perceptual Theory of Emotions* (2004), in which he puts forward a version of the affect program theory. Prinz's stated aim is to broker a reconciliation between the cognitivists (or intentionalists) on the one hand and the anticognitivists (or antiintentionalists) on the other by proposing that emotions involve both bodily responses and appraisals—but the appraisals are not really cognitive. Because he wants to get appraisal or meaning on the cheap, as it were, he thinks "informational semantics" can provide a plausible account of how this is achieved. The task of informational semantics is to give a nonintentionalist explanation of mental content by assuming that mental states carry information about the world in a reliably occurring way. The contents of our mental states and representations are thus understood as constituted by the lawful relations those contents bear to objects or elements in the external world: our dog concept, for example, is a mental state that is reliably caused by our encounters with dogs and has been acquired—by genetics or learning—for that purpose.[47]

Prinz's favorite example of an unlearned mental content is that of the snake, the perception of which, he suggests, reliably and naturally triggers a bodily fear response the further perception or representation of which connotes danger. For Prinz, the bodily response to snakes does not itself constitute the emotion of fear. Nor can fear be specified in terms of its particular object, the snake, as cognitivists might claim. Rather, the emotion is the mental state or content that reliably represents the property of something, here the snake, being dangerous *to us.* Emotions are therefore "gut reactions" that represent "core relational themes" through the perception of bodily changes, but the perceptions and representa-

[46] Paul E. Griffiths, "Emotion and Expression," *International Encyclopedia of the Social and Behavioral Sciences*, ed. Neil J. Smelser and Paul B. Baltes (Amsterdam and New York, 2001), 4433–37. In another article, Griffiths notes the possibility of refuting the experiments on "audience effects" by appealing to Ekman's notion of display rules, a notion that depends on the distinction between the emotion process itself, based on an affect program that is triggered automatically and takes no notice of display rules, and the social modulation of emotional expression according to various cultural norms. In this context, Griffiths again uncritically mentions the Ekman-Friesen study of the reaction of Japanese-American students without commenting on Fridlund's critique (Griffiths, "Basic Emotions, Complex Emotions, Machiavellian Emotions," in *Philosophy and the Emotions*, ed. Anthony Hatzimoysis [Cambridge, 2003], 39–67).

[47] Jesse J. Prinz, *Gut Reactions: A Perceptual Theory of Emotion* (Oxford, 2004); hereafter abbreviated *GR*. For the claims of informational semantics Prinz draws chiefly on Fred Dretske, *Knowledge and the Flow of Information* (Cambridge, Mass., 1981); and idem, "Misinformation," in *Belief: Form, Content and Function*, ed. R. Bogdan, (Oxford, 1986), 17–36. See also Prinz, "The Duality of Content," *Philosophical Studies* 100 (2000): 1–34; and idem, *Furnishing the Mind: Concepts and Their Perceptual Basis* (Cambridge, Mass., 2002).

tions don't involve semantically complex mental states or even cognitions of a more primitive kind. They don't involve cognition at all. Instead, the perceptions and representations are mental states comparable to states in our familiar sensory systems, such as vision: they are perceptions of our relationships to the world that can be explained in materialist-evolutionary terms. In a summary statement of his position Prinz observes:

> Consider the chain of events leading to fear. Something dangerous occurs. That thing is perceived by the mind. This perception triggers a constellation of bodily changes. These changes are registered by a further state: a bodily perception. The bodily perception is directly caused by bodily changes, but it is indirectly caused by the danger that started the whole chain of events. It carries information about danger by responding to changes in the body. That further state is fear. This is just like the somatic theories [of emotion] . . . with a new story about the semantic properties of the bodily perception.
>
> If this proposal is right, it shows that emotions can represent core relational themes without explicitly describing them. Emotions track bodily states that reliably cooccur with important organismic-environmental relations, so emotions reliably cooccur with important organismic-environmental relations. Each emotion is both an internal body monitor and a detector of dangers, threats, losses, or other matters of concern. Emotions are gut reactions; they use our bodies to tell us how we are faring in the world. (*GR*, 69)[48]

It would take me too far afield to offer a comprehensive assessment of Prinz's theory. But it can be argued that the above statement involves a large number of questionable assumptions and claims the failure of any of which would suffice to bring down the whole structure. For example, Prinz's position commits him to the idea that each emotion is accompanied by a distinct pattern of bodily change. In proof of this view he cites an experiment by Levenson, Ekman, and Friesen (1990) in which subjects were asked to deliberately assume or "pose" facial expressions that, it was stated, had been independently found to co-occur with emotional states (*GR*, 73). The subjects were then asked to report on their emotions while various of their physiological responses were measured. Levenson and his colleagues concluded that the discrete emotions the subjects reported experiencing were well correlated with distinct physiological patterns. But the

---

[48] Cf. Jesse J. Prinz, "Emotion, Psychosemantics, and Embodied Appraisals," in *Philosophy and the Emotions*, ed. Anthony Hatzimoysis (Cambridge, 2003), 69–86; and idem, "Embodied Emotions," in *Thinking about Feeling: Contemporary Philosophers of Emotion*, ed. Robert C. Solomon (Oxford, 2004), 44–58. Prinz argues against Griffiths that emotions constitute a single "natural kind" by suggesting, in terms derived from informational semantics, that the so-called higher or cognitive emotions, including shame, are evolved embodied appraisals that have been "recalibrated" by judgments to represent different relations to the environment, in rather the same way that coughing, which is used to clear the throat, can be recalibrated by a spy to serve as a secret code for communicating with an accomplice (*GR*, 99). Prinz appears to adopt a version of associationism to explain recalibration.

claim that the facial expressions the subjects were asked to pose had been independently found to correlate with distinct emotions was precisely the point at issue in Russell's 1994 critique of Ekman's judgment studies—a critique the validity of which in another section of his book Prinz appears partially to accept (*GR*, 111–15).[49] Moreover, Prinz continues to endorse Ekman's distinction between biologically given emotions and the display rules that influence their cultural expression, citing without critical discussion the very experiment by Ekman and Friesen on American-Japanese students that Fridlund has shown was misreported (*GR*, 137). When Prinz does mention Fridlund's critique of Ekman at a different point in his book it is only to rebut him by arguing that facial expressions may well serve to communicate our intended actions, as Fridlund proposes, but this is because they are naturally linked to the underlying emotions that typically accompany those actions—again the point at issue in Fridlund's critique (*GR*, 111). Finally, there is reason to think the materialist "informational semantics" theory on which Prinz's "embodied appraisal" theory centrally depends is incoherent, because it cannot help assuming the intentionalism or meaning it is trying to avoid.[50]

Objectless Emotions

All this may be summed up by saying that the affect program theory in various guises dominates American psychology and related fields today even though its fundamental assumptions and basic evidence cannot withstand critical scrutiny, which is to say that the antiintentionalist position on the emotions cannot be coherently sustained.[51] When we turn back to Sedgwick's views on

[49] Robert W. Levenson, Paul Ekman, and Wallace V. Friesen, "Voluntary Facial Action Generates Emotion-Specific Autonomic Nervous System Activity," *Psychophysiology* 27 (1990): 363–84. For a critique of the 1990 study by Levenson, Ekman, and Friesen, see appendix.

[50] For a valuable critique of informational semantics see Jason Bridges, "Does Informational Semantics Commit Euthyphro's Fallacy?" *Noûs* 60 (2006): 522–47. Bridges argues that informational semantics commits one of the most elementary of philosophical errors, discussed by Socrates, of simultaneously and contradictorily offering a constitutive and a causal analysis of mental content, such that its attempt to give a naturalistic or causal account of intention is doomed to failure. My thanks to the author for allowing me to read his paper before its posting on the web and for helpful exchanges on the topic of informational semantics. My thanks also to James Conant for alerting me to Bridges's work and for many fruitful discussions on topics relevant to my concerns.

[51] "[F]or certain classes of clearly dangerous or clearly valuable stimuli in the internal or external environment," neuroscientist Antonio Damasio writes, "evolution has assembled a matching answer in the form of emotion. That is why, in spite of the infinite variations to be found across cultures, among individuals, and over the course of a life span, we can predict with some success that certain stimuli will produce certain emotions. (That is why you can say to a colleague, 'Go tell her that: she will be so happy to hear it')." Antonio Damasio, *The Feeling of What Happens: Body and Emotion in the Making of Consciousness* (New York, 1999), 54. Damasio implies that the colleague's reaction will automatically follow

emotion, it might be argued that her endorsement of the affect-program theory is tactical, in that it serves as a useful corrective when it is directed against literary critics who treat the affects as a unitary category "with a unitary history and unitary politics" (*TF*, 110) and who automatically reject the existence of qualitative differences between the emotions. It might also be argued that her position is justified as a corrective to the tendency among today's literary critics and theorists, for which she also reproaches them, to adopt a reflexive or routine antibiologism that treats any neurobiological account of the affects as suspect and that again, to her mind, prevents them from accepting the idea that distinct emotions exist. More generally, it might be suggested that Tomkins's affect program theory serves Sedgwick's critical purposes because it provides her with a postmodernist theory of the subject as defined by multiplicity and contingency while also allowing her to step to the side of the tendency of deconstruction to analyze nonlinguistic phenomena, such as the affects, in linguistic terms, and above all to think past Foucault's "repressive hypothesis" by focusing on shame as an affect that according to Tomkins precedes prohibition and the Oedipus complex. Moreover, there can be no doubt that Sedgwick is genuinely attracted to Tomkins as a writer and is interested in drawing attention to the creativity of a thinker who was working at a time in the early development of cybernetics when the emotions were largely neglected. Nevertheless, Sedgwick's commitment to Tomkins's theory can hardly be allowed to stand unchallenged in the light of the many theoretical and empirical problems that as I have shown are encountered by the anticognitivist, affect program model.[52] As a matter of fact Sedgwick admits that she has

---

from the stimulus and won't depend on cognition or appraisal. But she won't be pleased unless she understands the information, and if she understands it, she's already doing cognition. In a similar spirit, Sedgwick (with Adam Frank) dismisses the cognitivist approach to the emotions, as represented by Schachter and Singer and, more recently, Ann Cvetkovich in *Mixed Feelings: Feminism, Mass Culture, and Victorian Sensationalism* (New Brunswick, N.J., 1992), by claiming that it is counterintuitive. "So ask yourself this," she writes: "How long does it take you after being awakened in the night by (a) a sudden loud noise or (b) gradual sexual arousal to cognitively 'analyze' and 'appraise' 'the current state of affairs' well enough to assign the appropriate *quale* to your emotion? That is, what is the temporal lag from the moment of sleep interruption to the ('subsequent') moment when you can judge whether what you're experiencing is luxuriation or terror? No, it doesn't take either of us very long, either" (*TF,* 113). But why does she assume that her reaction is not cognitive just because it happens fast?

[52] Isobel Armstrong adopts a view of Sedgwick's and Tomkins's affect theory not unlike mine in her interesting book, *The Radical Aesthetic* (New York, 1995), 105–7. In *The Secret History of Emotions: From Aristotle's Rhetoric to Modern Brain Sciences* (Chicago, 2006), Daniel M. Gross opposes a "psychosocial" account of the passions to modern scientific interpretations of the emotions. The terms of his analysis differ from mine, but his comments on the reductive scientism of the dominant emotion paradigm associated with the work of Paul Ekman and Antonio Damasio are welcome. For related criticisms of Ekman and Damasio, see John McClain Watson, "From Interpretation to Identification: Facial Images in the Sciences of Emotion," *History of the Human Sciences* 17 (2004): 29–51.

not asked herself whether she really believes Tomkins's hypothesis that there is a "kind of affective table of the elements, comprising nine components, infinitely re-combinable but rooted in the human body in nine distinctive and irreducible ways. At some level we have not demanded even of ourselves that we ascertain whether we believe this hypothesis to be true; we have felt that there was so much to learn first by observing the autonomic nervous system of a routinized dismissal of it in the terms of today's Theory" (*TF*, 117). She therefore justifies her interest in Tomkins's work on the grounds that she wants to use it to challenge what she views as the dead end of current postmodernist theory, not because she is sure Tomkins's claims are actually correct.

But what are the general implications of the antiintentionalist or anticognitivist theory of the emotions? In my view, what is most interesting about the theory is the way it makes it a delusion to say that you are happy because your child got a job, or sad because your mother died, for the simple reason that your child's get-ting a job or your mother's death are merely triggers for your happiness or sad-ness, which are themselves innate affect programs that could in principle be trig-gered by anything else. Tomkins, Sedgwick, and the other affect program theorists thus hold that the affects are inherently objectless because they are bodily responses, like an itch: I laugh when I'm tickled, but I'm not laughing at *you*. As Nathanson puts it, the affects "bear no intrinsic relation to any triggering source . . . If we are frightened, some other mechanism will have to tell us what has become not just too much, but more too much. Tomkins describes this char-acteristic of the affect system by noting that the affects are completely free of in-herent meaning or association to their triggering source. There is nothing about sobbing that tells us anything about the steady-state stimulus that has triggered it; sobbing itself has nothing to do with hunger or cold or loneliness. Only the fact that we grow up with an increasing experience of sobbing lets us form some idea about its meaning."[53]

Thus for Tomkins the paradigm of the affects is the miserable neonate who cries without knowing why or what can be done about it. For him, free-floating anxiety, of the kind one might attribute to the wailing newborn, is a paradigm of the affects precisely because it *is* free-floating and hence can be experienced as such, without relation to an object or cognition: though we may search to provide the anxiety with an object, there is no object to which it inherently belongs. For Freud, free-floating anxiety is only apparently free from the object, since the latter is not absent but only repressed. For Tomkins the anxiety really is free, and the at-tribution to it of an object is an illusion. The point for him is not to define the af-fects in terms of cognitively defined causes and consequences but as intention-less states. For Griffiths also the existence of so-called objectless emotions, such

[53] Donald Nathanson, *Shame and Pride: Affect, Sex, and the Birth of the Self* (New York, 1992), 66.

as certain forms of depression, elation, and anxiety, argues for the idea that the emotions are undetermined by beliefs (*WERA*, 28). As he puts it: "The affect program phenomena are a standing example of the emotional or passionate. They are sources of motivation not integrated into the system of beliefs or desires. The characteristic properties of the affect program states, their informational encapsulation, and their involuntary triggering, necessitate the introduction of a concept of mental state separate from the concepts of belief and desire" (*WERA*, 243). Or as he also writes: "The psychoevolved emotions occur in a particularly informationally encapsulated modular subsystem of the mind/brain. The processes that occur therein, the 'beliefs' of the system and the 'judgements' it makes, are not beliefs and judgements of the person in the traditional sense, any more than the 'beliefs' and 'judgements' of the balance mechanisms fed by the inner ear."[54]

So my ability to give a reason for my feeling something must be a mistake, because what I feel is just a matter of my physiological condition. This is a core materialist claim, and the affect program theory is therefore a materialist theory that displaces or suspends considerations of intentionality and meaning in order to produce an account of the affects as inherently organic in nature. So that if Sedgwick herself appears to offer a social-specular theory of shame based on the relations between self and other, the deeper significance of her adoption of the antiintentionalist or trigger model of affect seems to be that the subject does not need a world outside himself at all. Her theory of affect therefore appears to give primacy to the feelings of a subject without a psychology and without an external world.

Here an objection might be raised: Is this really an accurate account of Sedgwick's theory of shame? Doesn't Sedgwick say that "shame both derives from and aims toward sociability" (*TF*, 37)? And isn't the whole point of shame for her that it is an intersubjective state involving thwarted cathexes of interest in or desire toward the (m)other? It is certainly true that according to Sedgwick the affect of shame has features that distinguish it from most of the other affects. In particular, she suggests that shame is the exemplary affect for affect theory precisely because, like contempt and disgust but unlike the other primary affects, it requires or produces "figure/ground relations, the function of what Tomkins calls the 'cognitive antenna' of a theory" (*TF*, 116). By this she means that shame isn't activated by a certain "frequency of neural firing per unit time," represented by the straight line of some (positive, negative, or zero) slope, as are the affects of startle, fear, interest, anger, distress, and joy, but by the "drawing of a boundary line or barrier, the 'introduc[tion]' of a particular boundary or frame into an analog continuum.' That is, shame involves a Gestalt, the duck to interest's (or enjoyment's) rabbit." "Without positive affect," Sedgwick writes, "there can be no shame: only

---

[54] P. E. Griffiths, "The Degeneration of the Cognitive Theory of Emotions," *Philosophical Psychology* 2, no. 3 (1989): 298.

a scene that offers you enjoyment or engages your interest can make you blush" (*TF*, 116). Shame, Sedgwick thus suggests, provides the "'cognitive antenna'" for affect theory because of the capacity of its digitalizing mechanism to "'punctuat[e the system] as distinct,'" to serve as a "switch point for the individuation of imaging systems, of consciousness, of bodies, of theories, of selves—an individuation that decides not necessarily an identity, but a figuration, distinction, or mark of punctuation" (*TF*, 116–17).

But do these specific, brilliantly described features of shame pose a challenge to my general claim that Sedgwick's is an antiintentionalist, materialist account of the affects? I don't think so. It seems to me what remains crucial for her is the notion that the affects are inherently nonteleological and hence radically foreign to the means-end instrumentality of the drives. It is the radical contingency, indeed randomness of an emotion's relation to the object—our tendency to be wrong about our objects and wishes—that interests her politically, the way in which the affect program theory provides a site for "resistance to teleological presumptions of the many sorts historically embedded in the disciplines of psychology" (*TF*, 100). She is referring especially to the heterosexist teleologies so pervasive in American psychology, although she acknowledges that Tomkins's affect theory cannot guarantee resistance to such teleologies, as the continued heterosexism of some of his followers demonstrates.[55] If we are to take seriously her claim that the affects do not conform to the means-end instrumentality and teleology of the drives, we have to assume that this is also true of shame.[56] As Sedgwick puts it, shame is not a "discrete intrapsychic structure, but a kind of free radical that (in different people and in different cultures) attaches to and permanently intensifies or alters the meaning of—of almost anything" (TF, 62). In short, it seems that shame belongs to the same structure of nonintentionality as the other affects, and indeed to the same materialist paradigm.[57] And so apparently does guilt, since Tomkins treats the feeling of guilt not as an independent emotion involving the idea of unconscious intention, or identification with the aggressor, but as a modification or "phenotype" of shame and hence as independent of the intentionalist or means-end structure of the drives.[58] Survivor guilt, defined as "about do-

[55] See *TF*, 119, n. 3, where she criticizes the heterosexism of Tomkins's most prominent disciple, Donald Nathanson.

[56] In a recent interview Sedgwick has remarked that Tomkins's sense of the autotelic nature of "several important" affects "seems to have become a ground of my aesthetics, such as they are" (*RS*, 261), without saying whether she thinks shame belongs to this group. Presumably it does.

[57] See the appendix for some further comments on this aspect of Sedgwick's discussion of Tomkins's affect program theory.

[58] Tomkins says that shyness, shame, and guilt are not distinguished from each other at the level of emotion, but are one and the same affect. He suggests that it is the differences in the other components that accompany the experience of shame that make the phenomenological experiences of shyness, shame, and guilt different (*AIC*, 2:119; see also "QPM," 326–37).

ing, about what you have done," therefore tends under the influence of Tomkins's ideas, to be reinterpreted by trauma theorists as survivor shame, as a concern with "being, with what you are."[59]

And now it begins to become clear that what is at stake in the general valorization of shame and depreciation of guilt is a shift of attention away from questions of human agency to questions about the attributes of a subject, a subject that can incidentally attach itself to objects but which has no essential relation or intention toward them. The effect is to replace the idea of the meaning of a person's intentions and actions, which until now has informed theories of guilt, with the idea of the primacy of a person's affective experiences, or to put this slightly differently, the idea of the primacy of personal differences. The significance of such a development is the topic of my next and final section.

The Primacy of Personal Differences

In Tomkins's affect program theory, shame is induced when the subject's curiosity about another person is barred by that person's indifference or rejection, an indifference or rejection that draws the line between self and other and induces the subject's characteristic lowered face, averted gaze, and flush. Sedgwick's work on shame helps bring out the identitarian implications of Tomkins's ideas. Her approach is informed and indeed complicated by her "intransigent fascination" (*TF*, 3) with the concept of performativity as that notion has been elaborated by Jacques Derrida, Judith Butler, and many others, including herself. She observes in this regard that the "performative" carries the authority of two quite different discourses, that of the theater on the one hand, and that of speech act theory and deconstruction on the other. The stretch between theatrical and deconstructive meanings of the performative, she writes, spans the "*extroversion* of the actor (aimed entirely outward toward the audience)" and the "*introversion* of the signifier (if 'I apologize' only apologizes, 'I sentence' only sentences, and so on)" (*TF*, 7). She suggests that Michael Fried's opposition between theatricality and absorption seems "custom-made for this paradox about 'performativity': in its deconstructive sense performativity signals absorption; in the vicinity of the stage, however, the performative is the theatrical" (*TF*, 7).

However, in Sedgwick's analysis these oppositions do not line up in any simple way. In particular, the notion of absorption is itself conceptualized by her in dramaturgical terms, as when she describes Henry James's relation to his younger authorial selves, in his prefaces to the New York edition of his works, as one in

---

[59] Andrew M. Stone, "The Role of Shame in Post-Traumatic Stress Disorder," *Journal of Orthopsychiatry* 62 (1992), 133.

which James, the actor, interacts with his former selves as if they, too, were actors on a stage. That interaction, which takes place not along the "theatrical" axis between James and the audience in front of the stage, but along the "absorptive" axis between James and all the other personages behind the curtain, is described by Sedgwick as a shamefully engrossed, homoerotic performance in which James does not attempt to merge with his younger selves but preserves a spectatorial distance or difference from them. As she writes: "James certainly displays no desire whatever to become once again the young and mystified author of his early productions. To the contrary, the very distance of these inner self-figurations from the speaking self of the present is marked, treasured and in fact eroticized. Their distance (temporal, figured as intersubjective, figured in turn as spatial) seems, if anything, to constitute the relished internal space of James's absorbed subjectivity . . . The speaking self of the Prefaces does not attempt to merge with the potentially shaming or shamed figurations of its younger self, younger fictions, younger heroes; its attempt is to love them. That love is shown to occur both in spite of shame and, more remarkably, through it" ("QP," 8).[60] For Sedgwick, the shamefully pleasurable-erotic relation between James and his earlier selves, at once identificatory *and* identity-transforming, deconstituting *and* individuating, takes place on the basis of an antimimetic (or disidentificatory) sense of personal difference and distinction.

The importance of personal difference in Sedgwick's account of shame is made explicit in Douglas Crimp's discussion of her work when he takes her statement, "'People are different from each other,'" as axiomatic for all of her writing and what he has learned from it: "[T]he ethical necessity of developing ever finer tools for encountering, upholding, and valuing other's differences—or better, differences and singularities—nonce-taxonomies, as she wonderfully names such tools."[61] On this basis, Crimp contests the charge of voyeurism so often leveled against the films of Andy Warhol by claiming that the latter's movies don't set out to titillate the viewer by shaming and humiliating the film star (for example, Mario Montez, in *Blow Job* and other movies), but are ethical because they give visibility

---

[60] Similarly, in another passage she states: "The writing subject's seductive bond with the unmerged but unrepudiated 'inner' child seems, indeed, to be the condition of that subject's having an interiority at all, a spatialized subjectivity that can be characterized by absorption. Or perhaps I should say: it is a condition of his *displaying* the spatialized subjectivity that can be characterized by absorption. For the spectacle of James's performative absorption appears only in relation (though in a most complex and unstable relation) to the setting of his performative theatricality; the narcissistic/shame circuit between the writing self and its 'inner child' intersects with that other hyperbolic and dangerous narcissistic circuit, figured as theatrical performance, that extends outward between the presented and expressive face and its audience" (*TF*, 44).

[61] Douglas Crimp, "Mario Montez, for Shame," in *Regarding Sedgwick: Essays on Queer Culture and Critical Theory,* ed. Stephen M. Barber and David L. Clark (New York, 2002), 57; hereafter abbreviated "*RS*."

to "queer differences and singularities" (*RS*, 58). Central to Crimp's argument is the idea that the spectator's discomfort with Warhol's film techniques of cruelty and exposure is not a function of the viewer's unconscious identification or merger with the person on the screen but of the viewer's experience of difference. For according to Crimp, what one adopts in the contagion of shame is not the other's shame but only the latter's vulnerability to being shamed, so that the contagion works by highlighting personal difference. Treating this as the crux of the matter in Warhol's films, Crimp suggests that in the act of taking on the shame that is properly someone else's, I simultaneously feel my utter separateness from even that person whose shame it initially was: "In taking on the shame, I do not share in the other's identity. I simply adopt the other's vulnerability to being shamed. In this operation, most importantly, the other's difference is preserved; it is not claimed as my own. In taking on or taking up his or her shame, I am not attempting to vanquish his or her otherness. I put myself in the place of the other only insofar as I recognize that I too am prone to shame" (*RS*, 65). We might put it that the viewer does not identify or merge with the protagonist of the film but functions as a spectator or witness for the other's shameful mortification by preserving his distance intact. It is in these spectatorial, antimimetic terms that Barber and Clark appear to endorse Crimp's arguments: "In Montez's sad eyes, each viewer sees himself or herself; but this is no mirror-stage, and Montez is hardly a transparent medium of reflection. Instead, it is his radical opacity, his blazoning singularity that turns the viewer's gaze back upon itself. Caught up in this shaming nexus, Montez's 'difference is preserved,' his embarrassed indignity broadcasting another and finer dignity that Crimp names 'queer'" (*RS*, 29–30). For Sedgwick and her followers, then, the politico-ethical value of shame's contagiousness lies in its identity-transforming potential: whereas you can't feel guilty for another's actions (or fantasies), you can be changed by the shame of another, not because you share the other's shame *but because you don't*: what you share, rather, is a vulnerability to the triggering of a shame-induced identity-transforming experience that is all your own. Thus Crimp observes that when the viewer encounters the shaming of someone in Warhol's films, "we remain there with our disquiet—which is, after all, what? It is our encounter, on the one hand, with the absolute difference of another, his or her 'so-for-realness,' and, on the other hand, with the other's shame, both the shame that extracts his or her 'so-for-realness' from the already-for-real performativity of Warhol's performers, and the shame that we accept as also ours, but curiously also ours alone. I am thus not 'like' Mario, but the distinctiveness that is revealed in Mario invades me— 'floods me,' to use Sedgwick's word—and my own distinctiveness is revealed simultaneously. I, too, feel exposed" (*RS*, 67). (It's as if the uncanniness of the mimesis is fended off by a disidentificatory gesture and the assertion of difference. Indeed, some authors use Tomkins's work to theorize identification (or empathy) as a mode of "affective resonance" such that in the empathetic process one person's emotional experiences set up the requisite stimulus density to automatically trigger the same built-in affect in the other. Identification is thus defined antimimetically as a kind of emotional mirroring between two independent identities, not mimetically as an affective immersion that blurs the boundaries between self and other.) [62]

Shame thereby emerges for Sedgwick and her admirers as a means for ensuring each identity's absolute difference from the other.[63] It does this, moreover, by avoiding the moralisms associated with the "repressive hypothesis" on which the Freudian notion of guilt, including the concept of survivor guilt, depends. For Sedgwick, the "great usefulness" of thinking about shame comes from its "potential *distance* from the concepts of guilt and repression, hence from the stressed epistemologies and bifurcated moralisms entailed in every manifestation of what Foucault referred to as the repressive hypothesis" ("QP," 8).[64] The radical contingency of the shame experience—the capacity of shame, according to Tomkins's shame theory, to attach to any aspect of the self—means that shame avoids the

---

[62] See Michael Franz Basch, "The Concept of Affect: A Re-examination," *Journal of the American Psychoanalytic Association* (1974): 759–77; and idem, "Empathic Understanding: A Review of the Concept and Some Theoretical Considerations," *Journal of the American Psychoanalytic Association* 31 (1983): 101–26. Likewise Crimp in a discussion of AIDS observes: "[I]s empathy anything we would even want to strive for? Because it seems that empathy only gets structured in relation to sameness, it can't get constructed in relation to difference" ("'The AIDS Crisis Is Not Over': A Conversation with Gregg Bordowitz, Douglas Crimp, and Laura Pinsky," in *Trauma: Explorations in Memory*, ed. Cathy Caruth [Baltimore, 1995], 263).

[63] Thus for Probyn the value of Tomkins's and Sedgwick's model of the affects is precisely that it allows us to understand and reveal our personal singularities by showing us how human beings differentiate (Elspeth Probyn, *Blush: The Faces of Shame*, [Minneapolis, Minn., 2005], 21–22).

[64] In a discussion of the politics of shame that is informed by the work of Silvan Tomkins, Sara Ahmed shows how national declarations of shame for past wrongs not only play a role in the process of reconciliation, but can bring national identity into existence by subordinating notions of individual guilt and responsibility to the collectivity. She cites a passage from a speech by the Governor-General of Australia apologizing for crimes against the Aboriginal people: "'It should, I think, be apparent to all well-meaning people that true reconciliation between the Australian nation and its indigenous peoples is not achievable in the absence of acknowledgment by the nation of the wrongfulness of the past dispossession, oppression and degradation of the Aboriginal peoples. That is not to say that individual Australians who had no part in what was done in the past should feel or acknowledge personal guilt. It is simply to assert our identity as a nation and the basic fact that national shame, as well as national pride, can and should exist in relation to past acts and omissions, at least when done and made in the name of the community or with the authority of government.'" "But in allowing us to feel bad, does shame also allow us *to feel better*?" Ahmed goes on to ask, suggesting that the desire to feel better through the public discourse of shame displaces the recognition of injustice. Sara Ahmed, *The Cultural Politics of Emotion* (Edinburgh, 2004), 101–21. In other words, the apology functions as a technique for producing national identity for its members as individuals who feel shame yet also "feel better," and it does so by forestalling debate over what harms have been done, who or what has been responsible, and the nature of the injustice.

generational lockstep of the guilty oedipal scenario by allowing for the radical contingency and indeterminacy of experience (*TF*, 147).[65] Shame thus transforms and produces identity without any moralism and indeed without giving identity any specific content. Shame interests Sedgwick politically, because "it generates and legitimates the place of identity—the question of identity—at the origin of the impulse to the performative, but does so without giving that identity space the standing of an essence" (*TF*, 64). In short, shame is a technology for creating queer identity as the experience of pure difference: "Part of the interest of shame is that it is an affect that delineates identity—but delineates it without defining it or giving it content. Shame, as opposed to guilt, is a bad feeling that does not attach to what one does, but what one is [. . .] Shame is a bad feeling attaching to what one is: one therefore *is something*, in experiencing shame. The place of identity, the structure 'identity,' marked by shame's threshold between sociability and introversion, may be established and naturalized in the first instance *through shame*" ("QP," 12).[66]

Posthistoricism

All this suggests that Sedgwick's work on shame—and by extension the work of those others who also adopt a version of Tomkins's affect program theory—can be seen to conform to a posthistoricist logic, as the latter has recently been analyzed by Walter Benn Michaels in *The Shape of the Signifier*, a brilliant examination of developments in artistic, literary, and political theory during the past almost forty years. Michaels argues that when, as has happened in the deconstructive literary criticism and theory associated with the work of Paul de Man and others, an interest in notions of intention and belief gives way to an interest in what a text is without regard to the author's (conscious or unconscious) intention, the result is not only a commitment to the materiality of the text or signifier, but also, by way of that materiality, a commitment to both the subject position and the experience of the reader as the only factors that matter. In other words, the critique of intentionalism that we find in the work of de Man and others becomes the posthistoricist valuation of identity. Differences become intrinsically

---

[65] Although Sedgwick accepts the idea of the very early appearance of the shame response in infancy, she prefers not to emphasize the enduring effects of early shame experiences but the contingency of the affects' relation to objects, a contingency that appears to her to undo the infantile determinism of Freud's psychology (*RS*, 261).

[66] These passages bring out Sedgwick's commitment to an antiessentialist view of the self. She argues that Tomkins's own work is indeed "sublimely alien" to any project of narrating the emergence of a core self of the kind found in the self-help literature inspired by Tomkins's ideas. In short, she credits Tomkins with valorizing the "alchemy of the contingent" in identity (*TF*, 98).

valuable because a concern with disagreements over beliefs and intentions is replaced by a concern with differences in personal experience. The result is that when people have different experiences or feelings, they don't disagree, they just are *different.*

Moreover, Michaels crucially suggests that ideological disputes, or conflicts over beliefs, are inherently universalizing, because whereas we can't disagree about what we feel, we just feel different things, we can and do disagree about what is true, regardless of what we feel, or what our subject position is. Indeed, he suggests that it is only the idea that something that is true must be true for everyone that gives sense to disagreement: thus the belief that some social system is better than another, or that a certain political arrangement such as apartheid is unjust, is intrinsically universal. He notes in this regard that posthistoricist thinkers often treat the appeal to universality as a means to enforce agreement, insisting on the ethnocentric biases such appeals to the universal conceal, for standards of universality are only local. But, he replies, the "fact that people have locally different views about what is universally true in no way counts as a criticism of the universality of the true. Just the opposite; the reason that we cannot appeal to universal truths as grounds for adjudicating our disagreements is just because the idea of truth's universality is nothing but a consequence of our disagreement. The universal does not compel our agreement, rather it is implied by our disagreement; and we invoke the universal not to resolve our disagreement but to explain the fact that we disagree."[67]

The alternative to difference of belief is difference of subject position. The appeal to subject position, or personal feeling, eliminates disagreement because to see or feel things from a different personal perspective is to see the same thing differently but without contradiction. The result of the posthistoricist valorization of the subject position is thus that it dispenses with a universalist logic of conflict as difference of belief in favor of a posthistoricist logic of conflict as difference in subject position or primacy of identity and that accordingly, by disarticulating difference from disagreement, it eliminates disagreement altogether. Michaels's aim is to dismantle such a posthistoricist logic by showing, through readings of art-critical, literary, philosophical, fictional, and other texts, how the replacement of ideological disagreements, or conflicts over belief and meaning, with identitarian differences, or differences in our identities or bodies or histories or languages, produces an indifference to political (or ethical) dispute. Another way of putting

[67] Walter Benn Michaels, *The Shape of the Signifier: 1967 to the End of History* (Princeton, 2004), 31. As Michaels also emphasizes, his position does not involve a commitment to rationality on the model of what Habermas calls "'good reasons.'" According to Michaels, our reasons for believing something always seem good to us; that's what makes them our reasons. His commitment is, rather, to the difference between those things (beliefs and interpretations) that seem to us true or false and for which we can give some reasons and those things that seem to us to require no justification (188, n. 16).

this is to say that the posthistoricist logic Michaels is describing attempts to get rid of the notion of interpretation (or belief or intention) altogether, a collective tendency he regards as a mistake, to say the least.

Sedgwick's original contribution to this development is to show how Tomkins's affect theory lines up with the same posthistoricist logic because it defines the affects as inherently nonintentionalist and indeed materialist in nature. She is not alone among literary critics in defining the affects in this way. Rei Terada, for example, has recently put forward a similarly antiintentionalist or materialist account of the emotions by conjoining the affect program approach inspired by Tomkins with the antiintentionalism and materialism of deconstruction.[68] A similar tendency is at work in Giorgio Agamben's influential study of the ethico-political legacy of the Nazi camps. Agamben differs from Sedgwick and other theorists in that he does not pursue a psychological or postpsychoanalytic analysis of shame. Rather he offers an ontological analysis derived in part—so he claims—from the work of Emmanuel Levinas. Nevertheless, his hostility to the idea of survivor guilt and his privileging of shame depend on ideas about the absence of intention and meaning in shame and shame's concomitant materialization that we find much more brilliantly and indeed responsibly developed in Sedgwick's work. In the next and final chapter I offer a critique of Agamben's account of shame.

[68] "The content [or cognitivist] approach to emotion is currently under siege from many directions. Materialist cognitive science offers more epistemological sophistication . . . As Griffiths protests, [the content approach] has too often excluded feeling-based research on 'affect programs'—automated systems of chemical, reflexive, and other physiological responses that endanger concepts of emotional depth and the division between animal feeling and human emotion" (Rei Terada, *Feeling in Theory: Emotion after the "Death of the Subject"* [Cambridge, Mass., 2001]), 38. Terada links the poststructuralist shift from cognition to affect associated with the work of Paul de Man to the postpsychoanalytic shift from intentionalism to antiintentionalism associated with the work of emotion theorists Tomkins, Ekman, Griffiths, and others, work she uncritically embraces.

CHAPTER FIVE

The Shame of Auschwitz

The Gray Zone

THE ITALIAN philosopher Giorgio Agamben has won widespread recognition and esteem in Europe and the United States for his reflections on political philosophy, ethics, and the law. His *Remnants of Auschwitz: The Witness and the Archive* (1999) offers an analysis of life under extremity as epitomized by Auschwitz.[1] It has gone largely unremarked that a key move in the argument of his book involves the rejection of the notion of survivor guilt and its replacement by a conception of shame. Agamben differs from Sedgwick and the other theorists I have examined so far in that he does not pursue a psychological or postpsychoanalytic interpretation of shame. Rather, he offers an ontological conception of shame in his analysis of the ethico-political legacy of Auschwitz. We shall see that in spite of obvious differences, his approach shares certain features with the work of trauma theorists Shoshana Felman, Dori Laub, and Cathy Caruth, which is to say that, just as in the case of recent writings on PTSD, so in the case of Agamben's *Remnants of Auschwitz,* shame theory and trauma theory overlap.

In *Remnants of Auschwitz*, Agamben moves rapidly, less by way of close readings or sustained demonstration than through a series of formalist-logical-philo-

[1] Giorgio Agamben, *Remnants of Auschwitz: The Witness and the Archive,* trans. Daniel Heller-Roazen (New York, 1999); hereafter abbreviated *RA*. See also Agamben's "The Camp as the 'Nomos' of the Modern," in *Homo Sacer: Sovereign Power and Bare Life*, trans. Daniel Heller-Roazen (Stanford, Calif., 1998), 166–80, for Agamben's adumbration of his concept of the concentration camp as a biopolitical space that reduces humans to the condition of bare or "naked" life without mediation.

logical assertions based on brief analyses of a diverse body of philosophical, testimonial, and legal texts. His argument can be broken down into a number of key claims, which I shall proceed to examine more or less in the order in which they are developed.

As a commentary on the lessons of the Nazi extermination camps, Agamben's general assertion is that almost none of the familiar ethical-political principles of our age have stood the "decisive test" of Auschwitz, from which it follows that there is a need to clear away "almost all the doctrines that, since Auschwitz, have been advanced in the name of ethics" (*RA*, 13). These include ethical ideas associated with Nietzsche, Heidegger, Habermas, Apel, and others. This means that if shame is to emerge as the sentiment that defines the survivor's ethical experience, it, too, must be recast and rethought.

For Agamben, Primo Levi is the preeminent cartographer of this "new *terra ethica*" (*RA,* 69), if for no other reason than that his "gray zone" is an emblem of the breakdown of all the foundational categories and distinctions that have hitherto held sway. Agamben characterizes Levi's gray zone as an area that is "independent of every establishment of responsibility" (*RA*, 21) or "a zone of irresponsibility" (*RA*, 21) because it is one in which "victims become executioners and executioners become victims" (*RA*, 17), or, as he also puts it, "the oppressed becomes oppressor and the executioner in turn appears as victim" (*RA*, 21). It is a "gray, incessant alchemy in which good and evil and, along with them, all the metals of traditional ethics reach their point of fusion" (*RA,* 21). "It is about this above all that the survivors are in agreement," Agamben writes, citing Levi's statement "'No group was more human than any other'" (RA, 17), and Buchenwald survivor David Rousset's observation "'Victim and executioner are equally ignoble; the lesson in the camps is brotherhood in abjection'" (*RA*, 17). Agamben thus suggests that in the gray zone *the positions of victim and oppressor are reversible or interchangeable.*

A great deal in Agamben's analysis turns on this claim. But it is by no means evident that it accurately represents Levi's views. For Levi the gray zone is that zone of complicity or collaboration between the privileged prisoners and the SS in which the "two camps of masters and servants both diverge and converge." It is a zone where the oppressed collaborate through motives of "terror, ideological seduction, servile imitation of the victor, myopic desire for any power whatsoever, even though ridiculously circumscribed in space and time, cowardice, and, finally, lucid calculation aimed at eluding the imposed orders and order."[2] All those motives, Levi explains, come into play in the creation of the gray zone, "whose components are bonded together by the wish to preserve and consolidate established privilege vis-à-vis those without privilege" (*DS*, 43). Among that heteroge-

---

[2] Primo Levi, *The Drowned and the Saved* (New York, 1989), 42, 43; hereafter abbreviated *DS*.

neous mix of motives, Levi mentions the tendency of many of the oppressed to seek power by unconsciously striving to identify with their oppressors, thereby becoming contaminated by them. In a passage I cited in chapter 1 he states of such identification: "This mimesis, this identification or imitation, or exchange of roles between oppressor and victim, has provoked much discussion. True and invented, disturbing and banal, acute and stupid things have been said: it is not virgin terrain; on the contrary it is a badly plowed field, trampled and torn up" (*DS*, 48).

For Levi, the notion of the prisoner's unconscious identification with the aggressor becomes a badly plowed field when the victim-executioner dynamic is used to suggest an equivalence between the two roles. He refuses to judge the prisoners who identified or collaborated with the oppressor, even though, he states, they accrued a quota of guilt that might have been objectively serious. But he does not hesitate to define and judge the criminality of the Nazis. "I am not an expert on the unconscious and the mind's depths, but I do know that few people are experts in this sphere and that these few are the most cautious," he writes. "I do not know, and it does not interest me to know, whether in my depths there lurks a murderer, but I do know that I was a guiltless victim and I was not a murderer. I know that the murderers existed, not only in Germany, and still exist, retired or on active duty, and that to confuse them with their victims is a moral disease or an aesthetic affectation or a sinister sign of complicity; above all, it is a precious service rendered (intentionally or not) to the negators of truth" (*DS*, 48–49). In other words, Levi opposes the conflation between the roles of executioner and victim on which Agamben appears to insist.

Of Rousset's observation, cited by Agamben, that victim and aggressor were equally ignoble and that the lesson of the camps was a lesson in the fraternity of abjection, Levi once remarked that it was a "frightening proposition," adding that the statement was acceptable coming from Rousset, who had been there, but not from Cavani (the filmmaker) and other "aesthetes" who had subsequently explored the notion in their work. He noted in this regard that there was an element of truth in the claim "with due exception made at the level of moral judgment of course, since the executioner is the executioner and the victim the victim"—again suggesting that the two roles ought not to be confused.[3] Levi's remarks were made in response to an interviewer's query about the notion of identification with the aggressor. Levi gave as an example an experience of his own; for when he had returned to Italy after the war he had noticed with "a certain horror" but also

---

[3] Primo Levi, *The Voice of Memory: Interviews, 1961–1987,* ed. Marco Belpoliti and Robert Gordon, trans. Robert Gordon (New York, 2001), 252–53; hereafter abbreviated *VM.* Agamben cites Rousset's statement, in a slightly modified translation, from the Italian version of these interviews, *Converzationi e intervesti, 1963–1987* (Turin, 1997), 216.

some amusement that his spoken German was the German of the SS. He added:

> There was dehumanization on both sides: on one side imposed, on the other more or less chosen. It is a delicate subject, which is spoken about too much and too crudely, whereas it should be treated with extreme care. There is much more one could say, but I have given you some indications. For example, for practical reasons, there was a long chain linking together prisoners and executioners made up of all those prisoners who progressed, who in some way collaborated, and they were many, at least 10 per cent. There was an extensive hierarchy that went from the cleaners all the way to the barrack *Kapos*, who in some instances went over to the other side. This was rare among the Jews, but quite common amongst the criminal prisoners. The dividing line between victim and executioner was thus "blurred": there were executioner-victims and victim-executioners. We thought we were heading for a place of suffering, but one where there would be some solidarity, a united front against the Germans and this was almost never the case. National differences were exacerbated and Italians were treated by all Germans, whether Nazis or not, as *Badogliani* [turncoats or traitors]. The levels of the hierarchy were infinite, there was none of the clear-cut separation you might imagine. (*VM*, 253)

Nothing in this statement suggests to me that Levi saw in the camps a complete leveling of the roles of the SS and the victims. It says that there were "executioner-victims" as well as "victim-executioners," which I interpret to refer in both cases to the prisoners caught up in a system of terror, including the *Kapos*, but not to the members of the SS, who held absolute power and whose responsibility therefore remained clear. There is thus a considerable distance between Agamben's view of the gray zone as a zone of irresponsibility where all the traditional categories of ethics no longer apply and victim and perpetrator form a single homogenous group, and Levi's more nuanced position.[4]

---

[4] In a recent essay informed by Agamben's claim that Auschwitz marks the end of every ethics of conformity to the norm, Roberto Farneti suggests that in Primo Levi's collection of short stories, *I racconti: Storie naturali* (Turin, 1966), Levi imagines a world in which there is "no longer any room for such normative distinctions like the ones between freedom and authority, innocence and culpability, victims and perpetrators." See Robert Farneti, "Of Humans and Other Portentous Beings: On Primo Levi's *Storie naturali*," *Critical Inquiry* 32 (Summer 2006): 740. In my view, however, the opposition between normative, conscious, voluntary, and "fully responsible" human agency (whatever one takes this to mean) on the one hand, and the "mere event" or absence of human action on the other, which governs Farneti's discussion, is overly abstract, even "ideal," producing somewhat forced readings of Levi's subtle, and admittedly sometimes contradictory-seeming, fictional and other writings about life in extremity. Some of Levi's stories that Farneti analyzes appeared in translation in "*The Sixth Day*" *and Other Tales*, trans. Raymond Rosenthal (New York, 1990). I note in this regard that according to Levi's account, the gray zone included not just collaborators but also those in the resistance, such as Eugen Kogon in Buchenwald, whom Levi mentions (*DS*, 45–46). This point is also made by Philippe Mesnard and Claudine Kahan in *Giorgio Agamben á l'Épreuve d'Auschwitz* (Paris, 2001), one of the few works to criticize Agamben on historical, interpretive, and methodological grounds, and one that I have read with profit.

How are we to understand Agamben's representation, or rather misrepresentation, of Levi's thought? Presumably, he is far too intelligent not to realize the need for further clarification. In order to justify his position he insists on the need to distinguish between ethical and juridical categories. He suggests that although "it is not judgment" that finally matters to Levi, yet judgment must also be carried out (*RA*, 17) because when Levi speaks of the need to make the perpetrators pay for their crimes, he is speaking of the need for *legal* judgment. But according to Agamben the law does not exhaust the problem of truth and justice—he mentions the "failure" of the Nuremberg trials in this regard (*RA*, 19). He states that whereas the law is "solely directed toward judgment, independent of truth and justice" (*RA*, 18), the only thing that interests Levi is "what makes judgment impossible: the gray zone in which victims become executioners and executioners become victims" (*RA*, 17). The decisive point for Agamben is that there exists a "non-juridical element of truth" (*RA*, 17) concerning everything that places human action beyond the law—and beyond issues of guilt and responsibility as well, for according to him notions of responsibility and guilt are irremediably contaminated by law (*RA*, 20).[5] Levi's "unprecedented discovery," the gray zone, thus defines a zone of irresponsibility situated "not *beyond* good and evil but rather, so to speak, *before* them" (*RA*, 21). In other words, Agamben argues the need for a new post-Holocaust ethics because of what he views as a constitutive and irreducible impurity, derived from the law, that contaminates all the old ethical categories. It is as if for Agamben only an ethics devoid of the least trace of contamination will suffice—a position that relies on an absolute opposition between purity and impurity in order to condemn all previous moral concepts. This is not a position with which Levi would appear to have had any sympathy, and it is one, as I shall show, that serves several problematic ends.

---

[5] Agamben argues that in ancient times and to this day the gesture of assuming responsibility is genuinely juridical and not ethical: it expresses "nothing noble or luminous" (*RA*, 22) but simply legal obligation. Responsibility and guilt thus express simply "two aspects of legal imputability; it was only later that they were interiorized and moved outside the law. Hence the insufficiency and opacity of every ethical doctrine that claims to be founded on these two concepts" (*RA*, 22). (He claims that this criticism holds for Levinas, who, he suggests, transformed the legal gesture of the *sponsor*, or person who promises in the case of breach of contract to furnish the required service, into the ethical gesture *par excellence*.) To illustrate his point Agamben considers the example of Adolf Eichmann, who pleaded guilty "before God, not the law," whereas the assumption of moral responsibility, Agamben claims, has value only if one is ready to assume the relevant legal consequences. On this basis he asserts that "ethics is the sphere that recognizes neither guilt nor responsibility; it is, as Spinoza knew, the doctrine of the happy life. To assume guilt and responsibility—which can at times be necessary—is to leave the territory of ethics and enter that of law" (*RA*, 24). But this strikes me as an extremely—if not perversely—restrictive concept of guilt, one that depends for whatever force it may have on narrowly philological considerations. One of its effects is to exclude from discussion guilt feelings arising from fantasy, not actuality, and hence to ignore feelings of guilt that lack any relevant legal consequences.

"That Match Is Never Over"

For Agamben, an unusual event in Auschwitz, described by Levi, exemplifies the gray zone in all its horror: a soccer match that was organized one day in 1944 between the SS and the *Sonderkommando*, the special squad of prisoners forced to run the gas chambers and crematoria (*RA*, 25). Noting that this event would never have taken place with any other class of prisoners, Levi observes that it was as if with this particular group the SS could "enter the field on an equal footing, or almost. Behind this armistice one hears satanic laughter: it is consummated, we have succeeded, you no longer are the other race, the anti-race, the prime enemy of the millennial Reich; you are no longer the people who reject idols. We have embraced you, corrupted you, dragged you to the bottom with us. You are like us, you proud people: dirtied with your own blood, as we are. You too, like us and like Cain, have killed the brother. Come, we can play together" (*DS*, 55). Again, there is nothing in Levi's commentary to suggest that the soccer match reduced all the camp inmates to a single population, or that the SS became indistinguishable from the prisoners. What he describes is a scene in which the SS "almost" succeeded in placing a particular group of prisoners on an equal footing with themselves by dragging them down to their own corrupt level.[6] Ignoring Levi's qualifying words, "or almost," which suggest that the roles of the SS and the *Sonderkommando* could never be fully identical, Agamben instead treats the soccer match as an emblem of that conflation between victim and perpetrator which he regards as the true significance of the camps (*RA*, 26).[7]

[6] Deberati Saynal makes a similar point in her "A Soccer Match in Auschwitz: Passing Culpability in Holocaust Criticism," *Representations* 79 (Summer 2002): 1–27. Her criticism that Agamben risks erasing the historical specificity of the camps is well taken. Her emphasis, though, is different from mine. She ignores Agamben's critique of the notion of survivor guilt and his account of shame. Instead, she makes the question of identification the focus of her discussion by suggesting that since Agamben identifies too much with the gray zone, assuming a secondhand culpability for the Holocaust, he has the wrong sort of identificatory-transferential relation to the past. Her argument then takes the form of proposing, following Dominick La Capra's ideas, that Agamben should just adopt a less immersive or appropriative relation to the camps in order to arrive at a more "unbound" ethical engagement, one that recognizes the other's difference from oneself. It is as if she seeks to resolve the mimetic-antimimetic oscillation that, as I have argued, from the late-nineteenth century to the present has structured the modern theory of trauma, by favoring the antimimetic or nonimmersive pole of that oscillation.

[7] Levi's account of the soccer match is taken from the memoir of Miklos Nyiszli, published in English as *Auschwitz: A Doctor's Eyewitness Account* (New York, 1951). Agamben follows Levi in mistakenly identifying Nyiszli as a member of the last special team or squad of Auschwitz, implying that he was a member of the *Sonderkommando*. In fact, he was a Hungarian Jewish physician chosen by Mengele to be his assistant in his medical experiments and to serve as the physician to the *Sonderkommando*. Agamben also says that Nyiszli took part in the soccer match, but Levi merely reports that Nyiszli "attended it"—on these points and the position of Nyizsli in the camp, see Mesnard and Kahan, *Giorgio Agamben á l'Épreuve d'Auschwitz*, 36–40. These authors emphasize too that for Levi the situations of

Agamben makes a further striking yet problematic claim in this regard, which is that the soccer match of Auschwitz is not over—rather, it is still going on: "For we can perhaps think that the massacres are over—even if here and there they are repeated, not so far away from us. But that match is never over; it continues as if uninterrupted. It is the perfect and eternal cipher of the 'gray zone,' which knows no time and is in every place" (RA, 26). Hence the anguish and shame of the survivors is also *our* shame, "the shame of those who did not know the camps and yet, without knowing how, are spectators of that match, which repeats itself in every match in our stadiums, in every television broadcast, in the normalcy of everyday life" (RA, 26). This statement could be interpreted to mean, unexceptionably, that "here and there" versions of the gray zone are taking place today, reappearing in new guises and new sites, at the very center of "everyday" life. The rape camps in Bosnia, or the *zones d'attentes* in French international airports in which foreigners asking for refugee status are detained, are examples cited by Agamben.[8] But he seems to be proposing something far more radical. He appears to believe that if Auschwitz is not over, this is not because it is a historical event that occurred at an earlier time and whose repercussions are still with us, or because new instances of "Auschwitz" can be found in our world and time, but because the Auschwitz that occurred then is a continuing part of our *own personal experience.* The gray zone is *our* gray zone, "our first Circle, from which no confession of responsibility will remove us and in which what is spelled out, minute by minute, is the lesson of the 'terrifying, unsayable and unimaginable banality of evil'" (RA, 21), which is to say that the experience of Auschwitz is just as traumatic for *us* as it was for the original victims. Put slightly differently, Auschwitz for Agamben is a timeless event that we have not forgotten but that still haunts us today, as in our dreams. That is why he suggests that the traumatic nightmares which afflicted Levi and so many other survivors are *our* nightmares too. He writes in connection with Levi's report of his recurrent dream of being back in the camps:

---

the executioners and the victims were not interchangeable, as Agamben claims. They also stress that at the time of the soccer match, the members of the *Sonderkommando* were in fact planning to revolt, which suggests a more complex and ambiguous content to the gray zone than Agamben's homogenizing characterization of it would suggest. In addition, they point out that Nyizsli's position was quite different from that of the *Sonderkommando*: he could speak almost as an equal to Mengele, and his account of the match reveals an element of class snobbery toward the men involved.

[8] Agamben, *Homo Sacer,* 174. Similarly, Primo Levi associates the crimes of Algeria, Vietnam, the Soviet Union, Chile, Argentina, Cambodia, and South Africa with the crimes of Auschwitz (DS, 137). More recently, the journalist Seymour Hersh has invoked the concept of the gray zone to describe the scandalous treatment of Iraqi prisoners in Abu Ghraib prison (Seymour M. Hersh, "Annals of National Security: The Gray Zone," *New Yorker,* May 24, 2004, 38–44).

Auschwitz . . . has never ceased to take place; it is always already repeating itself. This ferocious, implacable experience appears to Levi in the form of a dream . . . [T]he ethical problem has radically changed shape. It is no longer a question of conquering the spirit of revenge in order to assume the past, willing its return for eternity [a reference to Niet-zsche's doctrine of eternal return]; nor is it a matter of holding fast to the unacceptable through resentment [a reference to Jean Améry's ethics of resentment]. What lies before us now is a being beyond acceptance and refusal, beyond the eternal past and the eter-nal present—an event that returns eternally but that, precisely for this reason, is ab-solutely and eternally unassumable. Beyond good and evil lies not the innocence of be-coming but, rather, a shame that is not only without guilt but even without time. (RA, 101–3)[9]

By redescribing Auschwitz not as an event that has passed but as one that is perpetually and eternally present because it has an "ontological consistency" (*RA*, 101) across time and place, Agamben seems to propose a version of the argu-ment proposed by Shoshana Felman, Cathy Caruth, and other trauma theorists to the effect that the trauma of one individual can haunt later generations, so that we who never directly experienced the camps are nevertheless imagined as con-tagiously experiencing or "inheriting" the traumatic memories of those who died long ago. In other words, Agamben appears to subscribe to the by now familiar tendency to collapse history into memory by redescribing, as Walter Benn Michaels has put it, "something we have never known as something we have for-gotten," thereby making the historical past "a part of our own experience."[10] Michaels is especially interested in the identitarian stakes involved in reconceptu-alizing history as memory in these terms, by which he means the way such a reconceptualization functions to make the Holocaust available as a continuing source of identitarian sustenance by imagining that we who were not there can nevertheless be marked by the trauma of the Jews and other victims. When the past of Auschwitz is reimagined as the fabric of one's own actual experience, Michaels suggests, then the past can become the key to *one's own* identity. The application of Michaels's insight to Agamben's ideas is clear, for by imagining that

---

[9] "Unassumable" and "assumable," key words in Agamben's lexicon, are Heideggerian terms from the word "assumption," meaning the free acceptance of something. My thanks to Hent de Vries for several helpful discussions about this and related aspects of Agamben's text.

[10] Walter Benn Michaels, "'You Who Never Was There': Slavery and the New Historicism, Deconstruc-tion and the Holocaust," *Narrative* 4, no. 1 (January 1996), 6. For a superb discussion of the current ten-dency to collapse history into memory and a review of the relevant literature see Kerwin Lee Klein, "On the Emergence of Memory in Historical Discourse," *Representations* 69 (Winter 2000): 127–50. I have criticized Caruth's de Manian account of how the intergenerational transmission of trauma is supposed to work in my *Trauma: A Genealogy* (Chicago, 2000), 284–92. For an impassioned reponse to my cri-tique, see Shoshana Felman, *The Juridical Unconscious: Trials and Traumas in the Twentieth Century* (Cambridge, Mass., 2002), 173–82.

the soccer match is not over for *us*, he is proposing that we who were never there can nevertheless be defined as survivors and inheritors of the trauma and shame of the camps. In other words, what is at stake for Agamben in his characterization of the timelessness of the camps is our alleged subject position as survivors, so that just as the question of our subject position emerged as central to the work of Sedgwick and the other shame theorists discussed in chapter 4, so it emerges as crucial to Agamben's account of shame as well. That is why Agamben can say that what we have survived, and what we today bear witness to, is a "shame that is not only without guilt but even without time" (*RA*, 103).

But what *is* shame for Agamben? How does he conceptualize it? And how is it transmitted? The answer to these questions can be found in what Agamben has to say about testimony, for we shall see that according to him the experience of testimony is also the experience of shame.

The Matter of Testimony

According to Agamben, the ethics that remains after Auschwitz is an ethics of testimony, and the fundamental task of such an ethics is to bear witness to the drowned, lowest, most marginal, barely surviving (and soon to die) type of prisoner, the so-called *Muselmann* or "Muslim" who reveals the horror of "naked life" stripped of all meaningful distinction.[11] His book thus belongs to the growing literature on testimony represented by the work of Felman, Laub, Caruth, LaCapra, and numerous others.

Levi famously stated that the true or complete witnesses to the horror of Auschwitz were not those who by good luck or for other reasons managed to survive, but the "Muslims," those who were the "submerged" or who "touched bottom," who could not speak. Agamben converts Levi's paradox, if we may call it that, into a claim about the inherent meaninglessness of all testimony. In Auschwitz, Levi had strained to understand a sound or word, *mass-klo* or *matisklo*, uttered by a paralyzed three-year-old child whom the prisoners called Hurbinek and who died just before the liberation. It was a sound or word the child repeated again and again but that no one in the camp could interpret. "'It was not, admittedly, always exactly the same word,'" Agamben cites Levi as writing, "'but it was certainly an articulated word; or better, several slightly different articulated words, experimental variations on a theme, on a root, perhaps even on a name'"

---

[11] "At times a medical figure or an ethical category, at times a political limit or an anthropological concept, the *Muselmann* is an indefinite being in whom not only humanity and non-humanity, but also vegetative existence and relation, physiology and ethics, medicine and politics, and life and death continuously pass through each other. This is why the *Muselmann*'s 'third realm' is the perfect cipher of the camp, the non-place in which all disciplinary barriers are destroyed and all embankments flooded" (*RA*, 48).

(*RA*, 38). Agamben observes that Levi and the other prisoners tried to decipher the sound, but that, despite the presence of the diverse languages of Europe in the camp, Herbinek's word remained "obstinately secret" (*RA*, 38). Again, he cites Levi: " 'No, it was certainly not a message, it was not a revelation; perhaps it was his name, if it had ever fallen to his lot to be given a name; perhaps (according to one of our hypotheses) it meant "to eat," or "bread"; or perhaps "meat" in Bohemian, as one of us who knew that language maintained . . . Hurbinek, the nameless, whose tiny forearm—even his—bore the tattoo of Auschwitz; Hurbinek died in the first days of March 1945, free but not redeemed. Nothing remains of him: he bears witness through these words of mine' " (*RA*, 38). For Levi then, in this mournful remembrance, *mass-klo* or *matisklo* was an unknown or difficult to interpret word (or cluster of words) said by a child in a foreign language whose meaning he and his fellow inmates tried but failed to decipher.

But for Agamben the child's sound simply has no meaning at all: "Hurbinek cannot bear witness, since he does not have language (the speech that he utters is a sound that is uncertain and meaningless)" (*RA*, 39). And precisely because it is without meaning—a piece of "non-language" (*RA*, 38)—Hurbinek's sound attests to what cannot be witnessed, to the untestifiable. The sound, *mass-klo* or *matisklo*, thus serves the same function in Agamben's theory of testimony that the breakdown of words in Paul Celan's poetry serves in what Agamben calls Shoshana Felman's "pertinent analysis" (*RA*, 36) of the trauma of the Shoah, which she defines as an "event without witnesses."[12]

But Agamben goes beyond Felman in certain respects. Rather than emphasizing the textual-performative dimension of testimony, as Felman does, he stresses instead the necessary role of the survivor's voice in the testimonial process by claiming that the drowned and the "saved"—those who died and those who survived—cannot be split apart but involve an "impossible dialectic" (*RA*, 120). In other words, survivor and *Muselmann* form an irreducible or inseparable couple. Hurbinek cannot bear witness, because he does not have language. But if Levi bears witness for

---

[12] Felman writes of Celan's poems: "Through their very breakdown, the sounds testify, henceforth, precisely to a knowledge they do not possess . . . But this breakdown of the word, this drift of music and of sound of the song which resists recuperation and which does not know, and cannot own, its meaning, nonetheless reaches a *you*, attains the hearing—and perhaps the question, or the answer, of an Other" (Shoshana Felman and Dori Laub, *Testimony: Crises of Witnessing in Literature, Psychoanalysis, and History* [New York, 1992], 37). Celan's poetry has the same status in Agamben's analysis as it does in Felman's, serving him as another example of the "inarticulate babble" or "background noise" or nonlanguage that constitutes testimony (*RA*, 37–38). Agamben observes: "This is the language of the 'dark shadows' that Levi heard growing in Celan's poetry, like a 'background noise'; this is Hurbinek's non-language (*mass-klo*, *matisklo*) that has no place in the libraries of what has been said or in the archive of statements" (*RA*, 162). However, Agamben accuses Felman of failing adequately to comprehend the structure of testimony, on the grounds that she aestheticizes it by imagining that testimony can speak to us beyond its words or melody, like the unique performance of a song (*RA*, 36).

Hurbinek by proxy by lending him his own voice, he does so, Agamben maintains, through words that are structured by the same irreducible aporia of language, since "not even the survivor can bear witness completely, can speak his own lacuna" (*RA*, 39). Testimony is thus defined by Agamben as the conjunction, or rather the "disjunction" (*RA*, 39), between two lacunae or impossibilities of bearing witness: "To bear witness, it is therefore not enough to bring language to its own non-sense, to the pure undecidability of letters (*m-a-s-s-k-l-o*, *m-a-t-i-s-k-l-o*). It is necessary that this senseless sound be, in turn, the voice of something or someone that, for entirely other reasons, cannot bear witness" (*RA*, 39). Testimony therefore involves a radical expropriation of subjectivity and language or meaning:

> To speak, to bear witness, is thus to enter into a vertiginous movement in which something sinks to the bottom, wholly desubjectified and silenced, and something subjectified speaks without truly having anything to say of its own [. . .] This can also be expressed by saying that *the subject of testimony is the one who bears witness to a desubjectification.* But this expression holds only if it is not forgotten that "to bear witness to a desubjectification" can only mean there is no subject of testimony . . . and that every testimony is a field of forces incessantly traversed by currents of subjectification and desubjectification. (*RA*, 120–21).

It is perhaps not surprising in this context that glossolalia, or speaking in tongues, in which the speaker "speaks without knowing what he says" (*RA*, 114), because he is in a state of radical desubjectification, when, as Heller-Roazen puts it in his presentation of Agamben's ideas, language is "sundered from its semantic and intentional ends," provides Agamben with a model for testimony, so that testimony begins where subjective intention and meaning leave off.[13] Poetic and hysterical depersonalization as well as simulation furnish Agamben with other examples of the same experience of that subjectification and desubjectivation he regards as intrinsic to testimony (*RA*, 112–13, 117–19).[14] Moreover, and this is crucial, according to Agamben the experience of glossolalia "merely radicalizes a

[13] Daniel Heller-Roazen, "Speaking in Tongues," *Paragraph* 25, no. 2 (2002), 93. Heller-Roazen, the translator of *Remnants of Auschwitz*, observes that glossolalia "furnishes Agamben with a fundamental example for the singular 'experience of language' . . . that he has defined as the basic *motivum* of his thought: that of 'the fact that there is language,' the fact that language, before or beyond determinate meaning, takes place" (93). Heller-Roazen notes in this regard that: "To 'speak with tongues,' therefore, is to speak without definite meaning and without even speaking oneself; it is, in every sense, simply to speak. But, for this very reason, it is simultaneously to speak without speaking, at least as long as speech is defined, in its classical form, as the bearer of sense and the instrument of a will. For glossolalia begins where the canonical determinations of language end: at the point at which speech is irrevocably loosened from both its significance and its subject, as one experiences, within oneself, 'barbarian speech that one does not know'" (93).

[14] That is why Agamben rejects an ethics based on communication, stating that "Auschwitz is the radical refutation of every principle of obligatory communication" (*RA*, 65).

desubjectifying experience implicit in the simplest act of speech" (*RA*, 115), be-cause in *every* act of enunciation the subject gains access to a "pure event of lan-guage" that is "independent of every meaning" (*RA*, 117), which suggests that for Agamben the aporia of Auschwitz has been determined in advance by the aporetic condition of language itself. Agamben therefore interprets Saussure's theory of the sign and Benveniste's structuralist theory of enunciation and the role of the shifter to mean that there is an absolute distinction between the individual's actual "discourse" on the one hand and "language" on the other, such that the act of enunciation, or entry into speech, always entails a kind of muteness owing to the radical expropriation of subjectivity and meaning in language (*RA*, 115). The speaker says "I," referring to herself, but the same word spoken by someone else will have a different reference. That is, unlike other words, the meaning of the pronoun "I" (and "you," and "this," and the adverbs "here," "now," etc.) arises only through reference to the situation or what Agamben calls the "event of discourse" (*RA*, 116) in which they are used. For Agamben, this points to an aporia, or fun-damental lacuna, between the word that is spoken (or discourse) and language. The result is that the very act of subjectification—the subject's attempt to speak—is simultaneously an act of desubjectivation such that the speaker gains access to being "always already anticipated by a glossolalic potentiality over which he has neither control nor mastery" (*RA*, 116). As Agamben also puts it,

> speaking is a paradoxical act that implies both subjectification and desubjectification, in which the living individual appropriates language in a full expropriation alone, becoming a speaking being only on condition of falling into silence. The mode of Being of this "I," the existential status of the speaking-living-being is thus a kind of ontological glossolalia, an absolutely insubstantial chatter in which the living being and the speaking being, subjec-tification and desubjectification, can never coincide. (*RA*, 129)

On this basis, he rejects as a "mythologeme" all attempts in Western reflections on language to bridge the aporia between the living being and the speaking be-ing, by imagining, for example, that an inner "I" or "Voice" of conscience ap-pearing to itself in inner discourse could be joined to language or the speaking voice (*RA*, 129).[15] Agamben even manages to make his claim regarding the in-

---

[15] "And yet in the final analysis this Voice is always a mythologeme . . . [N]owhere, in the living being or in language, can we reach a point in which something like an articulation truly takes place. Outside theol-ogy and the incarnation of the Verb, there is no moment in which language is inscribed in the living voice, no place in which the living being is able to render itself linguistic, transforming itself into speech" (*RA*, 129). On the one hand, this is a deconstructive insight or perspective: "It is in this non-place of articula-tion that deconstruction inscribes its 'trace' and its *différance,* in which voice and letter, meaning and presence are infinitely differed" (*RA*, 129–30). Agamben insists that this impossibility of conjoining the liv-ing being and language, "far from authorizing the infinite deferral of signification" (*RA*, 130), is precisely what allows for testimony. "If there is no articulation between the living being and language, if the 'I' stands suspended in the disjunction, then there can be testimony. The intimacy that betrays our non-co-incidence with ourselves is the place of testimony" (*RA*, 130).

herent meaninglessness of language and testimony the basis of a new ethics, on the grounds that the moment one attempts to speak or testify through language one is confronted with a radical loss of meaning that puts one in the very position of those, such as Hurbinek, who are unable to bear witness (*RA*, 161). Indeed, even as he observes that the lacuna of testimony calls into question the identity and reliability of the witnesses (*RA*, 33), he also claims that the impossibility of witnessing to which the survivor attests constitutes the *Muselmann* as the whole witness and that therefore Auschwitz is absolutely and irrefutably proven (*RA*, 164).[16]

What interests me is the way Agamben's commitment to the absence of intention and meaning in testimony parallels the commitment of Sedgwick and others to the absence of intentionality and meaning in shame. Moreover, Agamben's commitment to the absence of intentionality and meaning is, like theirs, also a commitment to materialism, since according to him the encounter with language is an encounter with the very matter of language divorced from meaning. "There where language ends," he writes, "it is not the unsayable which begins, but rather the matter of language. He who has never attained, as in a dream, that wood-like substance of language that the ancients called '*silva*,' remains, even when he is silent, a prisoner to representations."[17] Testimony for Agamben is thus the experience of the "pure exteriority" of language in which the subject is rendered mute by the pure event of language as such: "In the absolute present of the event of discourse, subjectification and desubjectification coincide at every point, and both the flesh and blood individual and the subject of enunciation are perfectly silent. This can be expressed by saying that the one who speaks is not the individual, but language; but this means nothing other than that an impossibility of speaking has, in an unknown way, come to speech" (*RA*, 117).

Another name Agamben uses for the double movement of subjectification and desubjectification in testimony is *shame*.

---

[16] Josh Cohen thinks that Agamben's claim that to bear witness is to bear witness to the impossibility of witnessing can be rescued from the "insuperable" aporetics of Jean-François Lyotard's *The Differend* or Maurice Blanchot's *The Writing of the Disaster*, to which it otherwise bears a close resemblance, by noting that Agamben's account founds an ethics based on "refusing to collude with biopolitics' linguistic and physical silencing of bare life." Cohen thus converts what Agamben views as the ineluctable or constitutive inability of the human witness to give voice to the inhuman into something like the survivor's resistance to power because the latter articulates the irreducible otherness that power would deny. "The impotence of the witness thus founds his very authority." Josh Cohen, review of Agamben's *Remnants of Auschwitz, Textual Practice* 15 (2001): 383.

[17] Giorgio Agamben, *The Idea of Prose* (Albany, N.Y., 1995), 37. Cited by Leland Deladurantaye, "Agamben's Potential," *Diacritics* 30 (Summer 2000): 7. Deladurantaye emphasizes the similarity between Agamben's and de Man's ideas about language as a pure event that possesses no meaning and is in a sense simply "the matter of language."

Shame

Agamben credits Primo Levi for having shown that "there is to-day a 'shame of being human'" which was and still is, Agamben goes on to suggest, "the shame of the camps, the shame of the fact that what should not have happened did happen."[18] For Agamben, however, shame is not a psychological state but an ontological sentiment. As it is for Levinas, so for Agamben, shame is the fundamental sentiment of Being, of "being a *subject*" (*RA*, 107).

To make the case for shame as the fundamental sentiment of the being of the camp victim Agamben first has to clear the ground by demolishing the concept of survivor guilt. He reviews the debate over the meaning of survival between Des Pres and Bettelheim in order to observe that the two adversaries are in fact not as far apart as they seem, not only because both end up reducing survival to the life drives (Des Pres to biological life as such, Bettelheim to the Freudian life drives or instincts) but also because both embrace an ethics of heroism that Agamben rejects (*RA*, 94). In that sense, Agamben's main criticism of the notion of survivor guilt is that it adheres to a model of tragic conflict, a model he feels is wholly inapplicable to Auschwitz. In ancient Greek tragedy an apparently innocent human being assumes objective guilt for what he or she has been fated to do. Although Oedipus marries his mother and kills his father without knowingly willing these acts, he nevertheless regards these as his own deeds and accepts responsibility for them. " 'The tragic heroes are just as much innocent as guilty,' " Agamben quotes Hegel as stating: " 'The right of our deeper consciousness to-day would consist in recognizing that since [Oedipus] had neither intended nor known these crimes himself, they were not to be regarded as his own deeds. But the Greek, with his plasticity of consciousness, takes responsibility for what he has done as an individual and does not cut his purely subjective self-consciousness apart from what is objectively the case . . . But they do not claim to be innocent of these [acts] at all. On the contrary, what they did, and actually had to do, is their glory. No worse insult could be given to such a hero than to say that he had acted innocently' " (*RA*, 96). In Freud's revision of the Oedipus story, which Agamben does not discuss, the survivor experiences feelings of guilt not just for evil acts that he may have performed without consciously willing them, but for virtual intentions and wishes that never go beyond unconscious fantasy. It is this insight that, as we saw in chapter 1, informs the concept of survivor guilt, which ascribes to the survivor-victim an unconscious wish or mimetic tendency to occupy the position of the aggressor by identifying with him—hence the victim's remorse. As I pointed out in chapter 1 Levi, too, posited the exis-

---

[18] Giorgio Agamben, *Means without End: Notes on Politics,* trans. Vincenzo Binetti and Cesare Casarino (Minneapolis, 2000), 131.

tence in the survivor of a non-contradictory combination of objective innocence and subjective feelings of guilt.

But for Agamben, such psychoanalytic considerations are irrelevant. This is because according to him every deportee was reduced to the condition of choicelessness seemingly captured by the German word *Befehlnotstand*, the state of compulsion following an order, a concept evoked by Levi when discussing the "limit" case of the members of the *Sonderkommando* (*DS*, 59). According to Agamben, it is this condition of *Befehlnotstand* that renders tragic conflict impossible in Auschwitz. "The objective element, which for the Greek hero was in every case the decisive question, here becomes what renders decision impossible" (*RA*, 97).[19] Agamben therefore seems to deny agency to every camp inmate, as if the entire population of the gray zone can be conceptualized on one model and one model only, that of the abject, absolutely suffering, anonymous, and mute limit-figure of "bare life," the *Muselmann*, who in passively submitting to his fate without resistance stands as an image or icon of horror at the threshold of the new ethics of shame.[20] Shame will take the place of survivor guilt in Agamben's post-Auschwitz ethics because, unlike guilt, it is an ontological sentiment that lies beyond or outside a thematics of agency.

This is what Agamben's discussion of Emmanuel Levinas's early work on shame, *De l'evasion* (translated as *On Escape*), is designed to confirm.[21] Levinas begins his discussion of shame by rejecting the idea that shame has anything to do with a specific unethical action. "On first analysis," he writes, "shame appears to be reserved for phenomena of a moral order: one feels ashamed for having acted badly, for having deviated from the norm. It is the representation we form of ourselves as diminished beings with which we are pained to identify" (*OE*, 63). Levinas repudiated this characterization of shame as insufficient, for it presents

---

[19] Mesnard and Kahan reproach Agamben for connecting the *Sonderkommando* and the SS into a single concept when he applies the notion of *Befehlnotstand* to both groups, whereas Primo Levi distinguishes between the compulsion to obey orders experienced by the *Sonderkommando* and the "impudent" appeal by the Nazis to the same concept as a way of excusing their conformist behavior, since the Nazis could always find a way out, but the *Sonderkommando* could not. As Levi writes: "The former [*Befehlnotstand* of the *Sonderkommando*] is a rigid either/or, immediate obedience or death; the latter [*Befehlnotstand* of the Nazis] is an internal fact at the center of power and could have been resolved (actually often was resolved) by some maneuver, some slowdown in career, moderate punishment, or, in the worst of cases, the objector's transfer to the front" (*DS*, 60). Moreover, Levi states his belief that "no one is authorized to judge [the *Sonderkommando*], not those who lived through the experience of the Lager and even less those who did not" (*DS*, 59), whereas one is right to judge the SS. But for Agamben, as Mesnard and Kahan note, "in both cases, judgement has already fallen away" (Mesnard and Kahan, *Giorgio Agamben a L'Épreuve d'Auschwitz*, 41).

[20] For a critique of Agamben's tendency to assimilate the suffering of the *Muselmann* to Christ's suffering, see Mesnard and Kahan, *Giorgio Agamben à l'Épreuve d'Auschwitz*, 63–66.

[21] Emmanuel Levinas, *On Escape* (*De l'evasion*), introduced and annotated by Jacques Rolland, trans. Bettina Bergo (1935; Stanford, Calif. 2003); hereafter abbreviated *OE*.

shame as a function of a "determinate act, a morally bad act. It is important that we free shame from this condition" (*OE*, 63). In his essay, Levinas is implicitly engaged in a struggle with both Husserl and Heidegger; specifically, he rejects the possibility of reading shame via the Husserlian phenomenological paradigm, which would make shame an intentional act. Rather, as Levinas puts it, shame "does not depend—as we might believe—on the limitation of our being, inasmuch as it is liable to sin, but rather on the very being of our being, on its incapacity to break with itself" (*OE*, 63). Thus like the shame theorists discussed in the previous chapter although in very different terms, for Levinas what is shameful does not concern our actions but our relation to the self, what he calls our "intimacy, that is, our presence to ourselves" (*OE*, 65). In Agamben's words, shame is "the most proper emotive tonality of subjectivity" (*RA*, 110).

Agamben also shares with many of today's shame theorists the idea that what we are ashamed of is our nudity. In this he follows Levinas, for whom "Shame arises each time we are unable to make others forget our basic nudity. It is related to everything we would like to hide and that we cannot bury or cover up" (*OE*, 64), a formulation that also links shame to the common theme of exposure and visibility. As Levinas also observes: "Nakedness is shameful when it is the sheer visibility of our being, of its ultimate intimacy" (*OE*, 64).[22] Not only can we not hide our shame from others, we cannot hide it from ourselves—we are spectators of the intimacy and nakedness of our total being which we would like to escape from but are unable to because we are chained to our being: "If shame is present, it means that we cannot hide what we should like to hide. The necessity of fleeing, in order to hide oneself, is put in check by the impossibility of fleeing oneself. What appears in shame is thus precisely the fact of being riveted to oneself, the radical impossibility of fleeing oneself to hide from oneself, the unalterably binding presence of the I to itself" (*OE*, 64). For Levinas, though, the body's nakedness of which we are ashamed is not that of a material thing but the "nakedness of our total being in all its fullness and solidity, of its most brutal expression of which we could not fail to take note. The whistle that Charlie Chaplin swallows in *City Lights* triggers the scandal of the brutal presence of his being; it works like a recording device, which betrays the discrete manifestations of a presence that Charlie's legendary tramp costume barely dissimulates" (*OE*, 65). In Agamben's summary of Levinas's views: "If we experience shame in nudity, it is because we cannot hide what we would like to remove from the field of vision . . . Just as we experience our revolting and yet unsuppressible presence to ourselves in bodily need and nausea, which Levinas classifies alongside shame in a single diagnosis, so in

---

[22] Agamben cites the analysis of shame in ancient Greece by Karl Kerenyi, according to which in ancient Greece shame or *aidos* "resembles the experience of being present at one's own being seen, being taken as a witness by what one sees. Like Hector confronted by his mother's bare chest ('Hector, my son, feel *aidos* for this!'), whoever experiences shame is overcome by his own being subject to vision" (*RA*, 107).

shame we are consigned to something from which we cannot in any way distance ourselves" (*RA*, 105).

Yet Agamben appears to depart from Levinas's meaning when, seeking to "deepen" (*RA*, 105) the latter's analysis, in an important passage he claims:

> To be ashamed means to be consigned to something that cannot be assumed. But what cannot be assumed is not something external. Rather, it originates in our own intimacy: it is what is most intimate in us (for example, our own physiological life). Here the "I" is overcome by its own passivity, its ownmost sensibility; yet this expropriation and desubjectivation is also an extreme and irreducible presence of the "I" to itself. It is as if our consciousness collapsed and, seeking to flee in all directions, were simultaneously summoned by an irrefutable order to be present at its own defacement, at the expropriation of what is most its own. In shame, the subject thus has no other content than its own desubjectification; it becomes witness to its own disorder, its own oblivion as a subject. This double movement, which is both subjectification and desubjectification, is shame. (*RA*, 105–6)[23]

But Agamben's analysis is at odds with Levinas's meaning because for the latter a desubjectified individual cannot feel shame. In a passage of Levinas's text not quoted by Agamben, Levinas writes: "When the body loses this character of intimacy, this character of the existence of a self, it ceases to become shameful" (*OE*, 65). He invites us to consider the naked body of the boxer, or the nakedness of the music hall dancer whose exhibition of herself is not necessarily the mark of a shameless being because "her body appears to her with that exteriority to self that serves as a form of cover. Being naked is not a matter of wearing clothes" (*OE*, 65). I take Levinas to mean that the naked music hall dancer doesn't feel shame, because her performance as a dancer necessarily entails the loss of that character of intimacy that is the condition of possibility for the experience of shame. For Levinas, it is our plenitude—the inescapable "fullness and solidity" of our total being—not our desubjectivation or lack, that is shameful.[24]

[23] In the light of his analysis of shame, Agamben clarifies the meaning of the term "passivity." "What does it mean to be passive with respect to oneself?" Agamben asks. "Passivity does not simply mean receptivity, the mere fact of being affected by an external active principle. Since everything takes place here inside the subject, activity and passivity must coincide. The passive subject must be active with respect to its own passivity; it must 'behave' . . . 'against' itself . . . as passive. If we define as merely receptive the photographic print struck by light, or the soft wax on which the image of the seal is printed, we will then give the name 'passive' only to what actively feels its own being passive, to *what is affected by its own receptivity*. As auto-affection, passivity is thus a receptivity to the second degree, a receptivity that experiences itself, that is moved by its own passivity" (*RA*, 109–10). Passivity, as the form of subjectivity, is thus "constitutively fractured into a purely receptive pole (the *Muselmann*) and an actively passive pole (the witness), but in such a way that this fracture never leaves itself, fully separating the two poles. On the contrary, it always has the form of an *intimacy*, of being consigned to a passivity, to a making oneself passive in which the two terms are both distinct and inseparable" (*RA*, 111).

[24] I thank Stefanos Geroulanos, who in a seminar of mine on guilt and shame pointed out Agamben's departure from Levinas in this regard.

It seems that Agamben distorts the meaning of Levinas's text on shame on this point because he wants shame to conform to his account of testimony, defined as the impossibility of witnessing and hence as structured by lack or lacuna. In other words, Agamben attributes to the sentiment of shame the same structure of desubjectification that he claims for testimony or enunciation, so that he can write: "It is now possible to clarify the sense in which shame is truly something like the hidden structure of all subjectivity and consciousness. Insofar as it consists solely in the event of enunciation, consciousness constitutively has the form of being consigned to something that cannot be assumed. To be conscious means: to be consigned to something that cannot be assumed" (*RA*, 128).[25]

Furthermore—and this is consistent with the materialism that informs his approach to language—Agamben defines the blush or flush that accompanies the shame of desubjectivation in materialist terms, characterizing it as a kind of "new ethical material" that, detachable from the victim of Auschwitz, can travel across time and space to reach us, the living, to bear witness to him. His account of the blush of shame depends on a reading of a moment in Robert Antelme's extraordinary account in *The Human Race* (1957) of his ordeal as a prisoner of the Nazis when, during a death march, he witnessed the arbitrary execution of a young Italian student. Agamben presents this episode as evidence that Antelme "clearly bears witness to the fact that shame is not a feeling of guilt for having survived another but, rather, has a different, darker, and more difficult cause" (*RA*, 103). In the last section of this chapter, I shall test the validity of Agamben's interpretation of that episode by examining Antelme's text more closely.

The Flush

The incident that interests Agamben occurred very near the end of the war, when Antelme and his fellow prisoners were being brutally marched toward Dachau by the SS as the latter were attempting to flee the oncoming Allies. Prisoners who straggled or couldn't keep up were shot; some were singled out for death for no discernable reason. Antelme relates that one day it was the turn of a young Italian student from Bologna, whom he knew. Agamben cites the following passage from Antelme's testimony [the elisions are his]:

> The SS continues: "*Du komme hier!*" Another Italian steps out of the column, a student from Bologna. I know him. His face has turned pink. I look at him closely. I still have that pink before my eyes. He stands there at the side of the road. He doesn't know what to

[25] In a rare reference to psychoanalysis Agamben adds: "Hence . . . the necessity of the unconscious in Freud" (*RA*, 128).

do with his hands . . . He turned pink after the SS man said to him, "*Du komme hier!*" He must have glanced about him before he flushed; but yes, it was he who had been picked, and when he doubted it no longer, he turned pink. The SS who was looking for a man, any man, to kill, had found him. And having found him, he looked no further. He didn't ask himself: Why him, instead of someone else? And the Italian, having understood it was really him, accepted this chance selection. He didn't wonder, Why me, instead of someone else? (*RA*, 103)[26]

Agamben begins his Levinasian interpretation of this scene by suggesting that the student's pink face (the adjective is *rose* in the French original) is a sign of the shame the victim feels on being confronted with the intimacy of his death: "It is hard to forget the flush of the student of Bologna, who died during the march alone at the last minute, on the side of the road with his murderer. And certainly the intimacy that one experiences before own's own unknown murderer is the most extreme intimacy, an intimacy that can as such provoke shame" (*RA*, 103–4). He thus interprets this scene as a paradigmatic scene of subjectivation (intimacy) and desubjectivation (loss of self), and hence as a scene of shame. As was noted in chapter 1, countless survivors have talked about feeling guilt for surviving when others have died, as if the latter had died in their place (as if the survivor had unconsciously wished for the death of the other). Agamben seems to be referring to this idea, which he rejects, when he goes on to observe: "But whatever the cause of that flush, it is certain that he is not ashamed for having survived" (*RA*, 104). Well, of course—the student is about to be shot, so he cannot feel shame for surviving. In fact, what Agamben wants to say, and does go on to say, is that the student feels shame for having to *die*—especially for having to die in such an arbitrary way: "Rather, it was as if he were ashamed for having to die, for having been haphazardly chosen—he and no one else—to be killed. In the camps, this is the only sense that the expression 'to die in place of another' can have: everyone dies and lives in the place of another, without reason or meaning; the camp is the place in which no one can truly die or survive in his own place" (*RA*, 104).[27] It is as though Agamben takes over the insight concerning the sheer arbitrariness of death and consequent feeling of survivor guilt but puts that insight to very different ends: "Auschwitz also means this much: that man, dying, cannot find any other sense in his death than this flush, this shame" (*RA*, 104).

[26] Robert Antelme, *The Human Race*, trans. Jeffrey Haight and Annie Mahler (Marlboro, Vt., 1992), 232; hereafter abbreviated *HR*. Agamben omits from the passage a sentence that might seem to support his thematization of shame. After the phrase "He doesn't know what do with his hands," Antelme adds a phrase that in the English translation of the text is given as "He seems embarrassed." In the French original the words are "Il a l'air confus," which can mean a number of things, such as "confused," "muddled," "crestfallen," or "abashed" but does not obviously warrant the word "embarrassed."

[27] This is an attempt by Agamben to rethink Heidegger's claim in *Being and Time* that no one can substitute for another's death.

Moreover, the young Bolognese's flush is further construed by Agamben in materialist terms. He materializes shame by divorcing it from considerations of intentionality and interpreting the pink color that suffuses the student's face at the moment of his death as a form of ethical matter, so to speak: "In any case, the student is not ashamed of having survived. On the contrary, what survives him is shame . . . Why does the student from Bologna blush? It is as if the flush of on his cheeks momentarily betrayed a limit that was reached, as if something like *a new ethical material* were touched upon in the living being" (*RA*, 104, my emphasis). The flush is a kind of ethical material because, in this scenario, it functions as a substance that can be imagined as traveling mutely from the victim to us today in the form of an address or call from which we "cannot turn away" (*RA*, 54) and which testifies to the space- and time-transcending desubjectivising shame of Auschwitz: "Naturally it is not a matter of fact to which he could bear witness otherwise, which he might also have expressed in words. But in any case that flush is like a mute apostrophe flying through time to reach us, to bear witness to him" (*RA*, 104).

In understanding the Italian student's flush as a sign of shame is Agamben being faithful to Antelme's own interpretive intentions? It is not at all evident that he is, to say the least. Attention to Antelme's own thematization of pink in the text suggests a different meaning, one that emphasizes not the issue of desubjectivation and shame but of human relatedness and responsibility. Very soon after the episode in which the student from Bologna's face turns pink on being selected for death, Antelme in a crucial passage ignored by Agamben describes how the remaining prisoners on the death march entered a quiet little tree-lined German town, Wernigerode, in which people were strolling down the sidewalks or heading home. "Yesterday morning, while the guys were being killed," Antelme writes, "these people were strolling about like this, on these sidewalks." And he adds in a passage that deliberately refers back to the murder of the Italian student and which I shall quote at length:

> The butcher was weighing the meat ration. Perhaps a child was sick in bed, and his face was pink, and his worried mother was looking at him. On the road, the Italian's face also turned pink; death slowly entered into his face and he didn't know how to behave, how to appear natural. The mother may be watching us go by now: prisoners. Five minutes ago they didn't know a thing about us. They didn't know a thing about us this morning, either, when we were afraid and some guys saw their mothers; and now this mother is looking at us, and sees nothing. The solitude of this little town, its torpor following the alert. They're losing the war, their men are dying, the women are praying for them. Who sees them blown to bits by the shells, and who saw those who'd just been machine-gunned, under the trees, in the Harz yesterday? Who sees the pink-faced little child in his bed and yesterday saw the pink-faced Italian on the road? Who sees the two mothers,

the child's mother, and the Italian's mother, in Bologna, and who can restore its unity to all that, and explain these enormous distances, and these likenesses? But does not everyone have eyes?

So long as you are alive you have a place in all this and you play a role in it. Everyone here—on the sidewalks, pedaling by on bicycles, looking at us, or not looking at us—has a part he's playing in this story. Everyone is doing something that relates to us. They may kick sick guys in the belly as much as they like, or kill them, or force guys with the shits to remain closed up inside a church and then shoot them because they shit, or yell *Alle Scheisse, alle Scheisse!* for the millionth time, between them and us a relationship nevertheless exists that nothing can destroy. They know what they are doing, they know what's being done to us. They know it as well as if they were us. And they are. You are us . . . They're going to ignore us; whenever we go through a town, it's a sleep of human beings that passes through a sleep of sleeping persons. That's how it appears. But we know; each group knows about the other, knows everything about it.

It's for those on the sidewalk that we're looking so intently as we go through Wernigerode. We are not asking anything of them; they just have to see us, they mustn't miss us. We make ourselves evident. (*HR*, 235–36)

"Who sees?" The traditional answer to this question is God. But this is not Antelme's response: God is conspicuously absent from this extraordinary passage. But nor is the answer every human being, despite Antelme's insistence on the ubiquity of the human capacity for vision. "But does not everyone have eyes?" (Mais tout le monde peut voir).[28] The central theme of this passage, in many respects the climactic passage in the book, is the absoluteness of the human relation; and the genius of the passage is to articulate that relation in terms of both seeing and not seeing. Put slightly differently, for Antelme the endpoint of the attempt of the Nazis to differentiate humans from nonhumans is an image of the absolute relatedness of all human beings, understood in terms of the success and failure of vision, that is, of both acknowledgment and avoidance. "Everyone is doing something that relates to us" (Tous, ils font quelque chose par rapport à nous), he writes, meaning that this is the case whether or not a particular person in the town actually was aware of the passage of the prisoners. (No adult person in the town could be unaware of the war, of the treatment of Jews and other prisoners, of the imminent collapse of the Third Reich.) At the same time, in contrast to those moments when the prisoners try to evade the gaze of SS in order to avoid being killed (*HR*, 52), Antelme positively wants the townspeople to see the victims, to take them in, to acknowledge their existence. The prisoners strive for visibility to force the issue of relatedness: "We make ourselves evident" (Nous nous montrons). Seeing thus becomes an operator for conviction as to the absoluteness of the human relation.

[28] Robert Antelme, *L'espece humaine* (Paris, 1957), 257.

Hence the inescapability of a certain moral failure on the part of the people in the town for refusing to acknowledge their part in the story of what is happening to the prisoners. The passage has nothing to do with shame. If anything, at a remove it has to do with human responsibility, with guilt. The implication, if there is one, is of the guilt of those who see but refuse to recognize what they see and the human relatedness of what they see. In this passage—as in Stanley Cavell's now classic reading of *King Lear*—seeing means acknowledgment.[29] The move from the Italian student to the sick child is crucial for Antelme in this regard. Pink, *rose*, emerges as the most vivid figure that Antelme can propose for the absolute similarity or likeness of human beings. It cannot be tied to any specific emotion. The fact that Antelme connects the pink face of the young Italian who is about to die with the pink face of the German baby who is perhaps sick is a rebuke to anyone who tries to link the color pink to a particular affect. All we are entitled to say is that in these pages pink appears to be an expression of a *threatened aliveness or vitality.*[30]

The passage thus insists on the prisoners' need to make themselves visible to the Germans. Antelme's account is at the farthest possible pole from the standard version of shame, since the emphasis falls not on the subject's wish to hide from the gaze of others but rather on the need to be seen. Antelme's stress on seeing and visibility would seem to make him an antimimetic writer, but the emphasis is in the service of an asserted identification: "You are us" (Vous êtes nous-mêmes!"). Nor does the passage appear to have anything to do with survivor guilt, not because Antelme replaces guilt with shame but because the implied guilt is that of the onlookers, not that of the survivors.[31] Moreover, at other moments in his book Antelme insists, against Agamben's reading of the camp as a zone of irresponsiblity, on the irreducibility of conscience. "The SS who view us all one and the same cannot induce us to see ourselves that way," he writes. "They cannot prevent us from choosing. On the contrary: here the need to choose is constant and immeasurably greater. The more transformed we become, the farther we retreat from back home, the more the SS believe us reduced to the indistinctness and to the irresponsibility whereof we do certainly present the appearance—the more distinctions our community does in fact contain, and the stricter those distinctions are. The inhabitant of the camp is not the abolition of these differences; on the contrary, he is their effective realization" (*HR*, 88). And speaking

[29] Stanley Cavell, "The Avoidance of Love: A Reading of *King Lear*," in *Must We Mean What We Say? A Book of Essays* (New York, 1969), 267–353. See also Cavell's "Knowing and Acknowledging," ibid., 238–66.

[30] In other places in the book, the pink and red of the skin and body variously signify health, vitality, strength, anger, power, and cleanliness (*HR*, 54, 62, 76, 113, 114, 139, 166).

[31] "No longer can you ever hope that we be at once in your place and in our own skin, condemning ourselves," he says to the Nazis. "Never will anyone here become to himself his own SS" (*HR*, 89).

directly to the Nazis he adds: "[O]wing to what you have done, right-thinking transforms itself into consciousness. You have restored the unity of man; you have made conscience irreducible" (*HR*, 89). Contrast this with the following statement by Agamben: "The survivor is therefore familiar with the common necessity of degradation; he knows that humanity and responsibility are something that the deportee had to abandon when entering the camp" (*RA*, 59–60). Agamben's interpretation of Antelme's text represents a distortion of the latter's meaning in the service of a commitment to a notion of shame that rejects the very questions of conscience and meaning that lie at the heart of *The Human Race*.

CONCLUSION ▐███████████████████████

IN THE PREVIOUS chapter, I ended on a somewhat ethical note, which is to say that my discussion of Agamben's views on shame turned out to be at least implicitly a critique of his position on moral as well as intellectual grounds. Nor do I wish to deny that there is an ethical component to my objections to his work. Not only do I disapprove of the partial and misleading way he has of reading certain crucial passages, expounding them in terms that are alien to the meaning of the texts in which they appear, as when he interprets Antelme as contributing to an antiintentionalist, materialist thematics of shame when in fact the latter's concerns are those of the absoluteness of the human relation and the importance of human responsibility. I also object to the fact that in substituting shame for guilt in his examination of the experience of the camps, Agamben offers a view of the human subject as completely lacking all attributes of intention and agency, with the result that a kind of traumatic abjection is held to characterize not only all the victims of the camps without differentiation but all human life after Auschwitz—including those of us who were never there.

But I do not want to let it appear that the only or indeed the main point of my book is an ethical critique of the antiintentionalist position on the affects. Rather, my aims in both the chapter on Agamben and the book as a whole are as much genealogical and analytic as they are ethical and political. I want to conclude here by reviewing the trajectory of my project and summarizing what I think its stakes are.

My project began as an inquiry into the history of the idea of survivor guilt. It originated in the intuition that there was something interesting and important about the fact that, although in the third edition of the *Diagnostic and Statistical Manual* of 1980 (*DSM-III*) survivor guilt was included in the list of "Miscellaneous

Symptoms" as an optional diagnostic criterion for the newly introduced Posttraumatic Stress Disorder (PTSD), it was dropped from that list when the manual was next revised in 1987 (*DSM-IIIR*). I thought I discerned the reasons for that development. Those reasons had to do with the fact that, since Freud, guilt had been defined as a relational bond between subjects. More precisely, the concept of survivor guilt had been theorized within the terms of psychoanalytic ideas about the relationship—the imitative or identificatory relationship—between the victim and the aggressor. The claim, as laid out by Freud and further elaborated by Sandor Ferenczi and Anna Freud among many others, was that one characteristic, indeed primordial, mode of defense against violence was for the victim to save herself by giving in to power and identifying with the threatening other.

As I explained in my previous book, *Trauma: A Genealogy*, and rehearse briefly in the Introduction to the present one, that emotional tie to the aggressor was sometimes imagined in "mimetic" terms as involving an imitative assimilation to the perpetrator on the model of a hypnotic immersion so profound that all distinction between self and aggressor was elided. We might put it that the mimetic model of trauma called into question any simple determination of the subject from within or without. The result was that the victim could not represent the violent other to herself but yielded to him in the mode of an unconscious-suggestive identification that was inaccessible to subsequent recollection. Trauma on this model was conceptualized as involving a kind of hypnotic-suggestive somnambulism: instead of remembering the event, the victim blindly repeated or imitated the scene of origin. The mimetic model was therefore capable of explaining the amnesia held to be typical of posttraumatic stress by understanding it as a type of posthypnotic forgetting. By the same token, because the victim was said to identify unconsciously with the aggressor, she was judged to be possessed by, and hence complicitous with, the violence directed at her. Survivor guilt thus found its explanation in the idea that the victim blindly incorporated the aggressivity of the unattackable authority into herself in the form of a distrustful superego that, now possessing all the aggressiveness the helpless victim would have liked to express against her tormentor, turned that aggressivity back against the subject's ego. Equating bad intentions with bad actions, the superego's harsh punishment for the subject's continuing fantasies and wishes was experienced by the ego in the form of an oppressive conscience.

An alternative, "antimimetic," model of trauma likewise conceptualized trauma in imitative terms, but it did so somewhat differently. On this model, the victim was imagined as imitating the aggressor in a mode that allowed her to keep a specular distance from the violent other because she remained a spectator of the traumatic scene, which she could therefore see and represent to herself and others. The result was that she was in principle capable of recollecting or recovering the traumatic memory of the event. The antimimetic model of trauma not only relegated the idea of immersive hypnosis to a secondary position, but it did so in ways that suppressed the mimetic-suggestive paradigm in order to reestablish a strict dichotomy between the autonomous subject and the external trauma. Instead of positing a traumatic-mimetic breaching of the boundaries between self and other, the antimimetic model enforced a rigid dichotomy between the internal and the external such that violence was imagined as assaulting the subject entirely from the outside. Passionate identifications were thus transformed into claims of identity, and the violence inhering in the mimetic relationship between victim and aggressor was expelled to the external world, from where it returned to the subject as an absolute exteriority. The value to proponents of this model of trauma was and continues to be that it served to forestall the possibility of scapegoating by denying that the victim participated in, or in any way colluded with, the scene of abjection.

The antimimetic model has also lent itself to various scientific or scientistic accounts of trauma. As I observed in *Trauma: A Genealogy*, scientists have recently conceptualized traumatic memory in neurobiological terms by proposing that the memory of the trauma is preserved in the victim's brain with a timeless accuracy that accounts for the long-term and often delayed effects of PTSD. In particular, some theorists have suggested that traumatic memory is encoded in the brain in a different way from ordinary memory. Unlike narrative or "declarative" memory that involves the ability to consciously tell the story of what has happened, researchers propose that "traumatic memory" involves modes of bodily memories, habits, and responses that lie outside verbal-semantic representation. At stake in the notion of traumatic memory is the idea that, precisely because the victim is unable to process the traumatic experience in a normal way, the event leaves a reality imprint in the brain that, in its insistent literality, testifies to the existence of a pristine and timeless historical truth undistorted by subjective meaning, unconscious suggestive or symbolic factors, or personal-social cognitive schemes. In my book on trauma, I suggested that such ideas are poorly supported by the evidence and arguments adduced in their favor. Yet they enjoy widespread support. The revision of the formulation of PTSD in 1987 around the mental image or icon, defined in strictly formal terms without regard to the question of its meaning for the patient, depends on just such a literalization of the traumatic event. It is as if a conception of traumatic memory as literal serves as a bulwark against mimesis by reinforcing a rigid polarization between the self and other.

In my book on trauma I proposed that, from the moment the concept of trauma was invented in the late nineteenth-century, these mimetic and antimimetic models of trauma have vied for supremacy. More precisely, I suggested that there has been a continuous tension or oscillation between them, so that even the most relentlessly mimetic theory has tended to resurrect the antimimetic theory, just as the antimimetic account has continued to haunt its mimetic alternative. The paradoxes and contradictions that have resulted from that tension or oscillation were the subject of my earlier study.

From the perspective of the issues I have just sketched, the vicissitudes of the notion of survivor guilt appear comprehensible. The demotion of survivor guilt from its position as one of the defining criteria of PTSD by the American Psychiatric Association in 1987 can be understood as a fallout of the recent antimimetic tendencies of contemporary American psychiatry. The recognition of PTSD in 1980 coincided with a major reorientation of official American psychiatry, as reflected in the third edition of its diagnostic manual (*DSM-III*) in which the new disorder appeared. Those in charge of that revision abandoned psychoanalysis as a template for understanding and organizing mental disease and reverted instead to the descriptive-nosological approach of an earlier, Kraepelinian psychiatry. The aim of the new orientation was to provide an inventory of mental disorders grouped according to distinct, differentiating diagnostic criteria and associated noncriterial features. Antipsychoanalytic and ostensibly atheoretical, *DSM-III* understood mental disorders by analogy with physical diseases and attempted to classify them according to principles that stressed both objective observation and opposition to etiological theories based on invisible psychic mechanisms. PTSD thus entered official American psychiatry in *DSM-III* as a disorder that could be defined in objective, empirical terms. Survivor guilt, which owed its original rationale to a now displaced psychoanalytic theoretical framework, was carried over into the new manual as one of a set of core criterial symptoms for posttraumatic stress, but one that now appeared as a "survivor" of an earlier, abandoned theoretical paradigm. The idea of survivor guilt had always aroused suspicion in some quarters largely because it appeared to suggest that the victim was psychically complicit with the enemy. Its subsequent demotion in *DSM-IIIR* (1987) to merely an associated and noncriterial feature of PTSD was not widely deplored.

It was clear to me at the outset of my new project that these historical themes would be the focus of the early chapters of the present book. Accordingly, the first three chapters trace the vicissitudes of the concept of survivor guilt, from its psychoanalytic formulations in postwar America and application to the Holocaust survivor, to its critique by Terrence Des Pres and others in the 1970s and later, to its 1987 demotion as one of the criteria for the diagnosis of PTSD. But I was also intrigued by the discovery that from the moment survivor guilt was downgraded in PTSD, trauma specialists began with almost missionary zeal to substitute shame as the emotion that best defined the traumatic state. Moreover, I realized that interest in shame extended far beyond the boundaries of American psychiatry, to fields as diverse as philosophy, literary-critical theory, queer theory, and legal thought. It further struck me that the terms in which shame was often theorized were at odds with those guiding the understanding of guilt. In particular, PTSD researchers, psychologists, psychotherapists, and literary theorists, such as Eve Kosofsky Sedgwick and others influenced by her, all exhibited a fascination with the work of psychologist Silvan Tomkins and his successors, who theorized shame in terms quite differently from Freud.

What impressed me in this regard was not just the fact that the shame theory inspired by Tomkins downplayed the unconscious-interpersonal-immersive dynamic central to the concept of survivor guilt—for historically, shame has always tended to be conceptualized in antimimetic-specular terms as an affect that is aroused when a person becomes conscious of being held in the humiliating (real or imagined) gaze of another. In this respect, the new interest in shame reflected the antimimetic tendencies of contemporary American psychiatry. But what also caught my attention was the fact that, under the influence of Tomkins's ideas, shame was being defined in postpsychoanalytic, antiintentionalist and materialist terms as one of a finite set of universal, preprogrammed, physiological responses of the body, responses that were held to be inherently independent of intentional objects. For according to Tomkins's affect program theory, the emotions can be triggered by what we call an object—but it turns out that the object is nothing more than a stimulus or trip wire for a built-in reflexlike, corporeal response. In other words, whereas guilt was conceptualized within an intentionalist framework in that the guilty subject was imagined as having fantasmatic identificatory intentions toward the aggressor, the new shame theory proposes an antiintentionalist account of the affects and an emphasis on the built-in responses of the body. Shame might appear to be a social, intersubjective emotion involving the interruption or refusal of the subject's curiosity and interest by the shaming strangeness of the gaze of the other. But since for Tomkins the relation of the affects to their triggering source is purely contingent, what one feels in shame is simply a matter of one's physiological state. Thus along with the other fundamental affects, shame is inherently independent of any particular object. It is defined instead as one of several organized sets of muscular, vascular, and glandular responses located in the face and body and activated at subcortical centers where the specific, genetically inherited, "programs" are held to be stored.

In sum, I began to discern that however disparate their intellectual agendas might seem to be, today's shame theorists can be seen to share a set of linked commitments:

1. *A commitment to antiintentionalism.* In the work of the recent trauma theorists I examined in *Trauma: A Genealogy* this commitment surfaced in certain claims about the inherently aporetic nature of language and representation. In the work of the shame theorists examined in the present book, it surfaces in their commitment to the "affect program theory" of the emotions, as well as in Agamben's discussion of the lack of intention and meaning in the language of testimony and shame.

2. *A commitment to materialism.* If you are a follower of Tomkins in the emotions field, you reconstrue the intentional object of the emotions as the cause or trigger of the affects defined as inherited, neural programs, and insist that the affects are intrinsically independent of any inherent meaning or association to their triggering source. If you are Agamben, you go so far as to depict shame as a material substance.

3. *A commitment to the primacy of personal experience or subject position.* According to shame theory, what matters in the experience of shame is not your conscious or unconscious wishes or intentions toward some object but your subjective feelings in all their difference from those of others: what matters is your subject position as an individual or personal identity. Just so, when Agamben, in rejecting the notion of survivor guilt, asserts that for all of us today Auschwitz is not yet over because it is an event that is perpetually and eternally present, he not only makes the experience of the concentration camp victims a part of our own experience but makes our alleged identity or subject position as survivors central to his discussion of shame.

The task of the final two chapters of the present work then became to demonstrate the ways in which modern shame theory coheres around those three commitments and to think through the latter's implications. What is it about these ideas that makes them alluring? Why do so many critics, theorists, and researchers in various fields find the affect program theory so compelling that they are prepared to ignore fundamental critiques that call it into disrepute? Indeed, why is Sedgwick—a truly brilliant critic—intent on foregrounding Tomkins's ideas when she admits she is not sure she really believes they are true?

One answer seems to lie in the new view of the subject that shame theory makes possible, one that is centered on an autotelic experience in which shame means not the experience of guilt for some real or imagined deed but simply some personal experience that is unique to you and that defines you as who you are. We might put it that the basic appeal of Tomkins's shame theory for its proponents appears to be that it provides a technology for guaranteeing each individual's absolute difference from every other and does so in terms that avoid the moralisms associated with the theory of guilt. For it is certainly true that the notion of guilt, however theorized, carries with it the notion of responsibility. And it is also the case that the notion of "survivor guilt" has consistently given rise to the objection that, however innocent she may be, the victim stands accused of complicity in the violence directed against her because she has unconsciously identified with power. But shame theory replaces such concerns about accountability with an emphasis on the question of our personal attributes. Indeed, according to my analysis, the value of shame as opposed to guilt for Sedgwick and her followers is that it is a technology for ensuring that one person's personal attributes will be different from everyone else's, indeed that it is a means for producing (queer) identity as the experience of pure difference. For Sedgwick, the further attraction of Tomkins's affect program theory seems to be that it conforms to the postmodernist critique of the idea of the sovereign subject: by defining the individual as lacking a consolidated core personality and constituted instead by relationships between a multiplicity of affect and other assemblies of various degrees of independence and dependence, Tomkins treats the subject as plural, contingent, and open to constant change. However, from my perspective, it makes no difference whether your view is that the subject is fixed and stable, or whether your position is that the subject is plural and mobile, because in both cases you are committed to the primacy of identity and difference.

But a focus on the value of personal difference also has problematic consequences. In particular, replacing an emphasis on what we have done or believe we have done with an emphasis on who we are changes the entire basis on which we can have arguments and debates. Indeed, it closes down the possibility of dispute altogether. For how can there be an argument about the meaning of an emotional situation if the issue for us is simply how we feel? Here it turns out that there is a deep convergence between my project and that of Walter Benn Michaels in his recent book, *The Shape of the Signifier: 1967 to the End of History.* Michaels argues that over a period that stretches from the 1960s to the present and coincides with the rise of postmodernism and posthistoricism, there has been a dominant tendency to replace an emphasis on ideological or political disagreement with an emphasis on identitarian difference. He claims that in the work of Paul de Man, Richard Rorty, and a host of other writers, the idea that what matters in interpreting the meaning of a text is the author's (conscious or unconscious) intention has been replaced by the idea that what matters is just what the text in all its materiality feels or looks like to each individual. In other words, when an interest in a person's intentions and beliefs—an interest that, Michaels argues, is inherently universalizing—gives way to an interest in what a person or text means without regard to authorial intentions, the result is not only a commitment to the materiality of the text or signifier, but a commitment also to the experience and hence the subject position of the reader as the only things that count.

Michaels's aim is to dismantle such a postmodernist and posthistoricist logic by demonstrating how, by trying to get rid of notions of intention, belief, and meaning, this development produces as one of its inevitable consequences a complete indifference to dispute. For on this logic, when people have different feelings or experiences, they don't disagree, they are just different. In my book I have approached these same issues from another perspective, that of the history of conceptualizations of survivor guilt and its displacement by a new theory of shame. On my account, the significance of current shame theory is that it mistakenly replaces intentionalist accounts of guilt, in which the meaning of one's real or fantasized actions is a central topic, with a nonintentionalist, materialist account of the emotions in which the issue of personal difference is the only question of importance.

APPENDIX ▬▬▬▬▬▬▬▬▬▬▬▬▬▬▬▬▬▬▬

Guide to the literature on the affect program theory, linked to the following notes in Chapter 4:

Note 34

For criticisms of the Schachter-Singer experiment see R. Plutchik and A. F. Ax, "A Critique of Determinants of Emotional State by Schachter and Singer (1962)," *Psychophysiology* 4 (1967): 79–82; R. M. Gordon, "Emotion Labelling and Cognition," *Journal for the Theory of Social Behavior* 8 (1978): 125–35; R. M. Gordon, *The Structure of Emotions: Investigations in Cognitive Psychology* (Cambridge, 1987), 94–109; R. Reisenzein, "The Schachter Theory of Emotion: Two Decades Later," *Psychological Bulletin* 94 (1983): 239–64; and Ronald de Sousa, *The Rationality of Emotions* (Cambridge, Mass., 1987), 53–57.

For texts by Lazarus on the role of appraisal in the emotions, see R. S. Lazarus, Allen D. Kanner, and Susan Folkman, "Emotions: A Cognitive-Phenomenological Analysis," chap. 8 in *Emotion: Theory, Research, Experience*, ed. Robert Plutchik and Henry Kellerman (New York, 1980), vol. 1, *Theories of Emotion,* 189–214; R. S. Lazarus, "Thoughts on the Relations between Emotion and Cognition," *American Psychologist* 37 (1982): 1019–24; R. S. Lazarus, "On the Primacy of Cognition," *American Psychologist* 39 (1984): 124–29; R. S. Lazarus, J .C. Coyne, and S. Folkman, "Cognition, Emotion, and Motivation: Doctoring Humpty Dumpty," in *Approaches to Emotion*, ed. K. R. Scherer and P. Ekman (Hillsdale, N.J., 1984), 221–37; R. S. Lazarus, *Emotion and Adaptation* (New York, 1991). Recent philosophical defenses of the cognitivist position include Andrew Ortony, Gerald L. Clore, and Allan Collins, *The Cognitive Structure of Emotions* (Cambridge, 1988); and Martha C. Nussbaum, *Upheavals of Thought: The Intelligence of Emotions* (Cambridge, Mass., 2001).

Note 37

For Paul Ekman's publications on the affect program theory, in a large oeuvre, see Paul Ekman, "Universals and Cultural Differences in Facial Expressions of Emotion." In *Nebraska Symposium on Motivation,* 4th ed., ed. J. K. Cole (Lincoln, 1971), 207–83; Paul Ekman and Wallace V. Friesen, "Constants across Cultures in the Face and Emotion," *Journal of Personality and Social Psychology* 17 (1971): 124–29; Paul Ekman and Wallace V. Friesen, *Unmasking the Face* (Englewood Cliffs, N.J., 1975); Paul Ekman, "Biological and Cultural Contributions to Body and Facial Movement in the Expression of Emotions," in *Explaining Emotions*, Amelie Oksenberg Rorty (Berkeley, 1980), 73–101; Paul Ekman, "The Argument and Evidence about Univerals in Facial Expressions of Emotion," in *Handbook of Social Psychophysiology*, ed. H. Wagner and A. Manstead (London, 1989), 143–64; Paul Ekman, "An Argument for Basic Emotions," *Cognition and Emotion* 6 (1992): 169–200; Paul Ekman, "Facial Expression and Emotion," *American Psychologist* 48 (April 1993): 384–92; Paul Ekman, "Basic Emotions," in *Handbook of Cognition and Emotion*, ed. T. Dalgleish and M. Power (Sussex, U.K., 1999), 45–61. For a recent popularization of Ekman's ideas see Malcolm Gladwell, *Blink: The Power of Thinking without Thinking* (New York, 2005). For Izard's contribution to the affect program theory see especially C. E. Izard, *The Face of Emotion* (New York, 1971); C. E. Izard, *Human Emotions* (New York, 1977); and C. E. Izard, *The Psychology of Emotions* (New York, 1991).

Note 41

For Ekman's replies to Russell's and Fridlund's criticisms of his work see especially Paul Ekman, "Strong Evidence for Universals in Facial Expression: A Reply to Russell's Mistaken Critique," *Psychological Bulletin* 115 (1994): 268–87; Paul Ekman, "Expression or Communication about Emotion," in *Genetic, Ethnological and Evolutionary Perspectives on Human Development: Essays in Honor of Dr. Daniel G. Freedman*, ed. N. Segal, G. E. Weisfeld, and C. C. Weisfeld (Washington, D.C., 1997), 315–38; Paul Ekman, "Should We Call It Expression or Communication?" *Innovations in Social Science Research* 10 (1997): 333–44; Paul Ekman, "Facial Expressions," in *Handbook of Cognition and Emotion,* ed. T. Dalgleish and M. Power (New York, 1999), 301–20; and Dacher Keltner, Paul Ekman, Gian C. Gonzaga, and Jennifer Beer, "Facial Expression of Emotion," in *Handbook of Affective Sciences,* ed., Richard J. Davidson, Klaus R. Scherer, and H. Hill Goldsmith (Oxford, 2003), 415–32.

Note 46

A critique of the 1990 study by Levenson, Ekman, and Friesen 1990 to which Prinz appeals in support of his arguments. In their 1990 paper, Levenson, Ekman and Friesen claim that the face leads the physiology, since the different facial poses are said to generate distinct physiologies. But this contradicts a claim made by Ekman in response to Fridlund's critique of the 1972 Japanese-American study. In that earlier Japanese-American study, the only time the Japanese students showed different faces from the American students was in the third phase of the experiment when, according to Ekman and Friesen, the Americans and Japanese felt the same negative affects in response to a stress film clip but the Japanese disguised their emotions more than the Americans by displaying smiles. Fridlund in 1994 complained that attributing the Japanese-American differences to display rules would, as the definition of display rules stipulates, have required verification that both cultures had equivalent emotions in the third phase of the experiment in which the facial movements of the two groups of students differed. He wondered in this regard why the data from self-reports that had been obtained through questionnaires after the experiment were not published. In a 1999 reply to Fridlund, Ekman stated that the reason the questionnaires were not published was that they would not have been of any use, since the same display rules that caused the Japanese students to mask their negative emotions in the presence of the authority figure (an interpretation questioned by Fridlund) would also have led them to mask their negative emotions on questionnaires given to them by the same authority figure. Instead, Ekman said, he and his colleague Wallace V. Friesen used a different strategy: they already knew that the films shown to the students produced the same emotional impact on both groups from the prior research of Richard Lazarus, who had found the same physiological response to the films among the Japanese and Americans.

But Ekman's reply to Fridlund exposes an incoherence in his position. According to the logic of the 1990 Levenson, Ekman, and Friesen paper, the Japanese students who displayed different faces in the third phase of the 1972 study must have experienced a different physiological response from that of the Americans because facial movements determine physiology. But according to the logic of Ekman's display rule thesis, the Japanese students actually felt the same negative emotions as the Americans and must therefore have had the same physiological response as they. Ekman can't have it both ways, a point overlooked by those, like Prinz, who cite this work in support of their position. The details can be followed in the 1990 paper by Levenson, Ekman, and Friesen cited above and in Paul Ekman, Robert W. Levenson, and Wallace V. Friesen, "Autonomic Nervous System Activity Distinguishes Among Emotions," *Science* 221 (1983): 1208–10; Fridlund, *Human Facial Expression*, 288–93; and Paul Ekman, "Facial Expressions," in *Handbook of Cognition and Emotion*, ed. T. Dalgleish and M. Power (London, 1999), 312–13. Finally, it is worth pointing out that Lazarus himself never claimed that emotional impact could be determined by physiology, since Lazarus was known for emphasizing the role of cognitive appraisal in determining emotional states, and for believing that physiology was just a backdrop or neutral context for the emotion experience. So Ekman is on very weak footing if he wants to claim by reference to Lazarus's work that the Japanese and Americans "felt" the same because they showed the same physiology. As a matter of fact, Lazarus and his colleagues reported striking and unexpected differences between the Japanese and Americans in their physiological reactions to the experiment as whole, results the authors attributed to the sensitivity of the Japanese at being observed by others in the experimental situation. They therefore suggested that this was what was threatening to the Japanese, rather than the specific content of the stress film ("SPS," 255–58). I thank Alan Fridlund for generously discussing these and many other related points with me.

Note 56

Shame and shame theory. The following points are worth making in connection with Sedgwick's remarks concerning shame's role as the exemplary affect for affect "theory":

1. Tomkins includes shame among the eight or nine inherited affects that according to him have innate activators and are triggered subcortically on the common basis of variations in the density of neural firing, that is, on the basis of the number of neural firings per unit of time. He posits three distinct classes of activators: stimulation increase, stimulation level, and stimulation decrease. In other words, the emotions are activated by whatever is new, whatever continues for any extended period of time, and whatever ceases to happen. Thus to take one example, joy will be activated when any sudden reduction of stimulation occurs from several disparate phenomena. On the one hand, as Tomkins explains, joy will be experienced at the sudden reduction of negative stimulation, such as pain, distress, fear, shame, or aggression. On the other hand, the theory explains the very different phenomenon of the enjoyment of the familiar. Thus when an "unknown but familiar" face is first seen, interest will be produced, with a sudden increase in stimulation; this will be followed by an equally sudden reduction of this stimulation when the familiar stimulus, the face, is recognized as familiar, thereby activating joy. Although the notion of the "recognition" of a familiar face would seem to implicate cognition in the affective response, Tomkins is committed to the idea that the affects are innate and have innate activators . See for example Tomkins's "Simulation of Personality: The Interrelationships between Affect, Memory, Thinking, Perception, and Action," in *Computer Simulation of Personality: Frontier of Psychological Theory* (New York, 1963), 24–31.

2. Tomkins states that the same type of mechanism at work in the activation of joy also operates in the affect of shame, except that in the case of shame the stimulation reduction owing to the interruption of the subject's interest in another person or object is incomplete compared with joy, and appears to be restricted to the reduction of positive affects themselves rather than just any kind of stimulation. It is because of the specificity of the activator for shame—the fact that shame is activated only by the reduction of the positive emotions and not by the reduction of simply any kind of stimulation—that shame can't be represented on the graph Tomkins uses to represent his theory of the innate activators of the affects, a graph in which the distinct emotions appear as straight lines on a positive, negative, or zero slope when plotted against the vertical axis of density of neural firing and the horizontal axis of time.

3. So shame does have certain distinct features in Tomkins's general theory of the affects, as Sedgwick observes. Sedgwick suggests that shame's distinction in this regard is that it works so as to punctuate the system as distinct in the sense of providing "cognitive antenna" for the affect system as a whole. It is important, I think, that this claim not be misunderstood to imply a cognitive-appraisal approach to the emotions of the kind associated with the work of Schachter and others, an approach to which Tomkins is in fact opposed. The "cognitive antenna" of which Tomkins speaks (*AIC*, 2.319) belongs not to the subcortical affect system itself, but to a central control or what he calls, in the cybernetic language that inspires him, the "central assembly" (*AIC*, 2.230). The role of the central assembly is to interpret "input information," or the traces of past experiences from various sources, including the subcortical affect system and memory, and to cognitively organize that information into a "theory" or "interpretation" of a large number of situations. The central assembly thus modifies responses through learning. The result is that whether or how intensely shame or distress or fear or enjoyment are experienced in a given situation will be in part a function of the individual's cognitive organization of past experience with each of the primary affects. The existence of a "shame theory" will thus guarantee that the shame-relevant aspects of any situation "will become figural in competition with other affect-relevant aspects of the same situations" (*AIC*, 2.231), which is to say that the individual's shame theory will guarantee that the shame-relevant aspects of any situation will compete for attention or dominance against the other affect-relevant aspects of the situation. The general result of the cognitive organization of experience into such "theories" is that individuals react in varying ways to situations according to the strong or weak affect theories they have developed. (Let me note an ambiguity in Tomkins's account—and in Sedgwick's discussion of Tomkins, as well as in my discussion of both of them—between the "theory" supposedly organized by an individual's "central assembly" and the standard definition of a scientific "theory" as something like "a proposed description, explanation, or model of the manner of interaction of a set of natural phenomena, capable of predicting future occurrences or observations of the same kind, and capable of being tested through experiments" [http://en.wikipedia.org/wiki/Theory]. What makes that ambiguity acceptable to Tomkins, and I guess to Sedgwick, is his notion that scientific theories in the standard sense of the term are analogous to those constructed by the central assembly, whatever that is taken to mean.)

4. Tomkins uses shame-humiliation to illustrate how different kinds of affect theory influence the individual, in ways suggesting that shame is indeed an exemplary affect for "theory," as Sedgwick suggests (*TF*, 115). But none of this alters the fact that for Tomkins the affects are discrete, inherited, self-rewarding or self-punishing responses of the body that can be and, in the early development stages, are activated by innate triggers. According to him, what is crucial for the design of the human machine is the existence of a critical gap between the conditions that instigate emotional responses and the affect system's "knowledge" of those conditions, for the affect system only knows that it likes some of those responses and dislikes others, not how to turn them on or off, or up or down, in intensity. It is the circuitry of the central assembly, or set of central assemblies, that slowly brings the affective responses under some sort of cognitive control, and it is the same set of central assemblies that provides the organism with knowledge, meaning, purposes, and intentions. For Tomkins, the operations of the affect system itself are inherently nonintentional or "blind," which is why humans never attain great control over their affects and why also the emotions are held by Tomkins to be revealed as innate and universal by Ekman's and Izard's cross-cultural studies, discussed in chapter 4, undertaken by the latter under the influence of Tomkins's ideas. For an especially vigorous critique of the cognitive theory of the affects and general discussion of his theories, see Tomkins, "The Quest for Primary Motives: Biography and Autobiography of an Idea," *Journal of Personality and Social Psychology*, 41 (1981): 306–29 (also cited at various points in my chapter 4).

INDEX